AMIGA™
ASSEMBLY LANGUAGE
PROGRAMMING

AMIGA™
ASSEMBLY LANGUAGE PROGRAMMING

JAKE COMMANDER

TAB BOOKS Inc.
Blue Ridge Summit, PA

FIRST EDITION
THIRD PRINTING

Printed in the United States of America

Reproduction or publication of the content in any manner, without express permission of the publisher, is prohibited. No liability is assumed with respect to the use of the information herein.

Library of Congress Cataloging in Publication Data

Commander, Jake.
Amiga assembly language programming.

Includes index.
1. Amiga (Computer)—Programming. 2. Assembler
language (Computer program language) I. Title.
QA76.8.A177C65   1987   005.265   86-1916
ISBN 0-8306-0711-9
ISBN 0-8306-2711-1 (pbk.)

TAB BOOKS Inc. offers software for
sale. For information and a catalog,
please contact TAB Software Department,
Blue Ridge Summit, PA 17294-0850.

Questions regarding the content of this book
should be addressed to:

Reader Inquiry Branch
TAB BOOKS Inc.
Blue Ridge Summit, PA 17294-0214

Cover photograph courtesy of Commodore Business Machines, Inc.

Contents

Introduction

Assembly language is the most challenging and rewarding kind of programming there is. It's challenging because, to be able to do it, you have to have a good grasp of both the processor being programmed and the machine that it's running on. It's rewarding because, when a program is finally completed and runs as planned, you have the most powerful implementation by which that program could have run on that machine, and you've demonstrated your mastery over the computer and its operating system.

The Amiga is a great machine to be able to program in machine code. The software interface to the Amiga has been extremely carefully designed and documented. Commodore has provided an incredible amount of software developer support. With other microcomputers in the past, finding out what was going on at the ROM level (where much of the prewritten machine code lies ready to use) was a matter of deduction based on disassembling ROM and finding where various routines were in order to avoid having to write them all over again in assembly language.

Commodore, however, has designed the Amiga to be used at the ROM level right from the start. This is accomplished without your even having to know anything about the whereabouts of code in ROM. For instance, if you want to draw a line across the screen, you won't have to write the routine from scratch. Neither will you have to disassemble and locate the routine in the Amiga's ROM. Routines, such as this one and any other conceivably useful routine, have already been written by Commodore and documented so that they can be called at the machine code level. For each routine, you simply supply a set of appropriate parameters, specifying such things as lengths and locations of lines, diameters of circles, and style and font of the text. This puts the incredible power of the Amiga hardware at your fingertips in assembly language.

To add even more to this developer-friendly scenario, the Amiga is driven by a Motorola 68000 microprocessor. This chip has a design as neat and logical as the Amiga itself, and seems to be the ideal "logic engine" for providing the power. Bearing in mind its power and the fact that it's probably the most successful of all 16/32 bit microprocessors, the 68000 is the best one to learn. This is the second reason why the Amiga is such a worthwhile machine to learn to program in assembly language.

So welcome to a journey that will introduce you first to the 68000 and then to the Amiga. Remember that the intention of this book is to provide an introduction. The first thing you'll want after finishing it is the Commodore-approved technical documentation for the Amiga. You'll need at least a copy of the AmigaDOS manual, the Amiga Intuition Reference manual, the Amiga ROM Kernel manual, and the Amiga Reference Manual:Exec. These manuals (and a few other optional ones) provide the definitive technical reference for the Amiga. They total several hundreds of pages in length—and they're not small pages either. My advice is to read this introductory book first.

Chapter

An Introduction
to Assembly Language

Welcome to what has to be regarded as the upper echelons of computer programming. For starters, let me put you at ease by telling you that machine-code programming is quite easy. Don't let the sight of thousands of hexadecimal digits convince you that something complicated is going on—a computer has to deal with those digits in exactly the same way a human would: namely, one at a time. Neither be dissuaded by the sight and appearance of many undernourished software hackers or shiny-headed computer boffins. Many computer programmers, just as many people in real life, sometimes appear to be a strange and overpriviledged crowd. You don't, however, have to have an IQ of 250, stare into a monitor for 15 hours a day, or be weird to program in machine code. There's nothing any more strange about the occupation than about driving a bus.

If you're totally new to computer programming per se, machine-code programming is probably the best place to start. I learned machine-code techniques on a hypothetical, nonexistent computer. Since that time, I've been lucky enough to be able to apply the same techniques and concepts to learning new computer languages with comparative ease. There's much more in common between computer processors (in our case, microprocessors) of different manufacturers than there is between the high-level computer languages that run on these processors. You, however, don't have to learn on a nonexistent computer. By learning machine code directly on the 68000 in your Amiga, you'll be armed with the knowledge of a very real microprocessor that shares characteristics with many other modern-day computer processors.

So what does the processor do? Understanding this is the key to understanding machine code. At its most fundamental level, you could say the function of a processor is to logically compute answers to questions posed by inquisitive human beings. The questions asked can range from the trivial, like "how much pay shall this employee take home?" to the grandiose, such as "what is the chemical composition of that star in Bega Minoris?" In either case, the processor has no innate or built-in knowledge of how to solve the problem. In fact, a processor of the current generation has no knowledge of anything. It's just a lump of inorganic matter waiting to be told what to do.

It is best to learn machine code before you learn high-level programming, because at this level you're at the very foundations of programming. You're at the heart of the computer when you program in machine code—at ground zero. Whatever drives the particular computer you're working on, you'll get the most power and speed from that computer by talking to the processor in its native tongue. This power and speed has a small price, however, and it's this small barrier that places machine-code programming at that upper echelon. The native language of a computer processor is, at first sight, very alien compared to a human language. This is one penalty. Another one is that at the machine code level, a processor can only carry out one tiny instruction at a time. Thus, building up a useful machine-code program always requires a large number of steps. This takes time and effort on the part of the programmer, so a good machine-code programmer is required to sacrifice time and use a high degree of skill. More time and skill is needed than would be needed when the programming is done in a high-level language, such as BASIC or COBOL. The skill is needed because the processor works in such small, discrete steps. For example, on a microprocessor, one single machine-code instruction is required to add two small digits together. If you wanted to add two high-precision numbers including a decimal point floating somewhere within the digits, you'd have to write a series of many machine-code instructions to perform the task. At the end of such a programming exercise, however, you will have an in-depth knowledge of the techniques required to perform that task. In other words, you will have gained expertise. Compare this with a programmer using a high-level language who simply has to use a plus sign to add two floating-point numbers together. It's obviously simpler, but the programmer remains totally ignorant about the techniques used to deal with floating-point numbers. Thus, by going through the learning process with assembly language, you'll acquire a degree of computing expertise over and above the norm. After that, high-level languages seem easy compared with the more careful, thought-out process of programming in machine code.

Computer operating systems have to be programmed (at least in part) in machine code. This is because the input/output functions of any computer involve hardware devices such as keyboards, video displays, and disk drives. "Driving" these devices requires the programmer to work as close to the hardware as possible—at the primitive processor level. Machine code is that primitive level. It's this code that is the processor's native tongue. When referring to microcomputer software, machine-code instructions can be thought of as atoms that can't be split into anything smaller. One machine-code instruction is the smallest possible operation that can be carried out. The operations that are performed by each processor instruction are determined within the hardware of the particular processor you're using. It's the differences between the hardware of one processor as compared to another that makes them appear different from one another at the software level. So, by using machine code, you can talk to the hardware directly if you so wish. This gives you the maximum power over your computer.

Computer languages, of course, aren't really languages at all, but because some method of communication is needed to let a computer know what you want it to do, the word *language* seems the most appropriate one to use while attempting to communicate with a computer. Compared with human language, a computer language is just a static set of rules that tell a computer what procedure to follow. The processor, which is at the heart of any and all computers, can be considered a stupid device—the only 'clever' thing a binary processor can do internally is add digits together. The only thing it really does is to plow through a set of electrically-encoded instructions that it senses at its inputs. Each input is either an on voltage or an off voltage. That's why computers are said to work in *binary*—the idea is that an on voltage represents the digit one, and an off voltage represents the digit zero. A processor can thus only distinguish between zeroes and ones (the binary system). A computer that only knows two numbers doesn't seem very useful, but things can be expanded somewhat by the simple expedient of allowing more than one binary input line to be *input* (or *read*) by the processor. So if you added just one more binary digit—called a *bit*—the processor, sensing both bits at once, would be able to recognize four possible combinations. The combinations that could exist with two input lines would be: both inputs zero, a zero and a one, a one and a zero, and both inputs one. This rudimentary computer would now be able to recognize four different external conditions. If yet another input line were added, the number of combinations would double to eight. Add another and it would double again to 16. The simplicity of the binary counting system starts becoming apparent. In fact, every extra input line added to the processor's electronics doubles the number of permutations of zeroes and ones recognized. It's an easy matter to work out the number of possible permutations from the number of bits input to any device. It's simply two to the power of the number of bits input or 2^n.

A device with eight input bits could detect two to the power of eight, or 256, different possibilities of input. A device with 16 bits can detect two to the power of 16, or 65,536. The number of permutations rises quicker than you'd think at first sight. You now have the rudiments of a binary system. You can count as high as you like just by representing numbers as different sequences of zeroes and ones.

The binary numbers that are presented on a processor can represent anything you want them to. They can represent simple whole numbers starting at zero and working up to the maximum attainable. Alternatively, you could count from zero up to half the maximum attainable and leave one unused bit that could be designated as a minus sign. This gives a possible way to represent negative numbers. You can represent characters of the alphabet by selecting certain numbers to represent alphabetic symbols. The addition of punctuation marks and numeric characters gives an entire, arbitrarily chosen, alphanumeric character set. If everyone sensibly chooses to agree which numbers represent which symbols (as with the ASCII character set), different computers can act on the same quantities, knowing they represent particular characters.

Another very important thing that can be done is to have the binary numbers represent actions to be taken by the processor. For instance, you could tell the processor to halt when it detects a combination of all ones on its input lines, or you could tell it to add two numbers when it senses all zeroes. In this way, numbers can represent actions or commands to be followed by the processor. All that's needed is for the processor to automatically step sequentially through a list of binary numbers in memory, and you have a sequence of predetermined events. In TV, radio, or theater, a program is used to determine or predict a sequence of events. Exactly the same is true of a computer processor. In any digital computer, a whole list of numbers stored in memory is scanned number by number, each one representing an action. Thus, the processor is simply a machine stepping one at a time through numbers that represent action codes. This is machine code. The set of numbers is the machine-code program. Notice that the computer only executes one action at any moment in time. The next action is taken only when the current one is complete. As a pure machine-code programmer (or, more strictly, from the point of view of this book an assembly-language programmer), the task is to know which numbers perform which actions and then string them together so some kind of sensible set of actions, known as a *program*, is executed.

In case this sounds a little scary, just remember that no sane person writes more than a few lines of a program in numeric machine code. If you were to do so, you'd need a list of every numerical action executable by any specific manufacturer's processor. This is by no means impossible, but to write a whole program, you'd need to look up and find the number that performed each action required in your program—a painfully long and error-prone process.

This description of machine-code programming is intended to illustrate the most primitive level of programming of any processor on any computer. If you've not been put off so far, you'll be pleased to know that the worst is over—things only improve from here on in.

A few definitions are in order at this point so that everyone knows what is being referred to as I go along.

The set of numbers representing every single action capable of being executed by a processor is called its *instruction set*. When a processor is designed, the manufacturer will decide what the instruction set will be and this becomes a permanent feature of that particular model of processor. It is possible on certain expensive and sophisticated mainframe processors to redefine some or all of its instruction set. This is known as microprogramming and is beyond the scope of this book.

Each number executed as an individual action is called an *opcode* (short for *operation code*) or an *instruction*.

The sequential list of opcodes or instructions that perform a single useful function (for example, reading a block of data from a disk or taking the square root of a number) is called a *routine* or *subroutine*. (The word *algorithm* is often used to refer to the particular method used to extract such quantities as square roots.)

The sequential list of opcodes or instructions that perform an entire task (a company payroll, for example) is called a *program*.

You've learned that a processor digests instructions in the form of a list of numbers (known as a program) stored in memory. Normally, execution is *sequential*, meaning that each instruction is found at the next higher location (or address) in memory. Certain instructions in a processor's instruction set can, however, change this sequential process. For instance, a processor might be plodding step by step (albeit at lightning speed) through a program starting at location 1000 in memory. The next instruction would be taken from location 1001, the next from 1002, and so on. But if the instruction at location 1003 were to say "jump to location 2000," the processor would duly take its next instruction from memory location 2000 and then go on from there. (*Locations* and *addresses* are numbers that refer to the particular memory cell being addressed.)

This type of instruction is usually called a *jump* or *branch* instruction, for obvious reasons.

In order to keep track of exactly where in memory the next instruction is to come from, all processors have a special internal register called a *program counter*. This points to the location (or, in other words, contains the address of) the next instruction to be executed. Thus, a jump instruction simply replaces the contents of the program counter with the destination of the jump. When the program counter is reloaded in this way, the processor continues onwards from this new address. This allows various routines that perform different functions to be kept separate from each other and then jumped to as appropriate by the program.

The program counter is by no means the only register to be found in a processor. There are other registers specifically designed to help with the handling of actual numbers by the computer. The most important of these registers is usually called the *accumulator*. There's always some kind of accumulator in every type of processor, because this is the main register used in the manipulation of data. Sometimes there's more than one accumulator in a processor; this allows the option of handling more than one number within the processor itself. In most computer processors the accumulator is referred to by its shortened name—the *A register*. A typical *mnemonic* (that is, an easily remembered form of an instruction, as explained at the end of the chapter) to load the A register might look like:

```
LDA     #7
```

which would load the accumulator (or A register) with the number seven. What that seven would be used for is entirely dependent upon the program—it could be the number of files in a disk's directory, for example.

No matter how many registers are inside a computer processor, they are all able to hold and manipulate numbers in some way, but some registers may have special uses. Usually, the A register is the only one that affects a set of special bits in the processor called the *condition flags*. Because they are no more than ordinary binary digits, these flags are either on or off and are used to indicate the status of the accumulator. For instance, the zero, or Z, flag will be set on if the accumulator contains a zero. Thus, you could test the A register and then jump to a new location if a previous number had been changed to zero.

Some other flags you're likely to find are the *sign flag*, to indicate whether the accumulator contains a positive or negative number, the *carry flag*, indicates if a carry-out was generated during an addition, and the *overflow flag*, which is set if a signed number becomes too large or small to fit in the accumulator. Remember that any register in a processor is finite in size: it has a definite number of bits that determine the maximum number that it can hold.

This gives a first overview of what machine code is all about. In nearly all cases, to program a processor in machine code, you solicit the aid of the computer itself. You would use a program called an *assembler*. This allows you to escape the drudgery of having to know and use the numerical instructions used by the processor. An assembler allows you to use such *mnemonics*, as the LDA #7 opcode referred to earlier. From machine code, you've now arrived at assembly language. This is the subject of the next chapter.

Chapter

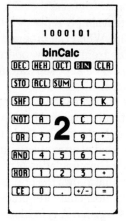

1000101

binCalc

DEC HEX OCT BIN CLR
STO RCL SUM
SHF D E F K
NOT A **2** C /
OR 7 9 .
AND 4 5 6 -
XOR 1 2 3 +
CE 0 . +/- =

An Introduction to Editor-Assemblers

To spare creative human beings such as ourselves from the mind-numbing drudgery of programming in machine code, assembly language was brought into existence. This removes the total dependence on numbers that's been enforced so far on both the computer and programmer. Up to this point, the term *machine code* has been used to refer to the numeric codes used by the processor. Note that although the term *machine language* is often used, it doesn't really have a precise meaning—there is no halfway point as such between machine code and assembly language. Nevertheless, the term *machine language* is still sometimes used, perhaps as an unconscious reference to machine code as achieved through assembly language.

Assembly language lets you forget all about those opcode numbers by providing names for each opcode instead of actual numbers. These names are kept intentionally short and are chosen to aid the programmer in remembering the opcodes available in a particular processor's instruction set. Thus, instead of having to remember the number 99, for instance, as a jump instruction, you'd simply write JUMP or JMP or whichever mnemonic is correct for that particular processor. Now you have something closer to a language than a set of numbers, and it's this that is referred to as *assembly language*. The processor itself still only understands numbers, however, so you have to introduce a means to translate these opcode mnemonics into the pure numerical opcodes that drive the processor. A special computer program exists for this exact purpose. Initially written in pure machine code by some hapless programmer, this program performs the translation from mnemonics to numbers automatically, quickly, and without errors. Such a program is called an *assembler*, attesting to the fact that it *assembles* a numerical list of opcodes from a list of mnemonics.

A program that is to be assembled is submitted in the form of line after line of mnemonics, which is called *source code*. The assembler takes the source code and churns out the equivalent numbers, which will perform the desired program. The computer has still been programmed to execute a machine-code program, but this program has been written in assembly language instead of pure machine code. To enter this assembly language program, you usually need some way of preparing, entering and storing the program code so that it is ready for presentation to the assembler. This is normally done using a program called an *editor*, which provides a programmer with various tools to ease the task of manually typing in programs that can sometimes grow to inordinate lengths. If you've used a word processor, you'll find an editor much the same, except that it encourages the input of text in tabulated columns and lacks some of the more typographical frills of a word processor. Many editors are included as part of the assembler program itself. These hybrid utilities are called, not surprisingly, editor/assemblers. The more sophisticated assemblers, due to their large memory requirements, often require the use of a separate editor.

Once a program has been entered using the editor, it can be saved as a file on tape or disk. This file is then input to the assembler, which generates the machine code back to tape or disk, or in certain cases, directly to memory. The assembler will also let you know what errors you made (such as using nonexistent mnemonics such as BUMP instead of JUMP). An assembly language program will almost always contain errors on the first try.

The main function of an assembler is as a pure tool for the machine-code programmer. This tool performs the same process you'd have to do if you wanted to put together a machine-code program by hand. It's not only the mnemonics that have to be translated to the correct numerical instructions, but the addresses used in your program. If done by hand, you'd have to cross-reference a table of mnemonics and opcodes. Then you'd have to work out the locations of other routines, to decide where to direct various jumps in the code. The result of this arduous hand-assembly process would be a machine-code program executable by the processor. It's unlikely that it would be free from errors in program logic flow, however. An assembler simply automates the process and leaves the programmer free to concentrate on program logic rather than the nitty-gritty of a processor's operation.

The lines of mnemonics that are submitted to and processed by the assembler are referred to as *source code*. The assembler churns through this to provide what is called *object code*. The object code is what is executed by the computer, although many assemblers produce a "halfway" object code. This halfway code can be linked with other halfway object codes to produce a final machine-code program. The source code written by the programmer has to follow a strict set of rules so that the assembler can perform its task correctly and unambiguously. In order to simplify things for the assembler, the source code is submitted one opcode per line in a known, specific format. This format is very similar for all kinds of assemblers, even those for different processors, and usually looks something like this:

line number   label   opcode   address   comment

A couple of real examples are:

```
00120 KVCTR    JMP      KBDIP    ;Key scan vector
01001 LBLX     JMP      LBLX     ;loop forever
```

The line number is not required by some assemblers. If it's there at all, it's merely to provide a reference to that line for editing purposes. In other words, it's more for the editor than the assembler, although the assembler can use it in pinpointing errors. The editor, in this case, would be able to reference any line by its number so that lines could be inserted, deleted, or corrected.

The label serves to reference the code generated at that point in the program by the assembler. If you wanted to jump to the opcode at a particular location, you'd label that opcode and jump to the label, rather than to a numerical address. That way you don't need to know anything about where your program will physically reside in memory—the assembler will do it for you. In this instance it would generate the op-code for a jump followed by the numeric address of the opcode you wanted to jump to. This leaves the assembler to worry about the physical addresses in the object code, relieving the burden on the programmer. Labels have a few rules of their own, although they're not very restricting. They always have to start with a nonnumeric character—most often a letter from A to Z, but sometimes a period, dollar sign, underline, or other special nonnumeric characters. This is required so that the assembler can distinguish between a label and a numeric address you might want to use. If you were to use the label 99, the assembler would have no way of distinguishing between the address 99 and the label 99. If you were to use the label L99, all ambiguity would be removed.

Labels are generally chosen, using a little common sense, to have a meaningful name. If you wanted to jump to a routine that scanned the keyboard until a key was pressed, you might want to label that routine GETKEY or something similar. It doesn't matter at all to the assembler, but it helps a programmer who has to read your code to understand the intent of any particular routine. Often that programmer will be yourself—assembly language is described as going "cold" after a couple of months. You can return to your own code after such a short time and hardly understand what you wrote. A sensible choice of labels can significantly help in the understanding of a program.

The next field required after the label is an opcode. This is the mnemonic, which represents the instruction to be performed at that point. The list of mnemonics available for use by a programmer is decided upon by the manufacturer of the processor being programmed. The assembler being used will probably also contain a list of these mnemonics in its documentation. That list is the entire repertoire of instructions that can be understood by the processor—it represents the entire instruction set. Thus, if a processor can perform the particular opcode you have in mind, it will be in that list somewhere. Some manufacturers' mnemonics are better than others' in that they're easier to remember (which, after all, is the purpose of a mnemonic). For instance, LDA is easily remembered as "load A," whereas XTHL is less easily remembered as "exchange top of stack with register HL." If you program more than one processor, you soon realize that mnemonics don't vary all that much from one type of processor to another. What is LDA #1 on one machine may be LD A,1 on another.

The address field, if used, lets the opcode refer to an address in memory. This can be an absolute physical address or a label that was used in the label field of another opcode. Thus, if you wanted to load the accumulator with the contents of location 3 in memory, you'd use an absolute address of 3. If you wanted to load the accumulator with the contents of a memory location labeled CELL in your program, you'd use the label CELL.

The address field doesn't necessarily have to contain just the address of a memory location; it may contain the name of another register in the processor, as in the example LDC B, in which B is a different register whose contents you want to load into register C. The address field may also consist of an *immediate* number, which is to be loaded into a register. An example of this is LDB #5, in which the number five is loaded into the B register. The # in this example serves to tell the assembler to generate the opcode that will load the number five immediately following the opcode into register B. This is as opposed to loading register B with the contents of memory cell number five. To do that, many assemblers require you to enclose the address (in this case location 5) in brackets. This is called *indirect addressing;* it's not the number five that is needed— it's the contents of memory cell number five. In the above example in which you wanted the contents of CELL loaded into the accumulator, you'd write LDA (CELL). The actual contents of the address field for any specific opcode will depend on the addressing modes available for that opcode. This will, in turn, depend on the capabilities of the processor being programmed. Most processors allow at least the types of addressing just described. These are called *indirect addressing, register addressing,* and *immediate addressing.* Other processors allow even more memory-addressing modes, thereby increasing the computing power available to the programmer.

The final field in a line of assembly language is the comment field. This does nothing as far as the assembler is concerned while generating code. The comment field is simply skipped over and ignored. Despite this ignominious end, however, the comment field can be as important as the actual code itself. While labels can help in documenting a program, the comments exist exclusively for that purpose. Unlike labels however, comments don't have to be cryptic. In fact, the clearer they are and the more often they're used, the easier it is for a stranger to your work to read your program. Remember, that will include yourself within a few weeks of completing a program. Comments are so important that most assemblers allow you to use the whole program line as a comment instead of using it for an opcode. Such lines often start with an asterisk or some other predefined character to let the assembler know to skip the entire line.

The layout of the fields that have been used up to now have been taken for granted. But how does the assembler know which field represents what? Many assemblers require each field to be aligned precisely at a particular position within the line. This *fixed-field* format is inherited from the days when each line was submitted on a punched card. Typically, you might have to start your label in column 10 and your opcode in column 19. Assuming at least one space after the label, that allows a maximum label length of eight characters.

Most modern assemblers allow a free-field format. This means that a field comes to an end when a space or tab character is encountered. Naturally, this means that a label or an opcode cannot contain a space or tab; these would confuse the assembler into assuming it had reached the end of a field. It doesn't matter how many spaces or tabs occur between fields.

Up to now, the opcode field has only contained the mnemonics in the processor's instruction set. However, it is possible to use the opcode field to tell the assembler something about how you want it to operate on your source code. The words that are used in the opcode field to do this are called *pseudo-ops*. A more accurate description that is used these days is *assembler directive*, and many currently-used assemblers refer to pseudo-ops by this name. A description of some of the pseudo-ops available with typical assemblers will give an idea of how useful they are.

The first pseudo-op to be encountered in many programs is ORG. This is a mnemonic for *origin* and tells the assembler where the assembly language is to reside in memory. It literally sets the origin of the code that follows the ORG directive. For instance, if the first line in a program were ORG 1000, then the next machine code byte to be generated by the assembler would be eventually stored in memory at location 1000. The creation of an entirely separate version of the program that loaded at location 2000 would simply involve changing the ORG line to ORG 2000, and then reassembling.

EQU is an important and often-used assembler directive. It is used to equate the label field with the address field. As an example, if you were writing a program that generated output on a video screen, you'd need to know how many text lines were available for display. Various parts of your program would probably need to check this maximum-line value to ensure that output was kept within the number of lines in the display. If the program were then changed to run on a screen with a different number of lines, you'd have to search for every occurrence of the old number of lines and change it to the new number. The EQU command lets you do it with one change. If the program started with MAXLINE EQU 16, then every time MAXLINE was used, the assembler would replace it with 16. Then if the program had to be reassembled for a 24-line display, that one equate would be changed to MAXLINE EQU 24. The assembler would then replace the occurrences of MAXLINE with 24. This is simpler for the programmer, but a sensible choice of label, such as MAXLINE, helps in documenting the program. You can use your intuition to guess what MAXLINE represents, whereas it would be difficult to figure out what a mysterious 16 or 24 meant.

Many pseudo-ops (or assembler-directives) exist to help in formatting a readable listing. LIST ON and LIST OFF tell the assembler whether or not you want a listing of the program at that point. If you were working on a small portion of a large program of which you already had a listing, you would use LIST OFF to switch off the listing. LIST ON would then be placed in the program at the point where you needed the listing. The EJECT pseudo-op sends a form-feed to the output device (most often a line printer) so that subsequent lines begin at the top of a new page. This helps separate the routines listed and immensely improves the readability of a program. As you should have gathered, readability is almost as important as the code itself.

Some pseudo-ops even allow you to control which parts of the source code will be assembled. Going back to the example of MAXLINE above, you might have a routine that is only required if MAXLINE is 16. You can have this routine automatically assembled or skipped over by using the IF pseudo-op and its relatives ELSE and EN-DIF. Imagine you have one routine you want assembled for a 16-line display and a different one otherwise. You'd write:

```
IF MAXLINE=16

(16-line routine)

ELSE

(other routine)

ENDIF
```

If MAXLINE wasn't equated to 16 within your program, the ELSE tells the assembler to assemble the second routine. The ELSE is optional, and is only used if you want one of two mutually exclusive routines to be assembled. The ENDIF tells the assembler that it has come to the end of the conditional assembly portion; at this point it continues to assemble the source code regardless of any previously required conditions.

The MACRO pseudo-op lets you generate whole sections of source code with a single word, and can save a lot of work. This can almost be used to define your own custom-made opcodes. Suppose you needed an opcode that multiplied the number in the accumulator by ten. This is unlikely to be included in the instruction set of the processor, so you would resort to defining a macro. First, you would decide on the name of your new opcode. MUL10 sounds like a reasonable choice. Then you'd have to write the source code that would be needed every time your program has to multiply register A by ten. The macro might look something like this:

```
MUL10   MACRO           ;Define name

        LDB     A       ;Hold number in B

        ADDA    A       ;Add A to itself (x2)

        ADDA    A       ;And again (x4)

        ADDA    B       ;Add original number (x5)

        ADDA    A       ;Add A to itself (x10)

        ENDM            ;Signal end of macro
```

Now, every time you would use the opcode MUL10 in your source code, the assembler would replace it with the lines between the MACRO and ENDM pseudo-ops. In effect, you invented a new opcode.

When the assembler is run, you have the choice of a listing. You might want the listing on the screen, on the printer, or perhaps on a disk. The screen is of limited use-

11

fulness with a long program, because most of it will have scrolled off the screen before you've had a chance to see it. Its main use is in examining small sections of code. You'll need a hard-copy printout at some point so you can scan to and fro within the code to determine where any changes need to be made. The listing consists of the actual machine code generated by the assembler, plus the original source code as entered using the editor. Part of an assembly-language listing looks as follows:

```
                  0001          ORG    0

0000 01           0002 BMORE    LDA    B       ;B into A reg

0001 0702         0003          ADDA   #2      ;+2

0003 180000       0004          JUMP   BMORE ;loop around

forever
```

The last five columns are the same as the source code that was input to the assembler. The columns before these are the work of the assembler itself, and represent a map of the machine code that was generated. The first column is the address of the opcode at that line. Because an origin of zero was specified in line 0001 of the source code, the first opcode (01) is assembled into memory location 0000. This is the machine-code instruction of LDA B. Notice that this opcode was labeled BMORE so that the jump opcode that is assembled into location 0003 (not at line number 0003) is assembled as 18—for JUMP—followed by 0000, which represents the address BMORE. If any further source code followed the jump, it would be assembled into location 0006—the next available address in memory.

From that example, which generated six bytes into memory, you can see the work done by the assembler in translating the source code contained in columns three and above into the machine code in column two. Column one tells you where this machine code is loaded into memory. A separate file would be produced containing the bytes in column two along with information as to where they should be loaded. It's sometimes possible to have these machine-code bytes assembled directly into memory; however, because many machine-code programs don't work the first time, it's wise to have it saved to a file, in case portions of it become overwritten. This is an unfortunate but favorite habit of new programs that have not yet been debugged.

The listing comes complete with another unpopular but important set of lines. These contain any error messages that the assembler decides you should know about. Unfortunately, the messages don't point out errors in the logic of your program—they only point out errors in the syntax or structure of the source code. For instance, if you tried to use the label 99 in the label column, the assembler would report that you had used an illegal label. It won't stop, though; it will continue until the end of the source code so you have an opportunity to check out any other errors. The total number of errors detected is printed at the end of the listing so you can dejectedly scan the listing until you've caught them all.

On some systems, it is possible to ask the assembler to stop whenever it spots an error during a listing to the screen. You can then make a note of the line number, press a key to continue the assembly, and check your source code while the listing continues. This is only one of a number of options you can call for when you instruct the assembler to start work. If you invoked the assembler with the option -LP for example, the assembler would ask you for the name of the file you wanted assembled, and then it would output its listing to the line printer. The hyphen before LP tells the assembler that you're requesting an option. The full list of these options is given in the assembler's documentation. They'll include such things as -NL to generate no listing at all, and -NO to generate no object code (useful for an error-scan of the source code). To get the assembler to pause when an error is spotted, you might use the -WE option to wait on errors. These options all help you in developing your own style of writing and debugging programs. Generally, the more options there are available, the greater the versatility in using an assembler.

The final thing that you can have generated by the assembler—and it's another of those options—is a cross-reference table. In a long program, this can be another invaluable aid. When your source code has been completely assembled, the assembler will have generated machine code with all your references to labels within the program replaced by the memory address where that label's code resides. It's useful to know where the assembler has placed each piece of labeled code. If you use the -XR option when you call the assembler, you'll get a cross-reference table after the source code listing. This will list every label you used in your program alongside its address as resolved by the assembler. Thus, when you add and delete lines, causing the addresses of labels to change, a cross-reference table will display their latest locations.

You have a choice. If you really want to, you can hand-assemble all the bytes of your program into memory. If you don't make any mistakes, you'll end up with a working machine-code program—and probably a nasty headache. Alternatively, you can use the assembler that will be available for the particular processor you wish to program. Not only will it prevent the headache, it will dramatically increase both your productivity as a programmer and the reliability of your program.

Now that you've had an overview of a typical assembler and machine code in general, let's step into the real world, where, at the heart of the Amiga, a processor awaits: the Motorola MC68000.

Chapter

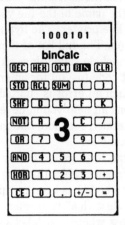

1000101

binCalc

DEC HEX OCT BIN CLR
STO RCL SUM ( )
SHF D E F K
NOT A **3** C /
OR 7 9 *
AND 4 5 6 -
HOR 1 2 3 +
CE 0 . +/- =

A Profile of the 68000

At the innermost depths of the Commodore Amiga microcomputer—in fact at its very soul—lies the integrated circuit that provides the brainpower of the machine: the Motorola MC68000 microprocessor. As a microprocessor chip, it has more in common with minicomputers than microcomputers. It could almost be described as a millicomputer. The 68000 has an ancestral background that goes back to the paleolithic days of computing. In the beginning were the first generation of mainframe computers. These beasts represented the dinosaur age—they were massive and slow by today's standards. The processor unit took up most of the space in a large room. The use of tubes as the electronic devices driving the logic circuits generated large amounts of heat, which consumed expensive amounts of electricity and literally required an air-conditioning plant to keep the thing at its proper operating temperature. Memory was comprised of tiny circular magnets called *toroids,* which were magnetized alternately clockwise or counter-clockwise to represent a zero or one.

Then the transistor was invented. This heralded a new dynasty in computing. Now the arithmetic and logical processing unit could be built to fit along a wall rather than taking up a whole room; however, computer peripherals, such as tape drives, still required tubes. Enough heat was generated to require keeping on the air-conditioning plant to enable the sensitive magnetic-core memory to function reliably. Meanwhile, the giants of the semiconductor industry were learning how to imprint transistors and other electronic components directly onto small squares of silicon. Now hundreds of transistors, diodes, and resistors could be etched onto a chip a mere one square centimeter in size. The building blocks of computers now came in plastic packages an inch long and a quarter inch wide. The third generation had arrived. This enabled the computer's central processing unit to be built into a cabinet only a few feet square. Air conditioning had also entered the computer age—it was now called *climatic control* and was even then required to operate these multimillion dollar beasts.

By this time, computers had proven their worth, but they were too expensive for all but the biggest businesses. The power of these third-generation megaliths, however, was such that they could easily deal with a number of terminals connected over a telephone line. Smaller businesses could afford to rent these, so computing as a tool at last started filtering down to the masses via engineering firms and accounting firms—in fact via anyone who used numbers.

Meanwhile, back at the semiconductor corporations, the scientists had not been idle. They had increased the number of components on a chip to such a density that now it was possible to manufacture a processor-on-a-chip. At first, only a 4-bit processor was available (compared with about 32 bits on a mainframe), but very shortly thereafter, 8-bit microprocessors appeared. Although this fourth generation of computers was initially a lot less powerful than mainframe computers, the mass of software that appeared gave them a power and versatility that at last brought computing to the general public.

Gradually, the 8-bit chips improved to a point where the only logical improvement was to increase the number of binary digits processed to 16. Presumably, the final step will be when a microprocessors' (micro now referring to their size, not their power) capabilities parallel those of a mainframe. That final step is not far off. The 68000 represents the current state in this process of microprocessor evolution. As a chip with a 16-bit bus, it leapfrogs the 8-bit microprocessors. As a chip with 32-bit processing capability, it matches some capabilities of mainframes. With the MC68000, Motorola has presented an electronic machine with a power and size that would have been considered impossible in the first generation of computing. This is the soul of the Amiga.

The 68000, in spite of its power, still has to deal with simple binary numbers. It does not have any floating-point instructions as do many mainframes, but the software already written to handle such quantities on other microprocessors can easily be modified, if so desired. In fact, the way the 68000 is laid out—its internal architecture—allows it to manipulate numbers like either a micro or minicomputer. Registers in the chip can deal with 8-bit quantities, which allows it to utilize any useful byte-oriented algorithms. It can also deal with words of 16 bits in length, or long words of 32 bits. This is the reason why the 68000 is sometimes referred to as a 32-bit chip. Actually, this is only true of the 68020—an upgraded version of the 68000. The 68000 gathers its information via a data bus of 16 bits, and it's this fact that usually determines how many bits a processor is judged by. Saying the 68000 is a 32-bit processor is equivalent to saying that the Z-80 or 8080 are 16-bit chips. (Both are capable of 16-bit arithmetic, but by consensus they are known as 8-bit chips.)

Motorola does have an eye to the future, and using the precedent already set for more bits per processor, they have the 68000 available in more than one version. The 68010 is a 68000 with a few enhancements that allow it to work in a virtual memory environment. The 68020 is a 68000 with a 32-bit data bus (and therefore is a true 32-bit processor). Finally, there's the 68008, which is a 68000 with an 8-bit bus. With a small sacrifice in speed, this allows for simpler interfacing with already existing 8-bit memory designs. With the existence of the 68020, it's comforting to know that the knowledge acquired in learning 68000 machine code will still be valuable as 32-bit technology consolidates its position in the marketplace.

The 68000 is generally regarded as having 17 internal registers for number manipulation. In fact, if you count the status register and the program counter, it has 19. However, it's probably most accurate to say it has 15 general-purpose and four special registers. The 15 general-purpose registers are split into two sections: eight 32-bit data

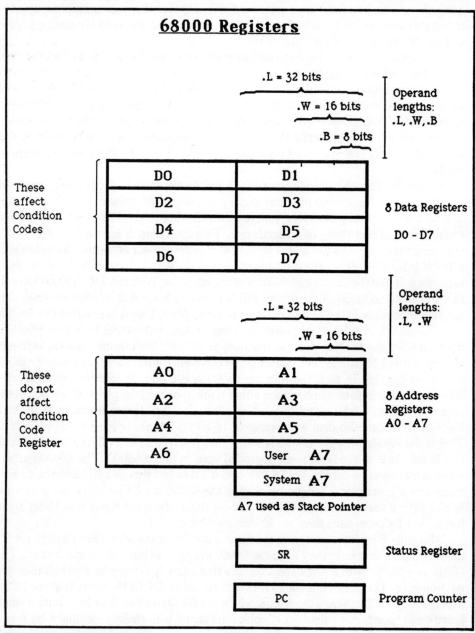

Fig. 3-1. The 68000 Registers.

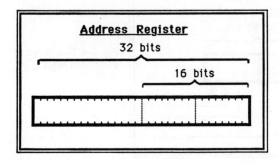

Fig. 3-2. The general layout of a data register.

Data Register

32 bits

16 bits

8 bits

registers named D0 to D7, and seven address registers named A0 to A6, also 32 bits in length. Another address register—A7—exists as a stack pointer and has two incarnations: the *system stack pointer* and the *user stack pointer* (more on these later). The 68000's register architecture is shown in Fig. 3-1. Each of the data registers, D0 to D7, bears a close resemblance to an accumulator except that with eight of them to manipulate, the processor's power is that much greater. The data registers have instructions available that allow the handling of 8-, 16-, and 32-bit quantities. The 8-bit quantities are dealt with in bits 0 to 7 of a register, the 16-bit quantities in bits 0 to 15, and the 32-bit quantities, of course, in the entire register (bits 0 to 31). All eight data registers are exactly equivalent to each other in the way they deal with numbers. It's just like having eight versatile 32-bit memory cells within the chip. Figure 3-2 shows the general layout of a data register.

Address registers can also be regarded as eight 32-bit on-chip memory cells. They differ from the data registers in that they can't handle data in 8-bit bytes using a single instruction. Opcodes do exist, however, to handle 16- and 32-bit quantities in address registers. Figure 3-3 shows the general layout of an address register. As in the data registers, bits 0 to 15 of an address register contain word-length numbers, and bits 0 to 31 hold long words. All 17 of these registers (remember there are two A7 registers) can pass quantities back and forth between each other, so if you wanted, 8-bit quantities could be dealt with to a limited degree within an address register by temporarily exchanging it with a data register.

The program counter is not a "normal" register, because it is only used to point to the next instruction to be executed. Its value is only changed to cause a jump in order to execute code from a different area of memory. Instructions are a minimum of one word (that is, two bytes) in length, so the program counter will always contain

Address Register

32 bits

16 bits

Fig. 3-3. The general layout of an address register.

an even number. Within the internal structure of the 68000, the program counter exists as a register 32 bits in length, although only 24 bits are physically connected to the outside world in order to address memory. This gives the 68000 the ability to address 2^{24}, or more than 16 million, bytes of memory. If Motorola ever decided to utilize the remaining eight internal bits of the program counter, the 68000 would be able to address a staggering 4 billion bytes.

The status register consists of various flags and mask bits. It is illustrated in Fig. 3-4. The status register is 16 bits in length, and is logically split into two bytes: the system byte and the user byte. The 68000 is always running in one of two modes: *supervisor* or *user*. The only difference between the two is that certain instructions can only be used in supervisor mode. These instructions would have a catastrophic effect within the computer if used carelessly, so they are restricted to use only while the processor is in supervisor (sometimes called *privileged*) state. Bit 13 of the status register—within the system byte—is used to place the 68000 in supervisor mode. Because the system byte itself is only accessible while in supervisor mode, it's quite easy to write an operating system that restricts normal programs to the user mode, thus denying access to the system byte containing the supervisor bit. This makes for a safer software environment that is less likely to crash due to an inexperienced or malevolent user doing the wrong thing. Bit 15 of the system byte sets the processor into *trace mode*. This facility is another one of the strong points of the 68000. When in trace mode, the processor will execute in single-step mode, thus allowing for easier debugging of machine-code programs. As more time is always spent in debugging than in actually writing code, any options that help in debugging will save time and money in program development.

Bits 8 to 10, still in the system byte, represent an *interrupt mask*. Any one of eight levels of interrupts can be set by these bits.

The first eight bits—bits 0 to 7—of the status register are known as the *user byte*. Only bits 0 to 4 have any significance. These bits are the condition flags, which act in pretty much the same way as on any processor. This is how they're arranged:

Bit 0 is the carry flag. This is set if an addition that causes a carry over from the most significant bit of the result is performed, or if a borrow is required during a subtraction. Shifts and rotates can also set or reset this bit according to whether a zero or one is shifted into it.

Bit 1 is the overflow bit. This is set if an addition or subtraction that causes the result to be too high or low to store in the register is performed on a signed quantity.

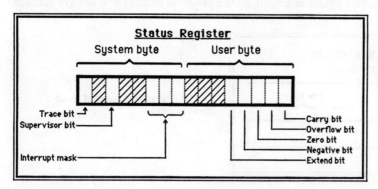

Fig. 3-4. The layout of the status register.

Bit 2 is the zero bit. It is set if the result of an arithmetic or logical operation is zero. It also returns the value of a bit during a bit-test instruction to see if a bit is zero or one.

Bit 3 is the negative or sign bit. If an operation results in a negative quantity (that is, with its most significant bit set), then the negative bit is set.

Bit 4 is the extend bit. This is simply a carry flag that is affected by fewer instructions than the carry bit. It is used to allow arithmetic of any degree of precision by allowing any carry bits to be extended from one operand to another.

Bits 0 to 3 of the user-status bits can be tested directly as conditions within the 68000's branch instructions.

The 68000 can directly access 16 megabytes of memory and has hardly any restrictions as to dedicated memory space. Only the first 1024 bytes of memory have a special function, as described below. In accessing a single byte, the 68000 can use any address within its memory space. A word or long word can only be accessed at an even address. If an attempt is made to reference a word or long word at an odd-numbered location, an exception process, which will cause a jump through location $00000C in memory, will begin. When accessing a word, the lowest-addressed byte (i.e., at the even location) is placed into the most significant part of the register. The same is true for long words; this means that registers are stored and loaded bit for bit the way they appear in memory. This is unlike many 8-bit processors, which load word-length registers in byte-reversed order from their order in memory. Remember, higher order bytes of a register are stored in lower memory locations, but so are higher order words. Thus, a long word is stored in memory as shown in Fig. 3-5. A word is stored as shown in Fig. 3-6. Finally, a byte is stored as shown in Fig. 3-7. This is worth remembering when long words might need to be accessed byte by byte.

As previously mentioned, the first kilobyte of memory serves as a dedicated memory area. Figure 3-8 shows the layout. Not all of this area has been commandeered for the 68000's system use; locations 100-3FF are available as user vectors. The system vectors are split into two main parts: the *trap vectors* and the *interrupt auto-vectors*. Each exception vector is called by the hardware of the 68000 and allows the processor to deal with exceptions, such as the address error described above, which uses location $00000C. These exception vectors run from location $000008 to $00002F and allow for the detection and subsequent processing of the following exception conditions:

A bus error.

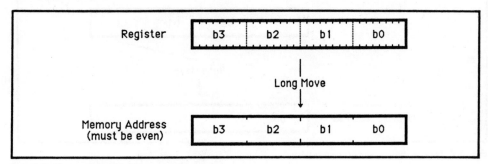

Fig. 3-5. How a long word is stored in memory.

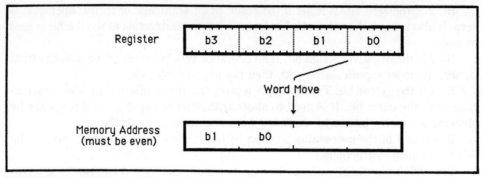

Fig. 3-6. How a word is stored in memory.

An address error.
An illegal instruction.
A divide by zero.
A CHK error.
An overflow.
A privileged instruction violation.
A trace after each instruction.

Two special traps are provided to allow for detection of opcodes beginning with bit patterns 1010 or 1111. This gives the facility of designing new opcodes that can be executed via these two trap vectors whenever the processor encounters any opcode starting with those bit patterns. Only four bits of the instruction word are required to cause one of these traps to occur, so the remaining 12 bits can be used at the discretion of the system programmer. These two opcode traps are often referred to as *A-traps* (for bits 1010) or *F-traps* (for bits 1111).

Locations $000060 to $00007F are provided to deal automatically with the eight possible levels of external interrupt. Locations $000080 to $0000BF are used by TRAP instructions by specifying a trap number from 0 to 15. The 68000 has two main ways of dealing with interrupts. Before taking a look at them, it will be helpful to see what happens when an external device demands the attention of the microprocessor. Three pins on the chip are assigned to the detection of interrupts. If a pulse appears on any of these pins, the 68000 might allow itself to be interrupted. This is dependent upon

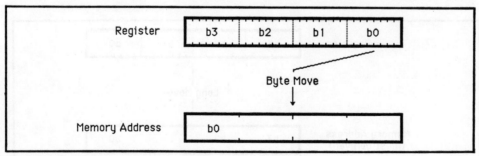

Fig. 3-7. How a byte is stored in memory.

Hex Address	Vector Number	Exception Type
0000	0	Reset: Initial System Stack Pointer
0004	1	Reset: Initial Program Counter
0008	2	Bus Error
000C	3	Address Error
0010	4	Illegal Instruction
0014	5	Division by Zero
0018	6	CHK Instruction
001C	7	TRAPV Instruction
0020	8	Privilege Violation
0024	9	Trace
0028	10	Unimplemented 1010 Opcode
002C	11	Unimplemented 1111 Opcode
0030	12	Unassigned (reserved for future use)
.	.	"
.	.	"
005C	23	"
0060	24	Spurious Interrupt
0064	25	Interrupt Auto-Vector Level 1
0068	26	Interrupt Auto-Vector Level 2
006C	27	Interrupt Auto-Vector Level 3
0070	28	Interrupt Auto-Vector Level 4
0074	29	Interrupt Auto-Vector Level 5
0078	30	Interrupt Auto-Vector Level 6
007C	31	Interrupt Auto-Vector Level 7
0080	32	TRAP # 0 Instruction
0084	33	TRAP # 1 Instruction
0088	34	TRAP # 2 Instruction
008C	35	TRAP # 3 Instruction
0090	36	TRAP # 4 Instruction
0094	37	TRAP # 5 Instruction
0098	38	TRAP # 6 Instruction
009C	39	TRAP # 7 Instruction
00A0	40	TRAP # 8 Instruction
00A4	41	TRAP # 9 Instruction
00A8	42	TRAP #10 Instruction
00AC	43	TRAP #11 Instruction
00B0	44	TRAP #12 Instruction
00B4	45	TRAP #13 Instruction
00B8	46	TRAP #14 Instruction
00BC	47	TRAP #15 Instruction
00C0	48	Unassigned (reserved for future use)
.	.	"
.	.	"
00FC	63	"
0100	64	User Exception Vectors
.	.	"
.	.	"
03FC	255	"

Fig. 3-8. The first kilobyte of memory.

the three interrupt mask bits in the system half of the status word. If all three bits are set, it will recognize any level of interrupt from the three interrupt pins. Otherwise, the processor will only recognize a level of interrupt at or above that reflected in the status register. This allows a clean and simple method of prioritizing maskable interrupts. A nonmaskable interrupt is always recognized and dealt with by the processor. (This happens if all three pins are pulsed at the same time.) No matter what the contents of the interrupt mask bits in the status register, such an interrupt will always cause the 68000 to honor the interrupt request.

The two ways that interrupts are dealt with when they occur are refreshingly simple. The first way is that the interrupting device can place a vector address (always 0 to 1K) on the address bus, causing the 68000 to jump through that address. The second method uses the interrupt auto-vectors at locations $000060 to $00007F. This can be requested by the interrupting device pulsing the VPA pin during the interrupt process.

Remember that the interrupt bits are set in the system byte of the status word, and this can only be done while in privileged mode. The whole point of having a status that allows or denies privileges is to prevent an undebugged program from causing a system crash. In a multi-user environment (for which the 68000 is well suited, due to its power) such a program only has to contain a STOP instruction to arrest the whole system—multiple users and all. By operating in user mode, such potentially dangerous instructions are not allowed to be executed. Instead, they are processed as an exception routine via those vectors in low memory. The operating system can then take steps to ignore the potential devastation and possibly issue a friendly warning message to the offending programmer. A master user will have a facility built into the operating system that allows access to the more sensitive opcodes.

On the Amiga, supervisor mode is reserved for traps, interrupts, and special system functions. Normal programs are expected to run in user mode. A machine-code program could break into supervisor mode by pointing a low-memory trap vector to one of its routines, and then triggering that particular trap. The routine pointed to would then take over in supervisor mode. This is not recommended unless you are writing advanced system software, because the whole instruction set of the 68000—sensitive opcodes and all—is at your disposal.

The trace mode of the 68000 is another of its strong points that is likely to leave other chip manufacturers looking on enviously. This single facility will, without exaggeration, save hundreds of thousands of dollars of program development time for developers of 68000 software. The trace mode works by causing an exception to occur at the end of each instruction if the trace mode bit is set in the status word. At that moment, the program counter and status word are saved on the stack, the trace mode is set off (to allow the exception to be processed without itself being traced) and the vector at location $000024 is entered. What happens from here on is the responsibility of the operating system, but it can be presumed that an entrance would be made into a debugging routine that would allow registers and/or memory to be examined or changed. Then the 68000 could single-step through a machine-code program with the debugger offering full control. If required, even though in trace mode, the program could continue unhindered (but slowed down a little) until a recognized breakpoint condition was recognized, causing the debugger to take over.

Notice that when the program counter and status word are saved during a trace or any other exception, they are saved on the stack. Where the stack is located in memory is completely arbitrary. Obviously it will have to be located somewhere safely away from any machine code, or else the many different kinds of items that are constantly saved on the stack will be saved all over the machine code. Naturally, this would cause a crash as soon as that portion of the program was executed. This is one reason why there are two stack pointers in the 68000. Only one is in use at one time, however, depending on whether the current operating mode is supervisor or user. Address register A7 is used as the stack pointer—one A7 is automatically used when in the privileged state and the other A7 comes into effect in the user mode. They are never available at the same time. There is no difference between the other seven address registers and the way that A7 is programmed or addressed. It's just that whatever value you place there becomes the stack pointer and will be assumed to point to a stack area, either by a machine-code instruction or by an incoming interrupt. The stack pointer is decremented and incremented automatically during a subroutine call, a return, or a TRAP instruction. The stack pointer always points to the next word to be used and works from high to low memory. It always saves to a word boundary and must contain an even address.

The program counter, being two words (32 bits) long, always requires four bytes if saved on the stack. This is true even though the top eight bits are not used. These bits may be used in the future, though. There are reports that Motorola might increase the address space available to the 68000. This could mean the possibility of addressing the whole potential 4 billion bytes or 2 billion words. In the meantime, though, the current generation of 68000 microprocessors don't use the upper eight bits of the program counter. So, if you copied the program counter from the stack into any 32 bit register, the upper eight bits could be used as private flags within your own software or to delineate sections of memory or whatever. If you elect to do this, remember that if Motorola does use those upper eight bits for addressing memory, your program will not work on such a machine without modification. In the meantime, until such an eventuality occurs, all Amiga owners can program these bits at their leisure.

The same cannot be said about the status register. The unused bits in both system and user bytes of this register will always be read as zero no matter what you try to store there by pulling a value from the stack. The user byte of the status register contains the usual flag bits, which will be familiar to anyone with previous machine-code experience. One point worth reiterating is that the condition codes are unaffected by any operation on the address registers. Only operations on the eight data registers will have any effect on the flags in the status register.

The 68000 has been designed to be interfaced with various peripherals in the 8-bit Motorola 68000 family. These peripherals have been tried and tested over the years since the introduction of the 6800 in 1974. Three pins on the chip: E, VPA, and VMA, are used to allow the 68000 to appear like a 6800 to various peripheral chips such as the 6821 peripheral interface adapter (PIA). Therefore, the 68000 has no problem talking to the outside world. Note that the 68000 has no instructions dedicated to input or output. All input or output is achieved through *memory mapping,* whereby the peripheral is connected to the address bus. The peripheral is then addressed and looks to the 68000 just as if it were a memory location.

The pinout of the 68000 is illustrated in Fig. 3-9. This information will only be of

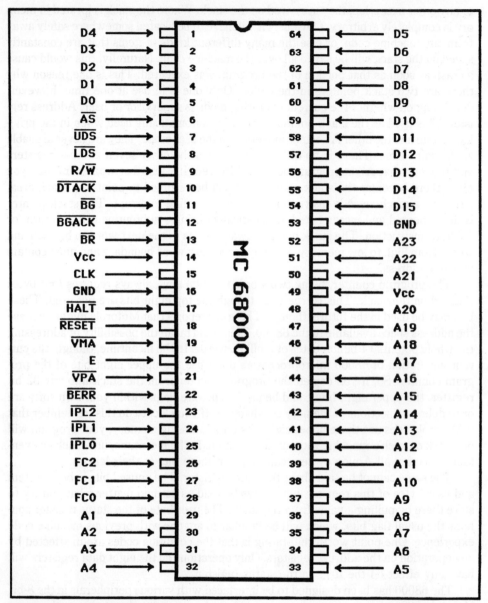

Fig. 3-9. The pinout of the 68000.

interest to those assembly-language programmers who want an idea of how the 68000 interfaces to the outside world at the hardware level. Here is a quick rundown of the 68000's 64 pins:

D0-15—the data bus. These are the 16 bits that are written and read as data words and read as program instruction words. This bus is used as both output and input to the processor.

A0-23—the address bus. This carries the address during both data and instruction accesses and is an output only from the chip. This bus is only used as an output from the 68000.

AS—Address Strobe. This lets memory or external devices know when a valid address exists on the address bus. It is an output signal.

R/W—Read/Write. This lets memory or external devices know when and in which direction data is expected. It is an output signal.

UDS—Upper Data Strobe. See LDS. This is an output signal.

LDS—Lower Data Strobe. UDS and LDS determine which 8-bit half of the data bus is being used. Both signals will be active during a word transfer (16 bits). This is an output signal.

DTACK—Data Transfer Acknowledge. This is an input to the 68000 to let it know that memory has read or written the data. Slow devices can thus hold the processor back until they have completed their data transfer. The 68000 automatically waits for this signal after every read or write. This is an input signal.

IPL0, IPL1, IPL2—Interrupt Inputs. These determine which level of interrupt is being requested. Theses are inputs to the 68000.

FC0, FC1, FC2—Function Code Outputs. These determine which kind of bus access is currently taking place. By external decoding, these outputs can be used to page memory in up to four banks. Thus, a 16 megabyte 68000 could be made to address 64 megabytes of memory. These are output signals.

BERR—Bus Error Input. This is used when an external device hasn't set the DTACK signal within a certain time limit. Circuitry external to the 68000 will determine what this time limit should be and then signal the BERR input if a time-out has occurred. This is an input signal.

HALT—As an input, it stops the 68000. As an output, it indicates that the processor has stopped due to a fault on the address bus. This is used both as an input and output signal.

RESET—This outputs a signal after a RESET instruction that can be used to reset external devices without resetting the 68000. As an input, it can optionally accompany the HALT input to provide a power-on reset. This is used both as an input and output signal.

CLK—Clock. This is the square wave train of pulses that drives the 68000 and determines its speed. It is an input.

BR—Bus Request. See BGACK. This is an input to the 68000.

BG—Bus Grant. See BGACK. This is an output from the 68000.

BGACK—Bus Grant Acknowledge. These three allow external devices that require direct memory access (DMA) to take control of the address and data buses from the processor. They are inputs to the processor.

E—Enable. See VMA.

VPA—Valid Peripheral Address. See VMA.

VMA—Valid Memory Address. These three signals allow for hardware interfacing between the 68000 and peripherals that were originally designed for use with the 8-bit 6800 microprocessor family.

Chapter

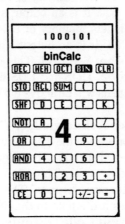

1000101

binCalc

DEC HEX OCT BIN CLR
STO RCL SUM
SHF D E F K
NOT A C /
OR 7 9 *
AND 4 5 6 -
HOR 1 2 3 +
CE 0 . +/- =

4

The 68000
Addressing Modes

The 68000 offers the assembly-language programmer over 300 different opcode combinations. There is no need to panic, however; of this 300 plus, only 56 separate opcode mnemonics are required, in combination with various addressing modes, to allow full access to the repertoire of the 68000. These mnemonics are listed in Fig. 4-1. It will be beneficial to take a close look at some of these opcodes to see what they can accomplish in a program. Before doing that, it's worth pointing out that Motorola has intentionally kept down the number of mnemonics specifically to help the assembly-language programmer. To remember all 56 mnemonics would be difficult enough—300 would be asking too much. In fact, even of the 56, only between 20 to 30 are likely to be used on a regular basis. The most common one you'll use, without a doubt, is the MOVE instruction.

MOVE is intended to be an all-encompassing opcode to be used when any kind of data needs to be transferred from one place to another within the computer. It doesn't matter if it's a transfer from register to register, memory to memory, or any combination of these. MOVE, in its various forms, will perform any data transfers on the 68000. Before looking at a few examples, note that the MOVE instruction, as well as many other opcodes, needs to know not only the source and destination of a data transfer, but also the data length involved. Bear in mind that the 68000 can deal with data in lengths of 8, 16, or 32 bits, referred to as bytes, words, and long words respectively. When writing an assembly language program, it's necessary to let the assembler know which length you intend your opcode to use. This is done by appending a letter to the opcode mnemonic. A period delimits this length from the opcode name. Thus, MOVE can exist in several variants, such as MOVE.B for move byte, MOVE.W for move word,

Mnemonic	Description
ABCD	Add Binary Coded Decimal
ADD	Add
AND	Logical AND
ASL	Arithmetic Shift Left
ASR	Arithmetic Shift Right
Bcc	Branch on condition
BCHG	Bit test and Change
BCLR	Bit test and Clear
BRA	Branch
BSET	Bit test and Set
BSR	Branch to Subroutine
BTST	Bit Test
CHK	Check against bounds
CLR	Clear
CMP	Compare
DBcc	Decrement and Branch Conditionally
DIVS	Divide (Signed)
DIVU	Divide (Unsigned)
EOR	Exclusive OR
EXG	Exchange registers
EXT	Extend sign
JMP	Jump
JSR	Jump to subroutine
LEA	Load effective address
LINK	Link subroutine
LSL	Logical Shift Left
LSR	Logical Shift Right
MOVE	Move data
MOVEM	Move Multiple
MOVEP	Move to peripheral
MULS	Multiply (Signed)
MULU	Multiply (Unsigned)
NBCD	Negate Binary Coded Decimal
NEG	Negate
NOP	No Operation
NOT	Logical complement
OR	Logical OR
PEA	Push Effective Address
RESET	Reset
ROL	Rotate Left
ROR	Rotate Right
ROXL	Rotate Left through Extend
ROXR	Rotate Right through Extend
RTE	Return from Exception
RTS	Return from subroutine
RTR	Return and Restore
SBCD	Subtract Binary Coded Decimal
Scc	Set conditionally
STOP	Stop
SUB	Subtract
SWAP	Swap data register halves
TAS	Test bit and Set
TRAP	Trap exception
TRAPV	Trap if overflow
TST	Test data
UNLK	Unlink subroutine

Fig. 4-1. The 68000 instruction set.

and MOVE.L for move long word. This is one of the reasons why those 56 mnemonics expand to over 300.

If you leave out the .B, .W, or .L suffix, the assembler will assume a default of .W, or a word-length operation, as the norm. Be careful, though—leaving off the suffix makes it less obvious what you mean in a program. By placing the qualifier after every opcode, not only is your meaning absolutely obvious, but it's an extra step towards a well-documented program.

The layout of the MOVE opcode is simple. In the operand portion of the opcode, you just specify a source and a destination separated by a comma. For instance, to transfer a byte from data register 0 to data register 1, you'd use:

```
MOVE.B    D0,D1
```

This reads exactly as it performs—"move byte data register zero to data register one." Note that this is a byte-transfer operation; only bits 0 to 7 of data register 1 will be affected. Bytes 8 to 31 are left unaltered. Similarly, the instruction:

```
MOVE.W    A1,A2
```

or, if you insist on leaving out the suffix:

```
MOVE      A1,A2
```

will move a word from bits 0 to 15 of address register 1 to address register 2 without affecting bits 16 to 31. Note that you can't move byte lengths when using address registers. A long word of 32 bits is manipulated with MOVE.L as in:

```
MOVE.L    A6,D0
```

which would move the entire 32 bits of address register six to data register zero.

Before you delve any further into the numerous variations of the MOVE instruction, along with the rest of the instruction set, you need to know about the addressing modes of the 68000. To fully understand what the opcodes are doing, you need to know what they are doing it to. The address mode of an opcode is what specifies this.

There are 14 addressing modes available on the 68000, but this should be no more confusing than those 300 plus opcodes. The 14 modes are in six groups, and of these, only two are used to address memory that is likely to contain data of relevance to your program. These are the six groups as they'll be described in this chapter:

Register direct
Immediate
Absolute
Address register indirect
Program counter relative
Implied

Of these, all except implied addressing have variations that account for the 14 modes in total. Wherever possible, the addressing modes are illustrated using MOVE opcodes.

REGISTER-DIRECT ADDRESSING

You've already seen register-direct addressing in the examples of the MOVE instructions given so far. As its name implies, any instruction that's performed using register-direct addressing addresses data directly in one of the registers. Any of the 16 data or address registers may be addressed in this mode (D0 to D7 and A0 to A7—these are generally referred to as Dn or An, where n is the register number). Remember that it's illegal to address any address register with a byte-length operand (those with suffix .B). An example of register-direct addressing is:

```
MOVE.W    A0,D0
```

IMMEDIATE ADDRESSING

The immediate addressing mode uses a value within the immediate opcode as the source operand. In other words, the machine code for the instruction will include a constant that is to be used in the actual operation. An immediate operand is specified by prefacing it with the # sign. To load data register 1 with a byte value of 100, you'd write:

```
MOVE.B    #100,D1
```

There is a variant of immediate addressing called *quick immediate*. This allows a smaller constant to be loaded more quickly than in the normal immediate mode. Also, quick immediate addressing allows this small value to be stored within the opcode itself, rather than in the bytes immediately afterwards. Thus, space is saved as well as time. The format of this variant is:

```
MOVEQ     #5,D2
```

This would load the number 5 into data register 2. The value is always taken to be a word length (by extending it), and is limited to the range one to eight.

ABSOLUTE ADDRESSING

The absolute addressing mode occurs in two forms: absolute short and absolute long. As its name implies, absolute addressing allows memory to be accessed at an absolute (or fixed) location. Because the memory space of the 68000 is 16 megabytes and requires 24 bits to address it, the 16-bit word version of this mode is sign-extended by carrying bit 15 of the operand into bits 16 to 31. Thus, the absolute short version can only be used to access the first 32 kilobytes or the last 32 kilobytes of memory. If you wanted to load the 32-bit value stored in location FFFF00, you could use either the long or the short form. The absolute long version would look something like:

```
MOVE.L    $FFFF00,A1
```

The assembler itself will choose which form to use. Normally, it tries to use the absolute short form, but you can specifically tell it to use absolute long addressing by using a pseudo-op in the source code prior to the relevant opcode. ORG.L tells the assembler to use absolute long form in any absolute memory references, whereas ORG tells it to try to use absolute short addressing if the operand is within the 32K at each end of memory (as in the above example).

ADDRESS-REGISTER INDIRECT ADDRESSING

The address register indirect addressing mode is the most powerful of the addressing modes available on the 68000 and includes five variants:

Register indirect
Register indirect with postincrement
Register indirect with predecrement
Register indirect with displacement
Register indirect with displacement and index

Each of these modes can be used to specify either the source or destination operand. All register indirect modes can only be used with address registers specifying the indirect address; data registers cannot be used for this purpose. If address register A7 is used, take care to leave its value as an even number at all times. Its use as a system stack pointer requires this to be so. Failure to observe this will cause a bus error to occur.

The Register Indirect Addressing Mode. The register indirect addressing mode uses whichever address register you want as a pointer to the memory location in question. If A5 contained 1000, the instruction:

```
MOVE.L    (A5),D0
```

would transfer 32 bits from memory location 1000 into data register 0. Notice that this would actually access bytes 1000, 1001, 1002, and 1003. This is the plain and simplest version of register-direct—using an address register to indirectly point to a memory location. The syntax of any address using register indirect is **(An)** where An is A0 to A7.

The Register Indirect with Postincrement Addressing Mode. This is only one step further than regular register indirect. Once again, an address register is used to point at a location in memory; however, as soon as the data at that location has been accessed, the address register being used will be incremented to point at the following item of data. This address register will have either a one, two, or four added to its previous contents. The actual amount of increment is decided by the type of data accessed before the increment is done. Accessing a byte adds one, accessing a word adds two, and accessing a long word adds four to the register. This is where A7—the stack pointer—once again behaves differently from the other registers. Because it must always contain an even value, it is never incremented by one after a postincrement. If a byte is accessed using both the stack pointer and postincrement addressing, A7 will be incremented by two rather than one in order to keep it an even number. A typical syntax for address register indirect with postincrement is:

```
MOVE.W    D4,(A3)+
```

which would move a word from data register 4 to wherever address register 3 was pointing to, followed by an addition of two to address register 3. Remember that the incrementing is done after the memory access, just as the word *postincrement* implies. To move a byte from one list to another, you could use two address registers, as in:

```
MOVE.B    (A1)+,(A2)+
```

which would copy the byte pointed to by A1 to the location pointed at by A2 and then add one to both registers.

The form is **(An)+** where An is A0 to A7.

The Register Indirect with Predecrement Addressing Mode. This acts just like postincrement except that the specified address register is decremented by the appropriate amount and it's done before the memory access is made. If you wanted to move a long word, the pointing address register should be four more than the address required. Similarly, a predecrement access of a 16-bit word would require an excess of two to be added, and a single byte, an excess of one. This addressing mode allows you to access lists of data that are aligned downwards in memory, like the stack. Once again, bear in mind that A7 will never be decremented by one; a byte access will decrement the stack pointer by two. An example is:

```
MOVE.W    #0,-(A7)
```

which would push a word of zero to the stack (pointed at by A7) leaving the stack pointer pointing at it.

The syntax is **−(An)** where n is 0 to 7.

The Register Indirect with Displacement Addressing Mode. This addressing mode lets you specify a displacement to be added to the address register before using it as an indirect pointer. The displacement is a 16-bit value that is sign-extended. Thus, the displacement can be any value between 32,767 and −32,768. The displacement word appears in the machine code immediately after the opcode word, so this form of addressing requires four bytes. An example is:

```
MOVE    D3,100(A2)
```

which would transfer a word from bits 0 to 15 of D3 into the memory location plus 100 pointed at by A2. This mode is useful when the address register contains a base address of an ordered area of data. By specifying displacements, any data within this ordered area can be easily accessed. Then if a different base address is loaded into the address register, once more the same ordered data can be accessed without changing the code to do it. Just changing the address register allows this access to a new data area.

The syntax of this addressing mode is **d(An)** where d is the displacement, and An is A0 to A7.

The Register Indirect with Displacement and Index Addressing. This is similar to register indirect with displacement, except that a displacement of only eight bits is allowed, and an additional register can be specified; this register is added to the address register and displacement before the final address is arrived at. This is the most powerful addressing mode of the 68000, because a single address is being computed from three separate elements: the address register, a displacement of -128 to 127, and an index register. The index register can be any of the 16 data and address registers. Normally, a sign-extended word is used from the index register, but adding the .L suffix to the index register forces the use of all 32 bits. A suffix of .W forces the default of 16 bits with sign-extension to be used. Using the appropriate suffix in all cases clears up any ambiguity and is preferred.

Register indirect with displacement and index allows for easy access of data within tables. In most cases, the displacement will be zero if you're accessing a simple sequential list of numbers. By specifying the table address in the address register, you can use the index register to provide an offset within the table. You can change to another table just by changing the address register. Because the index register is treated as a signed number, the index can be anywhere within the range $-32,768$ to $+32,767$ for a 16-bit index, or $-2,147,483,648$ to $+2,147,483,647$ for a 32-bit index. The index is treated no differently from the displacement; it is simply added to the address register before computation of the final address. Apart from their possible magnitudes, the only difference between the displacement and the index is that the displacement remains constant while the index can be altered by manipulation of the index register. Assuming 1000 in A1 and 100 in D2 the following example:

```
MOVE.W    D0,0(A1,D2.L)
```

would place the word from D0 into 1100 (0 + 1000 + 100). The statement:

```
MOVE.B    D0,-10(A1,D2.L)
```

would place the byte from D0 into 1090 ($-10 + 1000 + 100$).

Now assume -8 (hexadecimal FFF8) in bits 0 to 16 of D2. The following line:

```
MOVE.L    D0,20(A1,D2.W)
```

would place the long word from D0 into 1012 (20 + 1000 − 8).

The syntax for the address is **d(An,Ri.l)** where d is a displacement of -128 to $+127$, An is A0 to A7, Ri is D0 to D7 or A0 to A7, and l is .L for a long index or .W for a sign-extended word-length index. Leaving out .L or .W from the index register sets the assembler default to .W. The index and displacement are contained in a 16-bit word immediately following the opcode word. The most significant byte of this word (i.e., the byte immediately after the opcode) contains the index information. The least significant byte following the index byte is the 8-bit signed displacement.

PROGRAM-COUNTER RELATIVE ADDRESSING

The program counter relative addressing mode uses the program counter rather than an address register as the base from which to calculate an address. Whenever you specify any address in your program, the assembler will default to this addressing mode. Thus, program counter relative addressing will be used whenever possible for program control with jump (JMP) opcodes. It's therefore possible to use an instruction like JMP LOCN and expect to generate a relative address that will cause the jump to be a constant distance from the current opcode address, rather than to an absolute address. The same is also true of the MOVE opcode, as you'll see in the example that follows.

Program counter relative has two possible forms: one allows for a displacement and the other allows a displacement and an index. Both forms use the word following the opcode word in the same manner as address register indirect with displacement and optional index. The first form is displacement only. The 16-bit sign-extended word following the opcode is added to the program counter to form the effective address. The value of the program counter is the location of the word following the opcode, i.e., the extension word. An example is:

```
MOVE.B      DATA,D0
```

As long as memory location DATA is within the possible displacement area, the assembler will generate the proper program counter relative code—otherwise it will be absolute. The assembler being used will always first attempt to use program counter relative addressing if at all possible. By avoiding absolute addresses in this way, both program control instructions (such as jumps) and data transfer instructions (with the MOVE opcode) will remain independent of their physical location in memory. In this way, the 68000 provides the programmer with a transparent way to write position-independent code that can be executed anywhere in memory without being altered.

The second form of program counter relative addressing provides even more power by allowing an index to be used as well as a displacement. Any of the 16 registers can be elected to act as the index register containing either a sign-extended 16-bit index or a long index word of 32 bits. The displacement in the latter case is one byte in length and can contain a value between -128 to $+127$. This mode is excellent for implementing jump tables in which each jump in the table contains an equal number of bytes. The displacement would be used to point to the start of the jump table (within 128 bytes). Then the address register would be multiplied by the length of each jump in the table— this would be two, four, or six bytes according to the addressing mode of the jumps (address register indirect, short absolute, or long absolute). At this point you would be pointing at the indexed jump in the table at the displacement address. The jump in the jump table can then direct control to the appropriate address.

The syntax is d(An,Ri.l) where d is -128 to $+127$, An is A0 to A7, Ri is D0 to D7 or A0 to A7, and l is .L or .W and is taken to be .W if missing.

IMPLIED ADDRESSING

In implied addressing the 68000 uses a register whose use is implied in the execution of a particular opcode. It is not an addressing mode that can be invoked optionally as can all the others. For instance, a return from a subroutine always takes the return address using the stack pointer, A7. The only registers that are used implicitly in this way are the status register (SR), the stack pointer (A7), and the program counter (PC).

Chapter

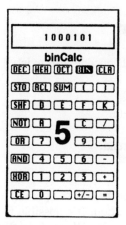

1000101

binCalc

DEC HEH OCT BIN CLR

STO RCL SUM ⬚ ⬚

SHF D E F K

NOT A **5** C /

OR 7 9 *

AND 4 5 6 –

HOR 1 2 3 +

CE 0 . +/– =

The 68000 Instruction Set

ABCD   Add Binary Coded Decimal

This is a specialized arithmetic instruction that adds together two bytes (and only bytes) containing binary-coded decimal numbers. (Each byte of BCD data contains two BCD digits.)

The addition can either be done between two data registers or between two memory locations. If performed on bytes in memory, only address register indirect with predecrement addressing can be used. This facilitates easy manipulation of multiple-precision BCD numbers. The extend bit is added along with the BCD bytes to allow this multiprecision data manipulation. Also note that the Zero flag is only changed if the result becomes non-zero.

Therefore, both the Extend and Zero bits in the condition code register should be present before the operation is performed. The Extend bit would normally be preset to a zero (to prevent extension on the first addition), and the Zero bit to a one (to preset a zero result prior to the first addition). A **MOVE #4,CCR** would setup these flags correctly.

Syntax: ABCD Dn , Dn
or   ABCD   –(An) , –(An)

where **Dn** is D0 to D7.
      An is A0 to A7.

Flags affected: The Extend, Zero, and Carry flags are affected as per the result of the operation. The state of the negative and overflow flags is undefined.
Instruction length: 2 bytes.

ADD   Add Binary

Four variants of the ADD opcode also exist:

ADDA   Add Address.
ADDI   Add Immediate.
ADDQ   Add Quick.
ADDX   Add with Extend.

These are described later.

The ADD instruction adds the source operand to the destination operand with the result appearing in the destination. It's possible to add bytes, words, or long words with this opcode by appending .B, .W, or .L to the mnemonic. Either the source or destination (or both) must be a data register. The source operand can be any memory location or data register, and the destination operand can also be any memory location or data register.

Syntax: ADD   Dn , Dn
or   ADD   address , Dn
or   ADD   Dn , address

Flags affected: The Extend, Negative, Zero, Overflow, and Carry flags are all affected as per the result of the addition.
Instruction length: 2, 4, or 6 bytes.

ADDA   Add Address

This variant of the ADD instruction only differs from ADD in that an address register is specified as the destination. As an address rather than data is being manipulated, the condition code flags are left unaltered. Only sign—extended words or long words can be added.

ADDI   Add Immediate

This variant of the ADD instruction is used to add a constant value to the destination. The immediate operand can be any 8-, 16-, or 32-bit value as specified by the .B, .W, or .L opcode suffix. The destination cannot be an address register or a program counter relative address.

Syntax: ADDI   #imm , Dn
or   ADDI   #imm , address

where **#imm** is an immediate value up to two to the power of 32.
      Dn is D0 to D7.
      address is any memory addressing mode except program counter relative.

Flags affected: The Extend, Negative, Zero, Overflow, and Carry flags are all set as per the result of the addition.
Instruction length: 4, 6, 8, or 10 bytes.

ADDQ   Add Quick

    This variant of the ADD instruction is used to add a small positive integer between one and eight to the destination. The destination can be a memory location, a data register, or an address register. If it is an address register, the condition code flags are unaffected and the operand length cannot be a byte.

    This operation takes the place of the increment instruction found on other processors.

Syntax: ADDQ   #imm , register
or   ADDQ   #imm , address

where **#imm** is an immediate value of 1 to 8.
      register is D0 to D7 and A0 to A7.
      address is any memory address mode.

Flags affected: The Extend, Negative, Zero, Overflow and Carry flags are all set as per the result of the addition unless the destination is an address register.

ADDX   Add Extended

    This variant of the ADD instruction adds two numbers plus the Extend bit from the condition code register. This allows multiple-precision additions to be performed. For this reason, the Zero flag is only affected when a nonzero result is obtained. This means that if multiple numbers are added together using ADDX, the Zero flag will stay reset if any of those numbers were nonzero.

Syntax: ADDX Dn , Dn
or   ADDX   –(An) , –(An)

where **Dn** is D0 to D7.
      An is A0 to A7.

Instruction length: 2 bytes.

AND   Logical And

The Logical And opcode also has one variant: ANDI — And Immediate.

This instruction logically ANDs bits in the source operand with the same number of bits in the destination operand where the result is left. The number of bits can be 8, 16, or 32 as per the .B, .W, or .L opcode suffix. One or both operands must be a data register.

Syntax: AND   Dn , Dn
                   AND   Dn , memory
                   AND   memory , Dn

ANDI   Logical AND Immediate

This instruction logically ANDs an immediate byte, word, or long word value with the destination. The destination address can be a data register, memory, or one of two special cases: the condition code register or the status register. If the destination is the condition code register, only a byte-length immediate value is allowed. If the destination is the status register, only a word-length immediate value is allowed, and the processor must be in supervisor mode or a privilege violation will occur.

Syntax: ANDI   imm# , Dn or memory
or   ANDI   immediate 8-bit # , CCR
or   ANDI   immediate 16-bit # , SR (privileged).

where **Dn** is D0 to D7.

Flags affected: The Overflow and Carry bits are reset, the Sign and Zero bits set as per result, and The Extend bit unaffected.
Instruction length: 2 to 10 bytes.

ASL   Arithmetic Shift Left

This instruction shifts the destination operand left by a specified number of bits. If you are shifting a data register, the number of bits to be shifted can be specified as an immediate value or as a value in another data register. The immediate value can be 1 to 8, whereas the data register value can be 1 to 64 (where zero acts as the 64 count). Data registers may be shifted as 8, 16, or 32 bit quantities. Only 16-bit word values can be shifted in memory and then only by one bit. As shown below zeroes are shifted in at the right hand side of the operand. As each bit is shifted out of the left of an operand, it is placed in the Carry and Extend bits in the condition code register. If the sign of the operand changes during the shift, the overflow bit is set in the condition code register.

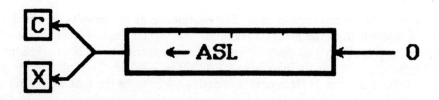

Syntax:
      ASL Dn , Dn
      ASL imm 3-bit value , Dn
      ASL memory   (1 bit only)

where **Dn** is D0 to D7.

Instruction length: 2, 4, or 6 bytes.

ASR Arithmetic Shift Right

This instruction shifts the destination operand right by a specified number of bits. If you are shifting a data register, the number of bits can be specified as an immediate value or as a value in another data register. The immediate value can specify a shift of 1 to 8, while the data register can specify a shift of 1 to 64 (where zero acts as the 64 count). Data registers may be shifted as 8, 16, or 32-bit quantities. Only 16-bit word values can be shifted in memory and then only by one bit. Each bit shifted out of the right hand side of an operand is placed in the carry and extend bits in the condition code register. As shown below the bit shifted in at the left hand side is the current sign bit (the most significant bit is therefore preserved throughout the shift).

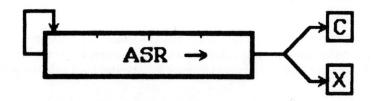

Syntax:
      ASR Dn , Dn
      ASR imm 3-bit value , Dn
      ASR memory   (1 bit only)

where **Dn** is D0 to D7.

Instruction length: 2, 4, or 6 bytes.

BRA Branch Always

This instruction changes the program counter register so execution continues at a different point in the program code. The destination of the jump is specified as a signed displacement to the program counter. This signed displacement can be an 8 or 16-bit quantity. With 8-bit quantities, this allows branches of +126 to −128 bytes; 16 bit quantities can specify branches of +32766 to −32768. The value of the program counter when the displacement is added is taken to be the first word after the BRA opcode. This is the actual opcode address plus two. Normally an assembler will assume a 16-bit quantity as the displacement, but if an opcode suffix of .S is appended to the BRA, a short 8-bit displacement will be used instead.

Other variants of the BRA instruction allow a branch to be made only if a certain condition is met in the condition code register. Here are the conditional branches and the conditions required for the branch to occur:

BEQ	branch if equal to
BNE	branch if not equal to
BMI	branch if minus
BCS	branch if carry set
BCC	branch if carry clear
BVS	branch if overflow set
BVC	branch if overflow clear
BHI	branch if higher
BLS	branch if lower or same
BHS	branch if higher or same
BLO	branch if lower
BGT	branch if greater than
BGE	branch if greater than or equal to
BLE	branch if less than or equal
BLT	branch if less than

The branch displacement is normally specified as a label within the program causing the assembler to automatically calculate the displacement required. However, an absolute displacement from the program counter may be specified as in the instruction

BRA   *+8

(which means branch to this location plus eight).

Flags affected: none.

BSR   Branch to Subroutine

This instruction causes control to be passed unconditionally to the specified program counter displacement as in the BRA opcode. However, before the branch is made, the address of the opcode following the BSR is saved on the stack so a return can later be made to that address to continue processing at that point. This is achieved as follows:

1. The 24-bit address following the opcode is stored as two words (highest word first) at the location pointed to by A7, the stack pointer.
2. The stack pointer is decremented by four to protect the two-word address on the stack.
3. The program counter is loaded with its new value and processing continues at the new address. Figure 5-1 shows the steps for a BSR.S *+100. (Note the .S causes the assembler to generate code for the short branch opcode of one word in length.)

BCHG   BCLR   BSET   BTST

These instructions allow the manipulation and testing of single bits. The bits are numbered from the right to the left starting with bit number zero. Thus a byte contains bits 0 to 7; a word, bits 0 to 15; and a long word, bits 0 to 31. The number of the bit to be tested is specified either in a data register or as an immediate value. The value of the bit is reflected in the Zero flag of the condition code register. This means that if the bit tested was a zero, the Zero flag will be set ($Z = 1$). Therefore the Zero flag is always the opposite of the bit being tested. Once the test is made and the Zero flag set up, then the tested bit is manipulated as follows:

BCHG   the bit is reversed.
BCLR   the bit is cleared to zero.
BSET   the bit is set to a one.
BTST   the bit is unchanged.

Syntax: BTST Dn , address
or   BTST   #imm , address

where **Dn** is D0 to D7.

Flags affected: Zero flag only.
Instruction length: 2, 4, 6, or 8 bytes.

CHK   Check Against Bounds

This instruction checks its first operand against a data register's word contents (that is, bits 0 to 15). If the data register contains less than zero or greater than its first operand, a trap occurs. The trap causes control to be passed to location 24 in memory (vector 6, hexadecimal address 18). Thus, CHK can be used to ensure that an element of an array is neither below nor above its boundaries.

Syntax: CHK   bounds , Dn

where **bounds** is anything except an address register.
       Dn is D0 to D7.

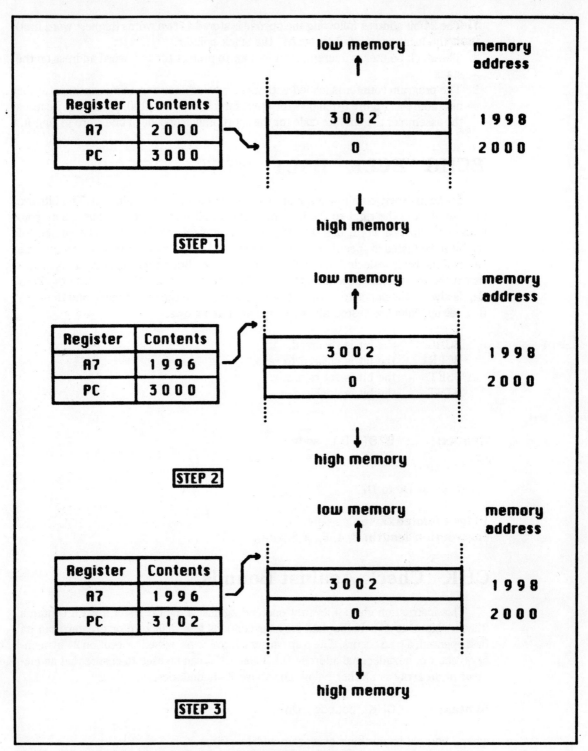

Fig. 5-1. The steps taken when a BSR.S ∗ +100 instruction is performed.

Flags affected: All flags are undefined after this operation.
Instruction length: 2 or 4 bytes.

CLR   Clear Destination to Zero

This instruction allows a byte, a word, or a long word to be cleared to zero according to the operand suffix .B, .W, or .L. The destination can be either a data register or memory. Address registers cannot be cleared with the CLR instruction (Use MOVE.L #0,An).

Syntax: CLR   Dn
or   CLR   address.

where Dn is D0 to D7.

Flags affected: Negative, Overflow, and Carry are all set to zero, the Zero flag is set to one, and the Extend flag is unaffected.
Instruction length: 2, 4, or 6 bytes.

CMP   Compare

Three other variations of the compare instruction exist:

CMPA   compare address.
CMPI   compare immediate.
CMPM   compare memory.

This instruction compares two operands and sets flags in the condition code register according to the result. Except for the Extend flag, the flags are set as if the source operand were subtracted from the destination. However, the result of this subtraction is not actually retained so the destination remains unchanged. The information about the comparison that is stored in the condition flags can then be acted upon by a conditional branch instruction. CMP may be used with byte, word, or long word source operands. Note that although any addressing mode can be used to specify the source operand, an address register can only be used if a word or long word comparison is performed.

Syntax: CMP   address , Dn

where Dn is D0 to D7.

CMPA   Compare Address

This variation of the CMP instruction is used to compare a source operand with an address register as destination operand. Only word or long word compares are allowed with CMPA. If a word is used as source, it is sign-extended to 32 bits before the comparison is made.

Syntax: CMPA   address , An

where **address** is any addressing mode.
       An is A0 to A7.

Flags affected: Same as CMP instruction.

CMPI   Compare Immediate

This variation of the CMP instruction is used to compare a source operand consisting of an immediate value with either a data register or memory. The comparison length can be byte, word, or long word as specified by the .B, .W, or .L opcode suffix.

Syntax: CMPI   #imm , Dn
or   CMPI   #imm , memory

where **Dn** is D0 to D7.

Instruction length: 2, 4, 6, 8, or 10 bytes.

CMPM   Compare Memory

This variation of the CMP opcode is used to compare sequential memory locations. These locations can be of type byte, word, or long word as specified by the .B, .W, or .L opcode suffix. To perform the sequencing automatically through memory, both source and destination operands must be specified using address register indirect with postincrement. Thus, after the compare is made, the address registers of both source and destination operands will have been incremented by the length of data compared.

Syntax: CMPM   (An)+ , (An)+

Flags affected: Same as the CMP opcode.
Instruction length: 2 bytes.

DBRA   Decrement and Branch

This instruction is used to control the program counter register in much the same way as BRA instruction is except that this allows greater power and versatility. By using DBRA, a specified data register is decremented and the branch made only if that register goes past zero. Thus, the count from a positive number will count down until zero and branch one more time. This allows loops where an index of zero is the last element. Note that as a result of this, the value left in the register will be −1 when an exit is made at the end of the loop. As an example, if eight locations were to be accessed, the data register specified in the DBRA instruction would be loaded with seven. The countdown, including the final zero, would go through eight cycles.

The program counter register is modified as in the BRA instruction whereby a sign-extended 16-bit displacement is added to the program counter. No short 8 bit form is available. Only bits 0 to 15 (that is, one word) of the data register is used. The destination of the branch is usually supplied as a label from which the assembler automatically calculates the displacement needed to branch to that label.

Syntax: DBRA   Dn , label

where **label** is a labeled opcode in the source code.

DBcc   Decrement and Branch Conditionally

This is a whole series of instructions that resemble the conditional versions of the BRA opcode. Conditional decrement and branch instructions work in a similar manner to the DBRA instruction except that one step is added to the execution process.

Before the decrement is performed as in DBRA, the condition specified in the mnemonic is tested (in the opposite order to that suggested by the opcode name). If the condition is true, control drops through to the next instruction—the branch is not made. This is opposite to the normal branch instructions where the conditional branch is made if the condition is true. Thus this mnemonic might more accurately be read as "decrement and branch unless condition".

Powerful loops can be constructed using the decrement and branch conditional instruction; an exit can be made from the loop either if the data register passes zero or if a pretested condition is met. The following list displays the conditions available for testing before the decrement and possible branch are made. This list is similar to that for the BRA opcode with the addition of the F (false) and T (true) conditions, which specify an always false or always true precondition. Therefore a DBF (decrement, branch false) is always false, so it will never drop through to the following opcode. Thus, the branch after the decrement will always be performed. Conversely, a DBT (decrement, branch true) is always true, so it will always drop through and never perform the decrement. (This would only be likely to be of use during program development.)

DBEQ   decrement, branch equal.
DBF   decrement, branch false. (Same as DBRA.)
DBGE   decrement, branch greater than or equal.
DBGT   decrement, branch greater than.
DBHI   decrement, branch higher.
DBLE   decrement, branch less than or equal.
DBLS   decrement, branch less than or same.
DBLT   decrement, branch less than.

DBMI	decrement, branch minus.
DBNE	decrement, branch not equal.
DBPL	decrement, branch plus.
DBRA	decrement, branch unconditionally.
DBT	decrement, branch true. (Branch never taken.)

Syntax: DBcc Dn , label

where cc is one of the above conditions.

Dn = D0 to D7.

label is a label within −32766 and +32768 bytes of the program counter.

DIVS   Divide Signed
DIVU   Divide Unsigned

These instructions allow a 16-bit divisor to be used as a source and a 32-bit destination to be specified as dividend in a divide operation. DIVS assumes both numbers are signed, whereas DIVU assumes both to be unsigned. The destination must be a data register. The source can be a memory location or another data register. The result is stored in the low word of the destination data register and the remainder in the high word of the same register. If the result will not fit in the 16 bits of the low half, the V (overflow) flag is set in the condition code register. It is possible that the overflow condition can occur during the internal processing of the divide, in which case the Negative and Zero flags will be undefined as will be the result. Either a conditional branch on overflow or a TRAPV can be placed after the divide opcode to act upon the error.

Another problem occurs if a divisor of zero is specified. In this case a divide-by-zero exception processing sequence is automatically initiated which causes a jump through memory location 20 (vector 5, hexadecimal address 14).

Syntax: DIVS Dn , Dn

or   DIVS address , Dn

where Dn is D0 to D7.

Flags affected: The Carry flag is always set to zero. The Zero, Overflow, and Negative flags are set as per the result. The Extend flag is unaffected.

Instruction length: 2, 4, or 6 bytes.

EOR   Logical Exclusive OR

There is one variation of this instruction, EORI. This instruction performs a logical exclusive OR of the source operand with the same number of bits in the destination operand where the result is left. The number of bits can be 8, 16, or 32 as specified by the .B, .W, or .L opcode suffix.

Syntax: EOR   Dn , Dn
or   EOR   Dn , address
or   EOR   address , DN

Flags affected: The Overflow and Carry (V and C) flags are reset. The Negative and Zero bits are set as per result, and the Extend bit is unaffected.

EORI   Logical Exclusive OR Immediate

This instruction performs a logical exclusive OR on a length of byte, word, or long word between an immediate value and a destination. The destination can be a data register, memory, or one of two special cases: the condition code register or the status register. If the destination is the condition code register, only a byte-length immediate value is allowed. If the destination is the status register, only a word-length immediate value is allowed, and the processor must be in supervisor mode or else a privilege violation will occur causing a trap through vector 8.

Syntax: EORI #imm , Dn
or   EORI #imm , memory
or   EORI #imm , CCR
or   EORI #imm , SR (privileged)

Flags affected: Same as the EOR instruction
Instruction length: 2, 4, 6, 8, or 10 bytes.

EXG   Exchange Registers

This instruction allows any of the 16 data and address registers to be exchanged. Only of type long, this always operates on the entire 32 bits of a register. The registers can be any combination of data and address registers. No flags are affected by this operation.

Syntax: EXG   reg , reg.

where **reg** is D0 to D7 and A0 to A7.

Flags affected: None.
Instruction length: 2 bytes.

EXT   Extend Sign

This instruction allows the sign bit (the most significant bit in a byte or word) to be extended up to the next higher size. Thus if an opcode modifier of .W is used, the bit in position 7 of the lower-order byte will be extended into the rest of the word (in bits 8 to 15). If an opcode modifier of .L is used, the bit in position 15 of the low-order word will be extended into the rest of the long word (bits 16 to 31, the remainder of the register). If a byte value has to be sign-extended to a long word, both an EXT.W and an EXT.L have to be performed on the data register.

Syntax: EXT Dn

where **Dn** is D0 to D7.

Flags affected: The Negative and Zero flags set as per the result. The Overflow and Carry are reset to zero, and the Extend flag is unaffected.
Instruction length: 2 bytes.

JMP   Jump

This instruction allows execution of the program to be transferred anywhere within the entire addressing space of the 68000. The jump address can be specified using any memory addressing mode except register indirect with postincrement or predecrement. It should be borne in mind that an absolute address specified in a jump instruction will load the program counter immediately with that value. Because absolute addresses are not position-independent, if the program is moved in memory it has to be reassembled if the label is contained within the program. The JMP instruction with an absolute address is more properly used for jumps to static locations such as ROM routines. To keep the jump position-independent, a program-counter-relative address should be specified.

Syntax: JMP address

where **address** is absolute, program counter relative, or address register indirect excluding (An)+ and −(An).

Flags affected: None.
Instruction length: 2, 4, or 6 bytes.

JSR   Jump to Subroutine

This instruction allows control to be redirected in a similar manner to the JMP instruction; however, before the jump is made, the address of the following opcode is pushed onto the stack. (See BSR for a description of the stack save process.) Thus a subroutine can perform a task, and when it finishes, it can execute a special instruction to return to the address saved on the stack. As far as the destination address of the JSR instruction is concerned, the same caveats apply as for the JMP instruction. Absolute addresses, even as labels inside your program, should be avoided where possible to avoid a program which is not position-independent. Unless using such things as ROM routines or memory-mapped hardware locations, which have absolute addresses, use program counter relative or address register indirect addressing.

Syntax: JSR   address

where **address** is absolute, program-counter-relative, or address register indirect excluding (An)+ and −(An).

Flags affected: None.
Instruction length: 2, 4, or 6 bytes.

LEA   Load Effective Address

This instruction provides a simple way of loading any address register with the address resulting from nearly any addressing mode. Only two such modes are excluded from the list of possibilities. Due to the fact that address register indirect with postincrement or predecrement represent a dynamically increasing or decreasing address, these two modes cannot be used with LEA. But any other address, no matter how complicated, (including address register indirect with displacement and index) can be loaded into the specified address register. This saves performing the address arithmetic within the program. The processor will automatically take the same value as the calculated address—or in other words "the effective address."

Only address registers can be used with this instruction, and the destination address register is loaded with a 32-bit long value even though the address will only be 24 bits long. No flags are affected by the result of the address calculation.

Syntax: LEA   address , An

where **address** is any memory addressing mode except postincrement and predecrement.
      An is A0 to A7.

Instruction length: 2, 4, or 6 bytes.

LINK   Link Subroutine

This instruction is a specialized data area allocation opcode for use by subroutines that require a temporary work area that will be relinquished after use. Normally, when a subroutine has been entered from a JSR or BSR instruction, the return address (that is, the address of the instruction after the JSR or BSR) has automatically been saved on the stack by the processor before transferring control to the subroutine. This is part of the regular linkage for a subroutine call, which is automatically performed by any computer processor. The LINK instruction adds another automatic-linkage option after control has been handed to the subroutine.

Assume the subroutine needs ten bytes of temporary storage in order to perform its function. The ideal place for this would be on the stack, which is the usual place for dynamic register saves during a program's operation. As the stack pointer saves numbers in a downward direction in memory, simply subtracting ten from the stack pointer register (A7) would reserve ten bytes of stack space with A7 pointing to it. However, A7 may not point to the ten bytes for long as other items may subsequently be pushed onto the stack changing A7 to point lower in memory. So ideally, another address register should be loaded with the contents of A7 before it was decremented by ten so we have a firm pointer to the stack before it is changed. This is exactly what the LINK instruction does.

An address register is elected to save the current pointer to the stack in A7; this assigned register will become the pointer to the temporary reserved stack space. The stack pointer A7 is then decremented by however many bytes are needed, but before being decremented, the assigned register itself is saved on the stack. This way, the called subroutine can perform a LINK to reserve space, knowing that it can call yet another subroutine, which can also perform a LINK with no registers being corrupted. The diagram in Fig. 5-2 shows what happens.

Note that because ten bytes are required on the stack going downwards in memory (as per normal stack practice), a negative displacement is specified in the LINK instruction. As the displacement is a signed 16-bit immediate value, a stack displace-

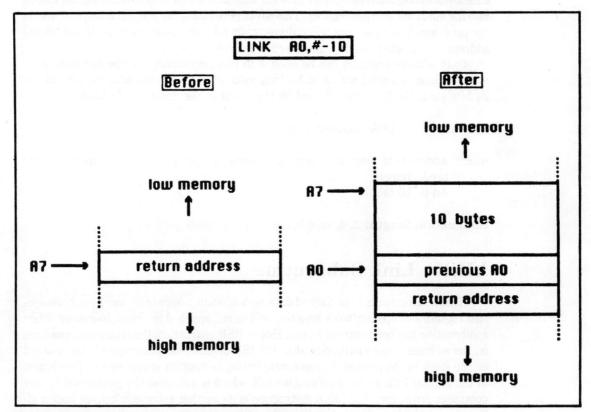

Fig. 5-2. The steps taken when a LINK instruction is performed.

ment of plus or minus 32K can be specified. The address register assigned to point to the top of the reserved space, or *stack frame*, is generally known as a *frame pointer* when used in this way. Note that as this register will be used with predecrement instructions, it initially points to one word above the frame.

Syntax: LINK An , #imm

where **n** is 0 to 6.
          #imm is plus or minus 32K.

Flags affected: None
Instruction length: 2 bytes

LSL   Logical Shift Left

This instruction shifts the destination operand left by a specified number of bits. If you are shifting a data register, the number of bits can be specified as an immediate value or as a value in another data register. The immediate value can be 1 to 8, whereas the data register value can be 1 to 64 (where zero acts as the 64 count). Data registers may be shifted as 8, 16, or 32 bit quantities. Only 16-bit word values can be shifted in memory and then only by one bit. Each bit shifted out of the left-hand side of an operand is placed in the Carry and Extend bits in the condition code register. As shown below, the bit shifted in at the right hand side is always a zero.

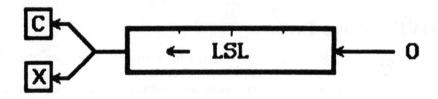

Syntax: LSL Dn , Dn
          LSL #immediate 3-bit value , Dn
          LSL memory (1 bit only)

Flags affected: The Carry and Extend bits are set as per the most significant operand bit before the shift. The Overflow flag is reset to zero. The Negative and Zero flags are set as per result.
Instruction length: 2, 4, or 6 bytes.

LSR   Logical Shift Right

This instruction shifts the destination operand right by a specified number of bits.

If you are shifting a data register the number of bits can be specified as an immediate value or as a value in another data register. The immediate value can be 1 to 8, whereas the data register value can be 1 to 64 (where zero acts as the 64 count). Data registers may be shifted as 8, 16, or 32 bit quantities. Only 16-bit word values can be shifted in memory and then by only one bit. Each bit shifted out of the right hand side of an operand is placed in the Carry and Extend bits of the condition code register. As shown below, the bit shifted in the left hand side is always a zero.

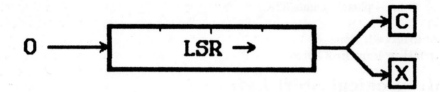

Syntax: LSR   Dn,Dn
            LSR   #immediate 3-bit value , Dn
            LSR   memory (1 bit only)

Flags affected: The Carry and Extend bits set as per the least significant bit before the shift. The Overflow bit is reset to zero. The Negative and Zero flags are set as per result.
Instruction length: 2, 4, or 6 bytes.

MOVE   Move Data

This is the 68000's general purpose data-transfer instruction. Using one single opcode, data can be moved from register to register, register to memory, memory to register, and memory to memory. A few variations of the instruction exist to perform more specialized data transfers. These are:

MOVEA   Move Address
MOVEM   Move Multiple
MOVEP   Move Peripheral data
MOVEQ   Move Quick

The general purpose MOVE instruction can also be used to move data to (but not from) the condition code register, thus explicitly setting a particular set of conditions. If you are in privileged (or supervisor) mode, the MOVE instruction can be used to move data to the status register and to or from the user stack pointer. (Privileged mode is not required to move data from the status register.)

With so many potential sources and destinations of data moves, the 68000 makes life easier by allowing all addressing modes to be used for the source. For the destination, all except program counter relative addressing modes may be used. With data transfers involving memory and/or data registers, the data transfer can be made using 8, 16, or 32 bit quantities and is specified by appending .B, .W, or .L to the MOVE mnemonic. If the high-order bits of a data register are not involved in the data move, those bits remain unaffected by the transfer. Care should be used when mixing lengths of operands during routines using MOVE; if a byte is moved from a location using MOVE.B and then stored back again using MOVE.W, it will be stored in a memory location one byte higher than it was fetched from. Similarly, storing it back with MOVE.L would store it three bytes higher than its original location.

If the destination operand of the MOVE is the condition code register, the length of the source operand can only be eight bits. If the status register is involved as either source or destination of the move, only 16-bit transfers are allowed. The instruction involving the user stack pointer is the only circumstance under which the 68000 allows optional access to either the user or the system stack pointer. Normally, the stack pointer is accessed as register A7. Whichever of the two A7 registers is in effect depends on whether the processor is in supervisor or user mode. However, the supervisor mode may have a need to access the user stack pointer even though it would normally only access the system stack pointer. This is why the privileged mode is required to access a normally unprotected register.

Syntax: MOVE source , destination

where **source** can be any addressing mode.

> **destination** can be any addressing mode except program counter relative and immediate. Either of the above can be CCR (condition code register), SR (status register), USP (user stack pointer—privileged mode only).

Flags affected: When the MOVE source, destination format is used, the Negative and Zero flags are set as per the data moved; the Overflow and Carry flags are reset to zero, and the Extend flag is unaffected.

When the MOVE source,CCR and MOVE source,SR formats are used, the flags are set directly from the data.

When the MOVE is done with the user stack pointer (USP) as an operand, no flags are affected.

Instruction length: 2, 4, 6, 8, or 10 bytes.

MOVEA   Move Address

This specialized version of the MOVE command is used when the destination is an address register. The instruction only allows transfers of 16 or 32 bits in length. Byte transfers are not allowed with an address register as the destination. Also note that unlike the normal MOVE command, no flag bits are affected.

Syntax: MOVEA source , An

where **source** is any addressing mode.

> **An** is A0 to A7.

Flags affected: none.
Instruction length: 2, 4, or 6 bytes

MOVEM Move Multiple

This variation of the MOVE instruction allows multiple registers to be saved and restored using a single operation. Any of the 16 data or address registers can be moved this way. At the source code level, the registers chosen to be saved or restored are specified to the assembler in a list separated by slashes. Thus, to save D0, D3, and A1, the register list would be specified as D0/D3/A1. If a consecutive number of registers are included in the list, they can be identified as such by a hyphen. So to save D0, D1, D2, D5, and A1, the register list can be specified as D5/D0-D2/A1. Notice that the order of registers between slashes is unimportant; however, when the 68000 saves these registers, it does so in a definite order. It also retrieves them in a definite (but opposite) order, so that if the registers are saved on a stack, they can be pulled off in a typical stack-like fashion (that is, last in first out). The order in which the 68000 saves registers is first A7 through A0, and then D7 through D0. Then in reverse order, D0 is restored first, and restoration continues all the way through to A7. As the registers are most often saved in a stack formation, normally an address register is chosen to point to that stack. Then a predecrement addressing mode is used to push the registers down onto the stack. Conversely, when registers are being restored, a postincrement addressing mode is used. As an example, to save two registers at a memory location pointed to by A3, the instruction MOVEM D1/A1, -(A3) might be used. To restore them at another point in a program, MOVEM (A3)+,D1/A1 would be correct. Note that registers can only be saved as words or long words. If they are saved as 16-bit words, then when they are restored, the upper half of the register is automatically sign-extended so that bit 15 fills the upper half of the register. Although less memory is used to save registers this way, such a loss of control of the upper 16 bits of every restored register may present problems unless you remain acutely aware of the possible corruption of an upper register half.

The MOVEM instruction may be used with addressing modes other than predecrement and postincrement. By specifying other addressing modes as the source or destination of the multiple transfer, registers can be saved and restored in ascending locations in memory. The same register order is used, but they will not be stacked in a last in, first out order. Note that no flags are affected by this operation. Thus a subroutine can affect the condition code register, restore multiple registers with MOVEM, and return with the condition code register still intact.

Syntax: MOVEM   register list , destination address
or   MOVEM   source address , register list
or   MOVEM   register list , -(An)
or   MOVEM   (An)+ , register list.

Flags affected: none.
Instruction length: 4 bytes with predecrement or postincrement; 4, 6, or 8 bytes with other addressing modes.

MOVEP   Move Peripheral Data

This variation of the MOVE instruction is used to transfer data between the 68000 and certain peripherals. As input and output on the 68000 is memory-mapped, certain addresses will not actually be memory at all but will instead be external devices. The 68000 has a special design to allow it to use the many hardware interfaces that exist for 8-bit microprocessors, in particular, the 6800. What this means to the programmer is that if a peripheral is interfaced to the 68000 and is normally addressed at consecutive addresses on an 8-bit microprocessor, it will be addressed at every other address on the 68000 due to the design of its peripheral hardware bus. Thus the MOVEP instruction was included to address such peripherals. A long word (four bytes) of data from a data register can be transferred high byte first to every alternate memory (peripheral) address with a single MOVEP to the first address.

This also works the other way round in that every other word will be addressed starting with the source address specified in the MOVEP instruction. Only word or long word transfers are allowed. (A normal MOVE would be used for a single byte.) The only addressing mode allowed to specify the memory location is address register indirect with displacement, and only a data register can be used as the other operand.

Syntax: MOVEP   Dn , disp(An)
or   MOVEP   disp(An) , Dn

where **Dn** is D0 to D7.
    disp is a 16-bit displacement.
    An is A0 to A7.

Flags affected: none.
Instruction length: 4 bytes.

MOVEQ   Move Quick

This variation on the MOVE instruction allows the quick loading of a data register with an immediate value. The MOVEQ variant works like a MOVE immediate value to data register except that MOVEQ is faster and only takes up two bytes in memory. The immediate value that is moved into a data register can only be in the range −128 to +127. This value is sign-extended into the entire 32 bits of the data register, so it is always of type long despite the small immediate value. As this instruction works so fast, it is quicker to clear a data register with a

                    MOVEQ   #0,Dn

than to use a

                    CLR   Dn.

MOVEQ cannot, however, be used with address registers (or numbers larger than eight bits).

Syntax: MOVEQ   #imm,Dn

where #imm is an immediate 8-bit signed value.
     Dn is D0 to D7.

Flags affected: The Negative and Zero flags are set as per the immediate value; the Overflow and Carry flags are reset to zero, and the Extend flag is unaffected.
Instruction Length: 2 bytes.

MULS   Multiply Signed
MULU   Multiply Unsigned

These instructions allow a multiplication to take place between a 16-bit source operand and the low order 16 bits of a data register. MULS assumes both numbers are signed, whereas MULU assumes both to be unsigned. The source can be a word from any memory location or the low-order 16 bits of a data register. The destination has to be a data register. The result is stored as a 32-bit signed or unsigned value in the destination register. The Negative flag in the condition code register is affected whether or not the operands are signed, and reflects the most significant bit of the result.

Syntax: MULS   Dn , Dn
or   MULS   address , Dn

where Dn is D0 to D7.
     address is any addressing mode.

Flags affected: The Negative and Zero flags set as per result. The Overflow and Carry are reset to zero. The Extend flag is unaffected.
Instruction length: 2, 4, or 6 bytes.

NBCD   Negate Binary Coded Decimal

This specialized arithmetic instruction allows a single byte containing two binary coded decimal digits to be negated. The byte can be contained in the low portion of a data register or in memory. If the number is in memory, any memory addressing mode except program counter relative may be used. If the number is in a data register, bits 8 to 31 are not affected.

Syntax: NBCD   Dn
or   NBCD   address

where **Dn** is D0 to D7.

Flags affected: The Negative flag is undefined. The Zero flag is set as per contents of register. The Overflow flag is undefined. Carry and Extend are set as per result of operation.
Instruction length: 2, 4, or 6 bytes.

NEG   Negate Binary
NEGX   Negate with Extend

This instruction negates its operand. The result is the same as if the operand were subtracted from zero. The operand may be 8, 16, or 32 bits long as specified by the .B, .W, or .L mnemonic suffix. All flags are affected by this operation. A variation of this instruction exists to facilitate the manipulation of multiple-precision quantities where data is handled in segments. This is achieved by using the Extend flag as set or reset from a previous arithmetic operation. The NEGX instruction works by subtracting its operand from zero then subtracting the Extend bit. All flags are affected by the result of the NEGX operation, but the Zero flag is only changed if the result becomes nonzero thus reflecting the nonzero state of a segmented number. For this reason, the Zero flag should be reset before performing code involving multiple use of NEGX.

Syntax: NEG   Dn
or   NEG   address

where **Dn** is D0 to D7.
        address is any memory addressing mode except program counter relative.

Flags affected: all.
Instruction length: 2, 4, or 6 bytes.

NOP   No operation

This instruction is a do-nothing opcode. It is used during program development to leave room in a section of code. This space can be patched with machine-code instructions as necessary during debugging to test new routines within a previously written section of code. Alternatively, pieces of code can be deleted at the machine code level by substituting NOP instructions for the instructions and operands.

Syntax: NOP

Flags affected: none
Instruction length: 2 bytes.

NOT   Logical NOT (One's Complement)

This instruction takes its operand and simply inverts all of its bits. (Each one-bit becomes zero and each zero-bit becomes one.) The operand can be either in a data register or memory and can be 8, 16, or 32 bits in length as per the .B, .W, or .L operand suffix.

Syntax: NOT   Dn
or   NOT   address

where **Dn** is D0 to D7.
        address is any memory addressing mode except program counter relative.

Flags affected: The Negative and Zero flags set as per result. The Overflow and Carry flags are reset to zero. The Extend flag is unaffected.
Instruction length: 2, 4, or 6 bytes.

OR   Logical OR

A single variant exists:

ORI - Or Immediate

The OR opcode performs a logical OR operation. A number of bits in the source operand are ORed with the same number of bits in the destination operand where the result is left. The number of bits can be 8, 16, or 32 as per the .B, .W, or .L opcode suffix. One or both operands must be a data register.

Syntax: OR   Dn , Dn
or   OR   Dn , address
or   OR   address , Dn

where **Dn** is D0 to D7.
        address is any memory addressing mode with the proviso that program counter relative may not be used as destination.

Flags affected: The Negative and Zero flags are affected as per result. The Overflow and Carry flags is reset to zero. The Extend flag is unaffected.

ORI   Logical OR Immediate

This instruction logically ORs a byte, word, or long word immediate value with the destination. The destination address can be a data register, memory, or one of two special cases: the condition code register and the status register. If the destination is the condition code register, only a byte-length immediate value is allowed. If the destination is the status register, only a word-length immediate value is allowed, and the processor must be in supervisor mode or else a privilege violation will occur.

Syntax:	ORI	imm# , Dn
or	ORI	imm# , address
or	ORI	immediate 8-bit # , CCR
or	ORI	immediate 16-bit # , SR (privileged).

Flags affected: The Overflow and Carry bits are reset. The Sign and Zero bits are set as per the result. The Extend bit is unaffected.
Instruction length: 2, 4, 6, 8, or 10 bytes.

PEA   Push Effective Address

This instruction takes the effective address of its operand and pushes it onto the stack as pointed to by the stack pointer A7. The operand can be nearly any addressing mode and is represented as a 32-bit long word. Only two addressing modes are excluded from the list of possibilities. Due to the fact that address register indirect with postincrement or predecrement represent a dynamically increasing or decreasing address, these two modes cannot be used with PEA. But any other address, no matter how complicated, (including address register indirect with displacement and index) can be pushed onto the stack. This saves performing the address arithmetic within the program. The processor will automatically push the same value as the calculated address—in other words, "the effective address." The destination address on the stack is loaded with a 32-bit long value even though the address will only be 24 bits long. No flags are affected by the result of the address calculation.

Syntax: PEA   address

where **address** is any memory addressing mode except postincrement and predecrement.

Flags affected: none.
Instruction length: 2, 4, or 6 bytes.

RESET   Reset External Devices

This instruction sends out a pulse from the RESET pin of the 68000. It is normally used when a system is first powered up to reset all devices to a known state. It is only likely to be used after that if a hardware fault-condition develops. Because it is such a powerful opcode, it is restricted to use in supervisor mode only.

Syntax: RESET

Flags affected: none.
Instruction length: 2 bytes.

ROL Rotate Left
ROXL Rotate Extended Left

These two instructions both rotate the destination operand left by a specified number of bits. If you are rotating a data register, the number of bits can be specified as an immediate value or as a value in another data register. The immediate value can be 1 to 8, whereas the data register value can be 1 to 64 (where zero acts as the 64 count). Data registers may be rotated as 8, 16, or 32 bit quantities. Only 16-bit word values can be rotated in memory and then by only one bit. As shown in Fig. 5-3, each bit rotated out of the left hand side of the operand is placed in the Carry bit of the condition code register, and in the case of ROXL, also in the Extend bit. The bit rotated in at the right is the most significant bit for ROL or the Extend bit for ROXL. Thus, one more bit is involved in the ROXL rotate than in the ROL rotate. Note that ROL does not affect the Extend flag in the condition code register.

Syntax:	ROL Dn , Dn
or	ROL #imm , Dn
or	ROL address.

where **Dn** is D0 to D7.
 # imm is an immediate value from 1 to 8.
address is any memory addressing mode except program counter relative.

Flags affected: The Negative flag is set as per most significant bit before the rotate. The Zero flag is set as per resultant operand. The Overflow flag is reset to zero. The

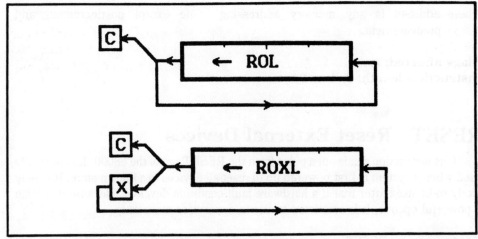

Fig. 5-3. The functions of the ROL and ROXL instructions.

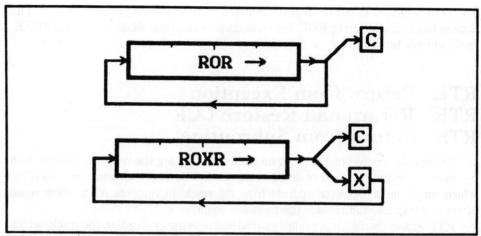

Fig. 5-4. The functions of the ROR and ROXR instructions.

Extend flag is unaffected by ROL, but contains the previous most significant bit for ROXL.

Instruction length: 2, 4, or 6 bytes.

ROR   Rotate Right
ROXR   Rotate Extended Right

These two instructions both rotate the destination operand right by a specified number of bits. If you are rotating a data register, the number of bits can be specified as an immediate value or as a value in another data register. The immediate value can be 1 to 8, whereas the data register value can be 1 to 64 (where zero acts as the 64 count). Data registers may be rotated as 8, 16, or 32 bit quantities. Only 16-bit word values can be rotated in memory and then by only one bit.

As shown in Fig. 5-4, each bit rotated out of the right hand side of the operand is placed in the Carry bit of the condition code register and in the case of ROXR, also in the Extend bit. The bit rotated in at the left is the least significant bit for ROR or the Extend bit for ROXR. Thus, one more bit is involved in the ROXR rotate than in the ROR rotate. Note that ROR does not affect the Extend flag in the condition code register.

Syntax:	ROR	Dn , Dn
or	ROR	#imm , Dn
or	ROR	address.

where **Dn** is D0 to D7.

 # imm is an immediate value from 1 to 8.

address is any memory addressing mode except program counter relative.

Flags affected: The Negative flag is set as per most significant bit before the rotate.

The Zero flag is set as per resultant operand. The Overflow flag is reset to zero. The Extend flag is unaffected by ROR, but contains previous least significant bit for ROXR.
Instruction length: 2, 4, or 6 bytes.

RTE   Return from Exception
RTR   Return and Restore CCR
RTS   Return from Subroutine

These instructions change program control by loading the program counter with an execution address previously saved on the stack. The most common version is RTS, which simply pulls the saved address from the stack, increments A7 to allow reuse of the stack space, and reloads the program counter.

RTE expects to find a previously saved status register word on the stack, which it pulls and restores prior to reloading the program counter. As RTE accesses the privileged byte of the status register, it can only be executed in supervisor mode or else a privilege violation trap will occur.

RTR expects to find a previously saved condition code register word on the stack, which it pulls and restores prior to reloading the program counter.

Syntax: RTS
                RTE
                RTR

Flags affected: No flags are affected by RTS. All flags are reloaded by RTE and RTR.
Instruction length: 2 bytes.

SBCD   Subtract Binary Coded Decimal

This is a specialized arithmetic instruction that subtracts one byte from another (only bytes) when each byte contains binary coded decimal numbers. (Each byte of BCD data contains two BCD digits.)

The subtraction can be performed either on two data registers or between two memory locations. If performed on bytes in memory, only address register indirect with predecrement can be used. This facilitates easy manipulation of multiple-precision BCD numbers. The extend bit is subtracted along with the BCD bytes to allow this multiprecision data manipulation. Also note that the Zero flag is only changed if the result becomes nonzero. Therefore, both the Extend and Zero bits in the condition code register should be preset before the operation is performed. The Extend bit would normally be preset to a zero (to prevent extension on the first subtraction) and the Zero bit to a one (to signify a zero result prior to the first subtraction). A **MOVE #4,CCR** would preset these flags correctly.

Syntax: SBCD   Dn , Dn
or   SBCD   –(An) , –(An)

Flags affected: The Zero flag is cleared if result becomes nonzero. The Carry and Extend flags are set if a decimal borrow is generated. The Negative and Overflow bits are undefined.
Instruction length: 2 bytes.

Scc   Set from Condition Codes

This instruction sets a single byte specified in the operand to all zeroes or all ones according to the condition codes. The condition codes which may be used are the same as for the decrement and branch opcode; that is EQ (equal to), NE (not equal to), MI (minus), PL (plus), CS (carry set), CC (carry clear), VS (overflow set), VC (overflow clear), HI (higher), LS (less than or same), HS (higher or same), LO (lower), GT (greater than), GE (greater than or equal to), LE (less than or equal to), LT (less than), F (false), and T (true). If the specified condition is true as reflected in the condition code register, the destination byte is set to all ones (hexadecimal FF). If it is not true, the destination byte is set to zero. Note that ST is always true and SF is always false.

The destination can be the low-order byte of a data register or a byte in memory. This instruction is of particular value in saving the status of a specific condition code.

Syntax: Scc Dn
or   Scc address

where **Dn** is D0 to D7.
      address is any memory addressing mode except program counter relative.

Flags affected: none
Instruction length: 2, 4, or 6 bytes.

STOP   Stop processor and wait

This is a privileged instruction that first copies its operand (which is an immediate word value) into the status register and then halts the processor. The processor will remain in this state until it receives an interrupt that is not masked by the interrupt mask placed into the status register.

Syntax: STOP   #imm

where **#imm** is a 16-bit word value

Flags affected: All flags are set as per the immediate value.
Instruction length: 4 bytes

SUB Subtract Binary

This instruction subtracts the source operand from the destination operand, leaving the result in the destination. One of the operands must be a data register. Four variants of the SUB opcode exist:

SUBA	Subtract Address.
SUBI	Subtract Immediate.
SUBQ	Subtract Quick.
SUBX	Subtract with Extend.

These are described later.

The SUB instruction subtracts the source operand from the destination operand with the result appearing in the destination. It's possible to subtract bytes, words, or long words with this opcode by appending .B, .W, or .L to the mnemonic. Either the source or destination (or both) must be a data register. The source operand can be any memory location or data register, and the destination operand can also be any memory location or data register.

Syntax: SUB Dn , Dn
or   SUB address , Dn
or   SUB Dn , address

Flags affected: The Extend, Negative, Zero, Overflow, and Carry flags are all affected as per the result of the subtraction.
Instruction length: 2, 4, or 6 bytes.

SUBA Subtract Address

This variant of the SUB instruction differs only in that an address register is specified as the destination. As an address rather than data is being manipulated, the condition code flags are unaffected. Only sign-extended words or long words can be subtracted.

SUBI Subtract Immediate

This variant of the SUB instruction is used to subtract a constant value from the destination. The immediate operand can be any 8, 16, or 32-bit value as specified by the .B, .W, or .L opcode suffix. The destination cannot be an address register or a program counter relative address.

Syntax: SUBI #imm , Dn

or   SUBI   #imm , address

where #imm is an immediate value up to two to the power of 32.
        address is any memory addressing mode except program counter relative.

Flags affected: The Extend, Negative, Zero, Overflow, and Carry flags are all set as per the result of the subtraction.
Instruction length: 4, 6, 8, or 10 bytes.

SUBQ   Subtract Quick

This variant of the SUB instruction is used to subtract a small integer between one and eight from the destination. The destination can be a memory location, a data register, or an address register. If it is an address register, the condition code flags are unaffected and the operand length cannot be byte.

This operation takes the place of the decrement instruction found on other processors.

Syntax: SUBQ   #imm , register
or   ADDQ   #imm , address

where #imm is an immediate value of 1 to 8.
       register is D0 to D7 and A0 to A7.
       address is any memory address mode.

Flags affected: The Extend, Negative, Zero, Overflow, and Carry flags are all set as per the result of the addition unless the destination is an address register.

SUBX   Subtract Extended

This variant of the SUB instruction subtracts two numbers and the Extend bit of the condition code register. This allows multiple-precision subtractions to be performed. For this reason, the Zero flag is only affected when a nonzero result is obtained. This means that if multiple numbers are subtracted using SUBX, the Zero flag will stay reset if any of those numbers was nonzero.

Syntax: SUBX   Dn , Dn
or   SUBX   −(An) , −(An)

where Dn is D0 to D7 and SS is A0 to A7.

Instruction length: 2 bytes.

SWAP   Swap data register halves

This instruction takes the lower 16 bits of the specified data register and swaps it with the upper 16 bits. It can only be used with data registers and only operates on the fixed word length in each half.

Syntax: SWAP Dn

where **Dn** is D0 to D7.

Flags affected: The Negative and Zero flags are set to reflect the 32-bit result. The Overflow and Carry flags are reset to zero. The Extend flag is unaffected.
Instruction length: 2 bytes.

TAS   Test and Set

This is a highly specialized instruction that is used to test a byte in memory or in a data register. When the condition codes are set as per the byte's contents, bit 7 (the most significant bit) of the byte is set to a one. This operation is achieved in an uninterruptible read-modify-write cycle. It is the only instruction on the 68000 that uses this method. Its importance lies in the fact that no interrupt can cause a read of the accessed byte before the operation is finished. If the operation were done in two steps, an interrupt could occur before the byte was changed, which would allow the interrupting routine to scan the byte and draw an erroneous conclusion as to its status.

Syntax: TAS Dn
or   TAS address

where **Dn** is D0 to D7.
    address is any memory addressing mode except program counter relative.

Flags affected: The Negative and Zero flags set as per the byte before modification. The Overflow and Carry flags are reset to zero. The Extend flag is unaffected.
Instruction length: 2, 4, or 6 bytes.

TRAP   Software Trap

This instruction causes a trap to occur in the same manner as if it had been caused by a hardware-detected condition. The processor will jump to one of the 16 special addresses set up in the first 1024 bytes of memory. The actual address that will be jumped to is determined by the operand supplied with the opcode. This will be a number from 0 to 15. The software trap vectors are 32-bit addresses stored in memory starting at location 128. Before the specified vector is taken, the status register and program counter are pushed onto the stack.

Syntax: TRAP #imm

where **#imm** is an immediate value from 0 to 15.

Flags affected: none.
Instruction length: 2 bytes.

TRAPV   Trap if Overflow

This instruction causes a trap to occur to the address in location 28 in low memory if the overflow flag is set in the condition code register. Before the overflow vector (vector #7) is taken, the status register and program counter are pushed onto the stack to facilitate a return via an RTE instruction.

Syntax: TRAPV

Flags affected: none.
Instruction length: 2 bytes.

TST   Test Operand

This instruction causes the processor to scan the operand and set the condition code flags according to its contents. The operand can be 8, 16, or 32 bytes as specified in the .B, .W, or .L opcode modifier. No registers other than the condition code register are changed. The operand can be either a data register or a memory location.

Syntax: TST Dn
or   TST address

where **Dn** is D0 to D7.
        address is any memory addressing mode except program counter relative.

UNLK   Unlink

This instruction is the reverse of the LINK opcode. It takes the address in the specified address register and loads the stack pointer (A7) with it. This removes any space allocated on the stack for temporary storage. The stack pointer then points at the previous contents of the address register (the frame pointer). These contents would have been placed there by a previous LINK instruction. The frame pointer is automatically reloaded by pulling the value from the stack. Both the frame pointer and the stack pointer are therefore returned to their values before the last LINK. This entire operation is performed automatically by a single UNLK instruction.

Syntax: UNLK An

where **An** is A0 to A7.

Flags affected: none.
Instruction length: 2 bytes.

Chapter

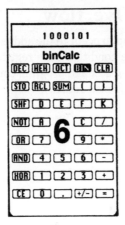

1000101

binCalc

DEC HEX OCT BIN CLR

STO RCL SUM ( )

SHF D E F K

NOT A **6** C /

OR 7 9 *

AND 4 5 6 -

XOR 1 2 3 +

CE 0 . +/- =

The Amiga System

The Amiga is a highly sophisticated microcomputer system. The word *system* implies a set of interconnecting hardware and software pieces, some of which don't even exist on other microcomputers. With the Amiga, what you have in front of you and what you'll be programming is a set of interconnecting parts—not just pieces of hardware like a keyboard, screen, and printer, but also pieces of prewritten software (such as the executive, disk operating system, and intuition routines), which interconnect with each other and the hardware. Before going any further, it's worthwhile to stand back and look at the definition of an Amiga, so you know exactly what it is you're intending to program. Given such a definition, all software writers will aim at the same goal— applications that will run on any Amiga regardless of any upgrades that come along. If you develop an application that will only work with a graphics tablet, you have only yourself to blame when nobody else can use it because they only have a standard configuration.

The standard Amiga setup is defined as:

- A main unit with a 68000 CPU running at 7.16 MHz containing a built-in 3.5 inch dual-sided minifloppy.
- A detached keyboard comprised of 89 keys.
- A two-button mouse.
- Memory capacity of 256K Kickstart write-protected RAM and 256K of user RAM. The built-in disk drive has 880K of space available.
- The video display has two resolutions. Low resolution is 320 dots wide by 200 dots high, each dot being any of 32 colors from a color palette of 4096. High resolution

is 640 dots wide by 200 dots high, each dot being one of 16 colors from a color palette of 4096. Vertical resolution can be increased to 400 dots by switching the display to interlaced mode.

This is the standard Amiga setup. Any program that will work on this configuration will work on any Amiga. If you want to program an application that uses something else, like a graphics tablet, you should make its use optional so that everyone can use your application even if they don't have the graphics tablet. Commodore-Amiga already offers a number of options, that will doubtless be augmented by the company itself and by third party suppliers in the near future. Current options from Commodore include up to three external floppy-disk drives (either 3.5 or 5.25 inch and 256K RAM expansion cartridge.

With these configurations in mind, you have a solid concept of what hardware is definitely hooked up, and what is possibly hooked up. Once again, if everybody is designing software to the same ends, greater consistency is achieved.

The sophistication of the system should not be perceived as a threat to an assembly-language programmer just starting out on the Amiga. The fact that all the interconnecting parts are made functionally available to a programmer makes the task of programming simple. With the 68000 Development System as supplied by Commodore, the effort involved in designing a program is reduced to its bare minimum. If you want your program to have such high-level facilities as windows, you don't have to write code to draw rectangles and title them. Those kinds of chores have already been undertaken by other programmers—you simply use their routines as if they were new opcodes in the 68000 instruction set. This not only simplifies program design, it makes your program fit in with the way other Amiga applications work. Thus, someone who isn't familiar with your new application won't be baffled by a bewildering set of brand new commands or menu choices—at least, not if your program uses the same windows, pull-down menus, and mouse-related features used in all the other Amiga software. This is what the software interface is all about: what's available in the way of building blocks and how to use them. A closer look at the actual building blocks will follow, in the next chapter. In this chapter, you'll get a feel for the Amiga system in general as it applies to the assembly-language programmer.

PROCESSES AND TASKS

When a program is run on the Amiga, it is run as a process by the *executive*. The executive is itself a process that, under the normal Amiga operating environment, never finishes. This is because one of its main purposes is to continually share the resources of the computer among processes that are trying to execute. Thus, while programs (processes) are being run, the executive will be there overseeing their execution and use of the machine. It's the executive that is loaded into memory from the Kickstart disk when you boot up the Amiga. Once loaded, the executive (often referred to as exec) is protected from external interference by being placed in write-protected RAM, which acts as ROM high up in the Amiga's memory map. (See Fig. 6-1.) This memory behaves as if it were ROM because it is hardware-configured to be read and not written once it has been loaded with the contents of the Kickstart disk following power-up of the machine. Thus, exec is safe from accidental overwrites by any crashing pro-

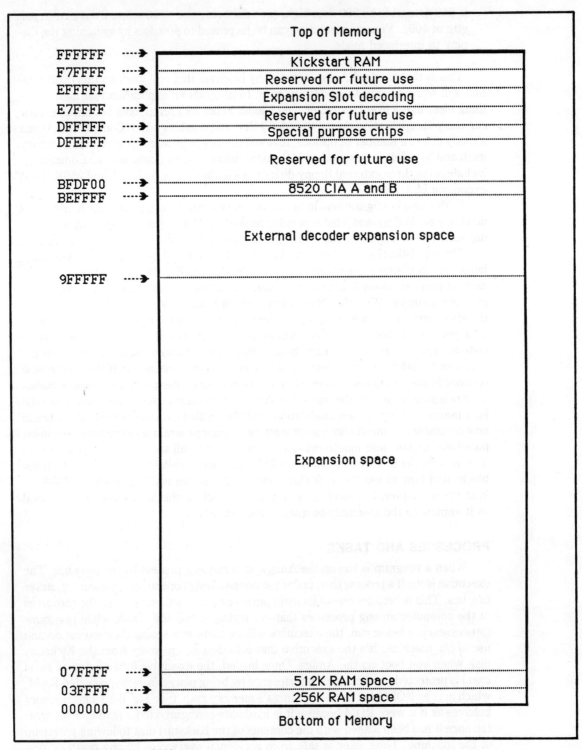

Top of Memory

FFFFFF ----➤	Kickstart RAM
F7FFFF ----➤	Reserved for future use
EFFFFF ----➤	Expansion Slot decoding
E7FFFF ----➤	Reserved for future use
DFFFFF ----➤	Special purpose chips
DFEFFF ----➤	
	Reserved for future use
BFDF00 ----➤	8520 CIA A and B
BEFFFF ----➤	
	External decoder expansion space
9FFFFF ----➤	
	Expansion space
07FFFF ----➤	
03FFFF ----➤	512K RAM space
000000 ----➤	256K RAM space

Bottom of Memory

Fig. 6-1. A simplified Amiga RAM map.

grams. (Further references to ROM, either in this book or in Commodore documentation, actually apply to this write-protected area of memory.) Apart from the inviolability of the executive process, using *pseudo*-ROM like this allows for updated versions of exec to be provided on a new Kickstart disk rather than having to open up the Amiga and replace a set of plug-in ROMs.

Processes that run on the Amiga can be split up into separate tasks, each of which can be run independently to improve the performance of the computer system as a whole. For instance, imagine that you have two tasks in the system, and one task wants to read some information from a disk. While the disk is being positioned for the read, the other task can take over the 68000 and perform its function, thus better utilizing the computer. Each task has its own environment, consisting of its program code and special task-related system information. A task runs as if it were a stand-alone program running on an independent 68000, and it might not even be aware of the existence of other tasks executing concurrently in the machine. Tasks have the option of communicating to each other using messages or signals. This same signal mechanism is used in the programs at the end of this book to detect user-selection of menus and gadgets.

The Executive

One of the main functions of the executive is to schedule the running of tasks on a priority basis. If one task has a higher priority than another, then the executive will let it have control of the 68000. If an executing task needs a resource that is currently in use, the executive will "steal" the 68000 from it and let the next priority task take over. If several tasks have the same priority, exec will allocate each one a limit called a *time-slice* and then swap between them as each limit runs out. The fact that multiple tasks can appear to be running at once is why the Amiga is described as a *multitasking* machine.

Don't worry if this setup seems complicated. Until the concept feels natural, just program the machine as if you were the only one running a program on the system. For the most part, this is how programs appear to execute anyway—both from the user's and programmer's point of view. Because of the importance of tasks within the Amiga, however, it's just as well to know of their existence at this stage.

As mentioned earlier, each task has an associated chunk of memory, in addition to that used by its program code, containing special system information that is used by exec. This will contain such data as the task's priority, where it resides in memory, how much memory it is taking up, and whether or not it is executing. Every task in the system will have its own independent task-control data structure. Each structure will have the same format, so that the executive knows where to find data it might need to deal with any task.

The software routines in the Amiga use many structures other than task-control data structures. For instance, one describes a window to be opened on the screen. This kind of structure contains information such as the window's size, its location on the screen, whether it can be sized, and other information appropriate to the opening of a window. This *NewWindow* structure, as it's called, always has the same layout, which, naturally enough, is why it's referred to as a structure. The use of predetermined structures in memory is central to the operation of many Amiga software routines. Other structures exist to describe the rendering of gadgets in windows, and the format and style of text—in fact, just about every manipulable object available in the Amiga software. The layout of each structure is described in the ROM Kernel Manual. You'll see some examples in the source code of the programs detailed in Chapters 11 and 13.

To keep track of the many structures that can appear in memory, exec maintains lists of them. Each item (or *node*) in these lists is linked together in such a way that the executive can access a structure easily. Thus, if a window is closed or a task removed, exec searches from the start of the list, finds the appropriate structure, acts upon data contained in that structure (perhaps reallocating memory used by a task), and then deletes the structure from the list. Often lists are maintained in no particular order, with items simply linked chronologically as exec-related events are kept track of. Whenever a list is ordered in a certain way (for instance, to keep track of tasks in order of priority), the list is referred to as a *queue*. This manipulation of items within lists and queues helps exec to deal with a constantly changing environment involving tasks, interrupts, messages, and other dynamically occurring events. Software routines are available to help manipulate items within lists, but you're not likely to need them unless you decide to write system software that interfaces deep down at the level of the executive.

AmigaDOS

Above the level of executive in software terms is the Amiga Disk Operating System, or *AmigaDOS*. This deals with the file system on disk and loads or saves programs and files on the disk hardware. AmigaDOS uses a special subset of software, referred to as the TrackDisk device, to interface with the disk hardware. Thus, you don't have to concern yourself as a programmer with the intricacies of disk seeks, reads, writes, or error detection. AmigaDOS has a whole set of routines available as part of the building blocks mentioned earlier. This makes the job of interfacing with the disk simply a matter of choosing the DOS routine to perform the task you need and letting AmigaDOS do the "donkey work."

Notice that AmigaDOS uses the TrackDisk software to perform disk input and output. It may also use various routines from within the executive while it carries out the functions of a disk operating system. The executive itself may schedule a different process if AmigaDOS becomes idle.

MODULE HIERARCHY

The reliance of software modules upon each other in the Amiga leads to a hierarchy that is shown in Fig. 6-2. In this diagram, the hardware of the Amiga is shown at the lowest level. This includes the 68000 microprocessor, which is assigned to tasks by the executive and thus is shown at the next higher level. The executive needs to be there to run AmigaDOS which, in turn, needs to be available to run the Workbench or the CLI (*command line interface*). The CLI and Workbench are shown at nearly the highest level, because they rely for their operation on all the levels below. The level at which programming is done in this book is equal to or above that of the CLI and Workbench.

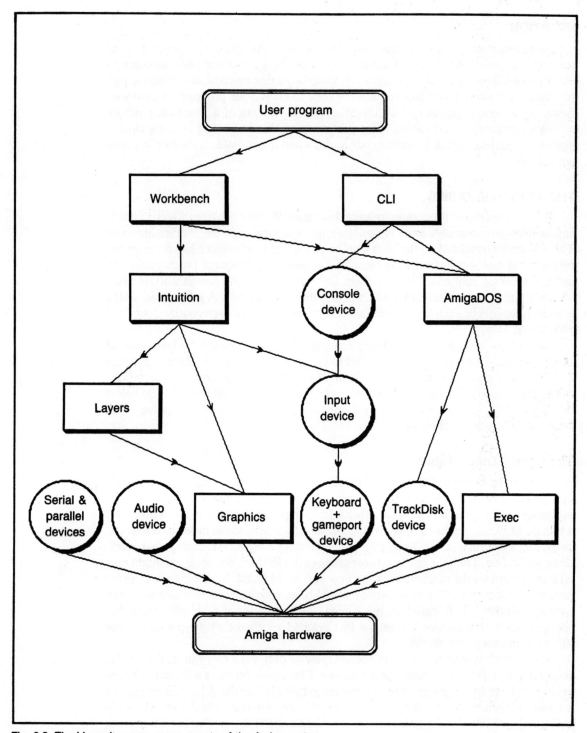

Fig. 6-2. The hierarchy among components of the Amiga system.

INTUITION

As shown in the figure, at about the same level as AmigaDOS, there is a set of software routines that goes by the name of Intuition. This important package contains many of the high-level graphic routines that give the Amiga much of its distinctive personality. The Intuition routines contain the code to allow your program to have windows, requesters, gadgets, and all the other accoutrements of a graphically driven software environment. By having these routines available as a set of building blocks, you're spared the effort of inventing code to draw and manipulate all the familiar Amiga objects.

THE AMIGA LIBRARIES

While all users and programmers have the Amiga Workbench from which to work, applications programmers have yet another metaphorical aid—the Amiga libraries. These libraries consist of all the high-level routines that Commodore has documented and made available to software developers. Any assembly-language programmer can use these library routines. Many of them are contained in the Amiga's ROM area, whereas others are loaded into RAM when a library is opened. A *jump table*, which is an integral part of each library, contains the whereabouts of each routine contained within that library.

Before you are able to use a library routine, you need to locate the base address of that particular library. This is provided to you when you open the library. (Further details of this procedure are given in the next chapter.) The jump table, containing actual jumps to each of the routines within the library, is located immediately below this base. Thus, to use a routine, you simply use a JSR opcode to a negative offset from the library base address.

The Library Offset Table

The call-by-library-offset is the kingpin around which the Amiga software interface works. Notice that this method eliminates the need to know exactly where the routines are located in memory. On other microcomputer systems, if you wish to use a routine in ROM, you have to know its absolute ROM address in order to use it. Initially, that's no problem; you write your program using those ROM routines and everything works fine. Then the manufacturer changes the ROM. Your program might now no longer work on the machine with the new version of ROM, because your program uses the old locations. The only remedy would be to rewrite your software for every new version that was released. In the Amiga, the library offset table eliminates that whole scenario. If a routine is changed by Commodore, then they simply update the library containing that routine.

Whenever any Amiga library is opened (new or old), each entry in its jump table is initialized to point to its constituent routines. Thus, your routines will always be executed at the proper locations because the jump table is initialized by exec whenever a library is opened. All this is totally invisible to your program, which executes without having to know if it's running on the old version of ROM—or whether it's running in ROM at all. Another useful thing about using a library vector table (as it is also called) in this way is that you can change the entries to point at your own custom routines, or you can even write your own libraries. This, however, is only for advanced machine-code programmers and is beyond the scope of this book.

Interaction Among Library Routines

Some of the higher-level library routines actually use routines from within other libraries, inferring a level of hierarchy and interaction among them. As an example, an Intuition routine that opens a window may use a routine from the graphics library to draw a gadget. As this suggests, the various routines available are separated into logically distinct libraries. For instance, most graphic functions—especially the lower level ones outside of Intuition—are handled by the graphics library.

Each library provides the assembly-language programmer with tools to achieve a definite purpose. To fully use the facilities provided by the libraries, you need the documentation for each one. This is currently available in the large volume published on behalf of Commodore called *The ROM Kernel Manual*. The various software routines, as referred to by their specific function names, are handled within a library specific to that kind of routine, such as the exec library, the math floating-point library, the Intuition library, and so on. Along with the appropriate function names, each routine is described as to its parameter requirements. Most routines need registers set up with appropriate values and/or addresses before being used. Many may have a value returned in data register d0.

Generally, register-driven routines have values passed in data registers d0 and up, while addresses are usually passed in registers a0 and up. There are exceptions to this rule, however, so the documentation should always be checked. A complete list of register requirements for each library routine is given in the appendix.

An example shows how easily a new window can be opened using a routine from the Intuition library:

LEA	IntBase,A6	Address of Intuition library
LEA	NewWindow,A0	Address of new window structure
JSR	_LVOOpenWindow(A6)	Call library routine

The routine named OpenWindow, which is part of the Intuition library, does the hard work. Following Amiga's conventions, the name of the routine is preceeded by _LVO to lessen the possibility of conflict with names within your program. All you have to do as an assembly-language programmer is ensure that the correct registers are loaded with the necessary values. In this instance, the Amiga's Intuition library has spared you the effort of having to write the great deal of code that would be necessary to draw a complete window on the screen. Of course, if you wish to write this kind of routine yourself, there's nothing stopping you, but you'll end up with software that deviates from the Amiga standards, and put yourself months behind on your project.

THE ADVANTAGES OF THE AMIGA SOFTWARE INTERFACE

You can deduce from this chapter that Commodore has put a great deal of thought into designing the software interface for the Amiga. The years of development that have been used to engineer this system save you, as an assembly-language programmer, from having to recreate that same effort. Thus, your program doesn't have to include things like how to draw a line or a box; it has already been done by Commodore and is right there in the library routines for your program to use.

By giving machine-code programmers the choice of using the system routines, Commodore has also encouraged a situation in which your program will share many characteristics of other Amiga programs. This is how they can be reasonably sure that many Amiga applications will have a high degree of consistency. Everybody's menus, for example, will work in the same basic ways, as long as everyone uses the documented library routines. You don't even have to worry about how you'd invent a menu from machine code—the weeks of work that would be involved in doing that have already been invested on your behalf. There is no reason, though, if you're a maverick-type programmer, why you can't bypass the entire operating system and program the Amiga directly at the hardware level. If you insist on doing this, however, you'll be on your own, and might end up with a program only you know how to use.

These building blocks, then, are the method by which you let the Amiga know what you want to accomplish. That doesn't mean your expertise in the 68000 is wasted—quite the contrary. Your application still has to perform its uniquely required task, which could be as diverse as running finances for a store or controlling the operation of a power station. Both applications will use the same methods of calling library routines to achieve the same results. To use each routine, you need to know the name of the function required to do it and the library in which it resides. Any information the function needs to know to carry out your requirements also has to be supplied. Some functions will return a quantity or an error number if what you asked can't be achieved. Many functions require you to direct their operation by specifying values in data and address registers of the 68000.

At this point it should be becoming clear that to remember all the potential routines available to a programmer (each performing a different task) would be as impossible as remembering the entire set of instruction codes of the 68000. To help simplify the problem, each routine has been assigned a unique name that is related to the job it performs. For instance, to help you in forming your own menu, there is a routine called SetMenuStrip. Names such as these will be connected into the library by the *linker*—the program that produces an executable version of your code after the assembler has produced object code from your source code. Whenever you specify an external library name as a subroutine address in your program, it will be replaced by a call to the library function. The characters _LVO are added to the beginning of the name to differentiate function names from other labels in your program.

AMIGA OBJECT DEFINITIONS

Some final definitions might help to clear up any remaining confusion when talking about the Amiga from a software development point of view. First, a *file* is a container of information. This can be a program, a picture, text, or whatever a user wants.

Other files may contain information the user doesn't even know about. Three major types of files are *projects, tools,* and *drawers*. Files containing tools are created by assembly-language programmers when writing an application program. Tools are application programs that contain code often used to manipulate files. Many tools have a menu bar that enables the user to see the available commands with which data can be manipulated. Each tool can have a window through which the user can view the information in a file. Windows can contain graphical objects called *gadgets*, which the user can select with the mouse to indicate a choice of some kind. *Projects* are the information that the user can access in a file via a tool. Most often, a project is associated with a principal tool, though this tool might not be the only one that can operate on the file. For example, an assembly-language program stored in source-code format will most likely be used by an assembler, but it will more often be used by an editor.

The Workbench Environment

There are two main environments in the Amiga from which your program may be launched. At the graphical level, the Workbench is the most fundamental level on the Amiga. It most closely approximates the operating system on other computers. Because it is graphic-driven instead of textual in nature, the user can accomplish work by using objects on this metaphorical "workbench" rather than by commanding the computer using its own rigidly defined set of command words. From the Amiga Workbench, you can throw a project in the trash rather than killing a file.

Windows are the most useful objects you can open in an application. Through them, you can view any information that a tool is capable of providing. All windows have similar attributes: they can be moved around, expanded or contracted, and sent in front of or behind other windows. If the tool being used allows its windows to be changed in size, it's always achieved in the same way, regardless of the tool. Windows lie in their own plane on the screen. Whichever one has its title bar highlighted is the *active* window—this is the one that is currently being manipulated and accepts input from the user. If any window overlaps another, it obscures the overlapped portion from view. Programs can have multiple windows open almost as easily as they can have a single one, although care should be taken, because multiple windows tend to confuse a user.

The CLI Environment

At the textual level, the Command Line Interface, or CLI, is the most fundamental level available on the Amiga. The CLI works like a more traditional (or old-fashioned) operating-system interface. Actions are invoked by typing in command words that have to adhere to a strict set of rules or syntax. If a user types a command using the wrong syntax, the program to execute that command has little choice other than to abort, perhaps giving the user a hint as to why it did so. Programs that are run from the CLI level can use the Amiga windows and requesters, but newcomers to the Amiga are still likely to find the CLI much less user-friendly than the Workbench.

As far as the programmer is concerned, it makes little difference whether the program is run from the CLI or the Workbench. If you decide that one environment or another suits your project best, it is possible to find out whether your program has been launched from the CLI or otherwise. This is demonstrated in the example programs in Chapters 11 and 13.

You now have a picture of the Amiga system as a whole. You have an overall picture of what it is you're programming, and also a rough idea of how to do it. The next chapter will take a closer look at what is available from the libraries when you are using the Amiga's software interface.

Chapter

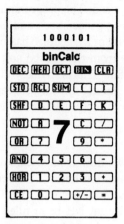

The Software Interface to the Amiga

The Amiga software interface consists of a number of libraries, each of which takes care of work under a logically distinct heading. An application interfaces with the routines in the library by supplying parameters described in the documentation for each routine. To be able to use any library effectively, you need to have a good idea of what it contains. This chapter takes a look at the contents of libraries, but doesn't delve deeply into the method of using them. The *ROM Kernel Manual* exists for this purpose. After reading this chapter, you'll know how the software interface is broken up and where to look to see if a library routine exists to accomplish something you need.

STRUCTURES

Before browsing through the libraries, we'll take a closer look at structures and how they are used in assembly-language programs. Structures are used by many routines throughout the Amiga's software libraries, and a good understanding of them is necessary to make these library routines function properly.

Structures are simply areas of memory of a definite size. Within this area, bytes, words, and long words are used to represent objects that the system needs to deal with. These objects will always be in the same place relative to the start of the structure. The location at which an object is placed within the structure is called its *offset*. Each member of a structure must be at a known offset; otherwise the routines that use them would have no way of knowing where a particular value is to be found. In keeping with the requirements of the 68000 in the Amiga, it is usual to find words and long words within structures aligned at an even address to prevent odd-address errors from occurring when they are accessed. This sometimes means padding with an extra byte to bring a structure member to an even location.

The layout of each structure and the meanings of each member are dependent upon whichever library routine is being used. The programmer of each routine decides which items of information are likely to be passed back and forth between an application and the routines it uses. Once the layout of a structure has been decided, its format is fixed.

Whenever you use a routine from the Amiga software library that uses a structure, its format is explained in detail. This is so that you, as a programmer, know which fields in the structure have any meaning in your program. This may sound like a headache, but in fact it makes things very simple. An example or two will make things clearer.

Macros and Windows

Whenever you open a new window from within a program, you use the routine called OpenWindow from the Intuition library. To function properly, the OpenWindow routine needs an address that it expects to find in register a0. This address will point to a NewWindow structure that has been filled with values determining what kind of window you want, where you want it to appear on the screen, and other options specified in the NewWindow structure. Figure 7-1 shows the format. It has been taken from the gadget display program in Chapter 11.

Whenever you open a new window, you simply initialize a structure (giving your window specifications) and pass the structure address to OpenWindow. In the example below, NewWind is the structure's address as yielded by equating the address (New-Window) with the current assembler location (*). It couldn't be simpler.

```
New Wind    equ     *
LeftEdge    dc.w    100
TopEdge     dc.w    50
Width       dc.w    200
Height      dc.w    60
DetailPen   dc.b    -1
BlockPen    dc.b    -1
IDCMPFlags  dc.l    CLOSEWINDOW!GADGETUP!MENUPICK
Flags       dc.l    WINDOWCLOSE!SMART_REFRESH!ACTIVATE
FirstGadget dc.l    Gadget0
CheckMark   dc.l    0
Title       dc.l    wtitle
Scren       dc.l    0
BitMp       dc.l    0
MinWidth    dc.w    0
MinHeight   dc.w    0
MaxWidth    dc.w    0
MaxHeight   dc.w    0
Type        dc.w    WBENCHSCREEN
```

Fig. 7-1. The format of the NewWindow structure used in the Gadget Box program.

Despite this simplicity, there's something of a disadvantage in the method used to declare the NewWindow structure above. By giving each member of the structure a unique name (such as TopEdge), it's easy to address it directly from within a program, but if there happens to be two or more NewWindow structures in a program, there will have to be a unique name for each "TopEdge" member of every structure. You could use TopEdge1, TopEdge2, and so on, but this can become tedious with so many structures to keep track of. For instance, the calculator program in Chapter 13 has to be able to address 40 gadget structures.

It would make much more sense to be able to refer to a structure member as an offset from the structure start. Not only is this less tiresome, but you can use one of the addressing modes of 68000 that lends itself perfectly to this situation—address register indirect with displacement. If TopEdge were defined to be a displacement instead of an absolute address, it could be used anywhere in a program to access the proper location within the structure. In the above example, there is a two-byte word (dc.w) preceding it, so TopEdge would be equated to the number 2—it is set two bytes into the structure. Thus, if register a1 contained the address of the NewWindow structure, the following instruction:

```
MOVE.W   d0,TopEdge(a1)
```

would move the 16-bit word from d0 into the top edge value of the NewWindow structure. If register a1 were changed to contain the address of a different NewWindow structure, the very same opcode would access two bytes into that structure. This method of labeling using offset names is how structures are defined and accessed in the Amiga. When you use structures, as long as you access values at their preordained offsets from the structure start, you will be using a known parameter.

As another example, consider the structure defining a gadget that may be used within a window (Fig. 7-2). Aside from a few comments, this appears exactly as it is defined in the include file—intuition.i—that is provided with the Amiga Macro Assembler package. You'll notice what appear to be some strange storage declarations in the opcode fields. These are, in fact, predefined macros taken from another include file called types.i. These storage macros allow a structure to be defined much more easily, and allow each member of the structure to be referred to by a named offset into the structure. In this structure, predefined macros allocate structure storage according to the length of the data type for each structure element. These macros, as defined in the types.i file, are used extensively throughout other include files. A perusal through types.i shows which data-type macros have been predefined. The ones used in this example are as follows:

WORD—a 16-bit data word, two bytes long.
LONG—a 32-bit data word, four bytes long.
APTR—an address pointer, four bytes long.
STRUCTURE—a macro to define the start of the structure and some space at the start so that it can be linked into a list or queue.
LABEL—this macro defines a label that is the size of the entire structure.

```
        STRUCTURE  Gadget,0

        APTR     gg_NextGadget        ;next gadget in the list
        WORD     gg_LeftEdge          ;"hit box" of gadget
        WORD     gg_TopEdge           ;"hit box" of gadget
        WORD     gg_Width             ;"hit box" of gadget
        WORD     gg_Height            ;"hit box" of gadget
        WORD     gg_Flags             ;see below for list of defines
        WORD     gg_Activation        ;see below for list of defines
        WORD     gg_GadgetType        ;see below for defines


    ;appliprog can specify that the Gadget be rendered as either as Border
    ;or an Image. This variable points to which (or equals NULL if there's
    ;nothing to be rendered about this Gadget)

    APTR    gg_GadgetRender

     ;appliprog can specify "highlighted" imagery rather than algorithmic
    ;this can point to either Border or Image data
    APTR    gg_SelectRender


    APTR    gg_GadgetText        ;text for this gadget


    LONG    gg_MutualExclude     ;set bits mean this gadget excludes that


    ;pointer to a structure of special data required by Proportional, String
    ;and Integer Gadgets
    APTR    gg_SpecialInfo


    WORD    gg_GadgetID          ;user's ID field


    APTR    gg_UserData          ;ptr to g.p. user data


    LABEL   gg_SIZEOF
```

Fig. 7-2. The intuition-library gadget structure.

Other Macros

Many useful macros are defined in other include files. For instance, the include file alert.i contains a macro called ALERT. By including this file in your source code, you can have the code generated to cause an alert simply by using the ALERT macro and specifying some parameters that you want passed to the alert library routine. The library macros, used this way, can save a lot of coding effort.

Equates

In addition to structure and macro definitions, the include files contain many labeled *equates*. These equates allow you to use names in place of absolute quantities in your program. This makes your program infinitely more readable.

For instance, when specifying a gadget to be used in a window, a flag field (called gg-Flags) exists within the gadget structure; it determines how the gadget is to be highlighted when selected by the user. Imagine you want your gadget to have a box drawn around it when it is selected. This is accomplished by setting the bit in position zero of gg__Flags to one. For you as the programmer, it is far more enjoyable and readable, and much less prone to cause an error, if you achieve this by using a value called GADGHBOX rather than the number 1, even though each is equivalent to the other.

Many such equates exist within the include files. The usefulness of these equates, wherever they are available, cannot be exaggerated. Take a look at the portion of the intuition.i include file shown in Fig. 7-3. Once again, this has been extracted from the part of the file dealing with gadgets. Notice that the third value equated is the GADGHBOX value mentioned above. You can see that it would be almost impossible to do without the numerous equates defined in this file. There are so many values—all with different meanings—that your program stands only to gain by their use; not only in readability, but in accuracy. You're much less likely to make a mistake when using a mnemonic such as GADGHBOX rather than having to remember which bit it represents.

Fig. 7-3. A portion of the intuition.i include file.

```
; - - - FLAGS SET BY THE APPLIPROG

; combinations in these bits describe the highlight technique to be used
GADGHIGBITS      equ    $0003
GADGHCOMP        equ    $0000    ;Complement the select box
GADGHBOX         equ    $0001    ;Draw a box around the image
GADGHIMAGE       equ    $0002    ;Blast in this alternate image
GADGHNONE        equ    $0003    ;don't highlight


; set this flag if the GadgetRender and SelectRender point to Image imagery,
; clear if it's a Border
GADGIMAGE        equ    $0004


; combinations in these next two bits specify to which corner the gadget's
; Left & Top coordinates are relative. If relative to Top/Left,

; these are "normal" coordinates
GRELBOTTOM       equ    $0008    ; set if rel to bottom, clear if rel top
```

```
GRELRIGHT        equ   $0010   ; set if rel to right, clear if to left

; set the RELWIDTH bit to spec that Width is relative to width of screen
GRELWIDTH        equ   $0020

; set the RELHEIGHT bit to spec that Height is rel to height of screen

GRELHEIGHT       equ   $0040


; the SELECTED flag is initialized by you and set by Intuition. It
; specifies whether or not this Gadget is currently selected/highlighted
SELECTED         equ   $0080

; the GADGDISABLED flag is initialized by you and later set by Intuition
; according to your calls to On/OffGadget( ). It specifies whether or not
; this Gadget is currently disabled from being selected
GADGDISABLED  equ   $0100


; - - - GADGET TYPES

; These are the Gadget Type definitions for the variable GadgetType.
; Gadget number type MUST start from one. NO TYPES OF ZERO ALLOWED.
; first comes the mask for Gadget flags reserved for Gadget typing
GADGETTYPE       equ   $FC00   ; all Gadget Global Type flags (padded)

SYSGADGET        equ   $8000   ; 1 = SysGadget, 0 = AppliGadget

SCRGADGET        equ   $4000   ; 1 = ScreenGadget, 0 = WindowGadget

GZZGADGET        equ   $2000   ; 1 = Gadget for GIMMEZEROZERO borders

REQGADGET        equ   $1000   ; 1 = this is a Requester Gadget

; system gadgets
SIZING           equ   $0010

WDRAGGING        equ   $0020

SDRAGGING        equ   $0030

WUPFRONT         equ   $0040

SUPFRONT         equ   $0050

WDOWNBACK        equ   $0060

SDOWNBACK        equ   $0070
```

```
        CLOSE            equ    $0080

; application gadgets
        BOOLGADGET       equ    $0001

        GADGET0002       equ    $0002

        PROPGADGET       equ    $0003

        STRGADGET        equ    $0004
```

THE INCLUDE FILES

Altogether, there are about seventy include files listed in Commodore's *ROM Kernel Manual*. The few outlined here will give you a feel for what's available to the assembly-language programmer, and when certain files might be used. Here is a brief rundown of some of the include files available:

alerts.i

This file contains a useful macro called ALERT, which simplifies the code that has to be written to invoke an alert box on the Amiga screen. When such an alert is displayed, it is shown with some "magic" numbers describing the cause of the alert. These special alert numbers are all defined within this file.

dos.i

As its name implies, this file contains information of relevance to the disk operating system. Some DOS structures, such as FileInfoBlock, are defined here. Of particular interest are the equates that define the DOS error codes returned by the IoErr library call.

dosextens.i

This file extends the usefulness of the dos.i include file. It is intended for programmers who need more in-depth features than provided in dos.i. Many structures, such as the DOS process structure and the command line interface structure, are defined here.

intuition.i

This file contains all the structures and definitions required to use the Intuition user interface. It will be used by any application programmer who needs to use windows, menus, gadgets, and so on. Any of the objects associated with the graphical user interface will have their equates and data structures defined here.

Another useful thing about intuition.i is the inclusion of many descriptive comments throughout the file. These help to clear up any misunderstandings that might arise regarding the internal use of intuition.

libraries.i

The libraries.i include file contains some definitions that are useful when you are writing your own libraries. More useful, though, are the macros provided to simplify library calls and external definitions. These are described in detail in the next section.

lists.i and nodes.i

These files are used to help deal with the lists and queues used by exec. The list.i file contains many macros that generate list-manipulation assembly code. Some useful node identification values are defined in nodes.i.

ports.i

This file defines the message and message port structures required when using the message-passing mechanisms of the executive.

startup.i

This include file contains structures useful for a program that has been started up from the Amiga Workbench.

tasks.i

This file is included if your program (which runs as an Amiga task) needs to know anything about its runtime environment. It contains task-related structures and equates.

types.i

The types.i file contains the definitions of various basic data types. These definitions are subsequently used by other include files. Whenever another include file defines a data-structure specification, it will do so using data types defined here. For that reason, most other include files themselves need to include types.i. Consequently, types.i is likely to be the first included file in many programs.

THE LIBRARY CALL

So far, you've taken a look at the tools provided in the form of named equates and structures. Now, a closer look at the mechanism used to perform useful work on the Amiga—the library call—is needed.

As explained in the last chapter, the library routines are called by executing a JSR to an offset from a library's base address. This base address is only known to a program after the library in question has been opened. Thus, before using any library routine, the library must have already been opened and its base address pointer saved. The open is accomplished by using an exec library call appropriately named Open-Library. You need to know the exec library base before you are able to use this call. Apparently, a special situation exists at this point. It seems as if you need exec's library base in order to open the exec library to find its library base! In fact, you don't need to open the exec library to find its base address. A location exists in the Amiga's memory that always contains exec's library base pointer. This is absolute location 4, more properly referred to by the name _AbsExecBase.

Suppose you wanted to open a window on the Amiga screen. As you've already seen, this is performed by using the OpenWindow routine available from the Intuition library. Before you can use the routine, you have to open the Intuition library. To open Intuition requires the OpenLibrary call to be available. This is part of the exec library, which therefore must itself be located first. Thus two main steps are required before using OpenWindow:

1. Find the exec library's base pointer. The OpenLibrary procedure will then be available.
2. Open the Intuition library. The OpenWindow procedure is now available.

Obviously, location 4 is a very important address in the Amiga and should never be changed by any program.

To call a routine within a library, its base address is loaded into an address register and a JSR made to a negative offset from this base. By convention, the address register used is usually a6, but it can be any 68000 address register, if so desired. From assembly language, all library routines on the Amiga are called by using the routine name preceded by __LVO. The characters LVO stand for library vector offset. Every single assembly language library call is performed this way. The exec library routine Disable, for example, would be called as follows:

```
MOVEA.L    _AbsExecBase,a6

JSR        _LVODisable(a6)
```

In the above example, __AbsExecBase would have previously been defined as four, but what about __LVODisable? None of the __LVO names are equates, even though they only represent a negative offset from a library base. Each one of them has to be individually defined as an external quantity by your program prior to its use. The actual value assigned to each offset is determined not by the assembler but by the linker after the assembly has been completed. The linker program will link your assembled object code with any library you specify. It's this library that lets the linker know what values to assign to the __LVO offsets. When the library was put together, its __LVO names were defined as externals using the assembler XDEF directive. When your program wants to access them, they will be defined as external references by using the assembler's XREF directive. Thus, the assembler knows to leave such symbols to the linker, which gets their values from the library you specify.

To recap the library call mechanism: first, the required library must be opened to obtain its base address. This base address should be saved as it will be needed whenever you are using that library. Then, when a routine from a library is needed, the appropriate library base address should be in register a6. Finally, at the source code level, a JSR __LVOName(a6) is executed. It performs the subroutine call.

A few useful macros exist within the include file libraries. These macros are named LINKLIB and CALLLIB. Another useful macro, called EXTERN__LIB, is defined in types.i. These macros are provided for assembly language programmers as a shortcut to the regular protocol of declaring and calling library routines. When you declare a library routine as external, you do so using a line such as:

```
XREF   _LVODebug
```

By using the macro EXTERN_LIB, you can simply type:

```
EXTERN_LIB   Debug
```

When expanded by the assembler, this would generate the XREF line above but would spare you the clutter of the _LVO prefix.

Most assembly-language library calls are performed using code such as:

```
JSR   _LVOName(a6)
```

The CALLLIB macro allows you to omit the (a6) register specification. The above JSR could then be coded as:

```
CALLIB   _LVOName
```

This assumes that register a6 already contains a valid library address. If not, you could preserve the contents of a6 on the stack before loading it with the proper library address. After making the library call, you would then restore a6 from the stack. All this would look something like this:

```
MOVE.L     a6,-(sp)

MOVE.L     lib_base,a6

JSR        _LVOName(a6)

MOVE.L     (sp)+,a6
```

Using the LINKLIB macro, this entire four lines of code can be replaced by typing:

```
LINKLIB    _LVOName,lib_base
```

REGISTER CONVENTIONS

All Amiga system functions use a consistent set of register conventions. By knowing and following them, you'll have a chance of following the same protocol within your own code. You'll also know which registers might or might not be corrupted by any routines.

Data registers d0 and d1, and address registers a0 and a1 are always available as "scratch" registers. Other routines you call are allowed to change these registers without saving them. Your routines may do the same. Therefore, if any of these four registers contain valid data before a call, they should be saved before you make the call and then restored afterwards. If you pass any parameters in these registers, they might not be there after a function call. All other registers will be kept intact.

If a routine yields a result, it is returned in register d0. If more than one result is returned, the most important will be in d0, and others will be stored in data structures.

Address register a6 is used by the Amiga system functions as a library base pointer. Its use as a parameter register is therefore discouraged.

THE LIBRARY ROUTINES

With this description of the mechanism of the Amiga software interface, it remains only to know what routines are available to perform the work required by your program. This is once again where the *ROM Kernel Manual* comes in. It describes in detail what each function does, which library it is found in, what parameters need to be passed, and what results may be returned. You can find some of these details in the appendix, which gives a list of these functions and the registers used by them. Here is a quick rundown of the libraries available and the kind of routines they perform:

clist.library

This library contains routines that deal with the manipulation of character lists, which contain variable-length strings of bytes that can be dynamically allocated and deallocated in discrete blocks of the Amiga's RAM.

diskfont.library

This contains two routines, AvailFonts and OpenDiskFont, which provide information about fonts stored on disk.

dos.library

In dos.library, you'll find all the routines concerned with file handling. All kinds of files are supported by this library, not just disk files. Routines exist to open, close, lock, position, read, and write files. Disk directories are also handled by this library. Routines are provided for process handling as well as loading and unloading program code. The Execute routine allows you to run a CLI command from within your program.

exec.library

This important library contains all the routines necessary to run tasks on the Amiga. It consists of nearly 90 separate routines that perform various system duties. Some routines deal at the low level of the 68000 microprocessor, while others deal at the Amiga library level. The routines fall under the following headings:

Devices
Interrupts
Libraries
Lists
Memory Allocation
Messages
Resources
Tasks

The exec library, among a few other miscellaneous routines, contains the code to perform an alert. Also included is the Debug routine, which provides the interface with the machine-code debugger.

graphics.library

This large library contains the code that allows you to use the Amiga's graphic capabilities right down to the hardware level. This library, however, doesn't deal with high-level entities such as gadgets or windows—the intuition library serves that purpose. The graphics library is used more for dealing with the graphics hardware than dealing with user-interface graphics such as menus or pointers. There are routines that deal with pixels, image areas, text, gels, sprites, and blitter objects. In all, nearly 100 routines are available for graphic programming of the Amiga.

icon.library

This library contains routines that deal with the Workbench icons and the entities they represent.

intuition.library

This is another library that ranks in importance alongside the exec and graphics libraries. The routines in this library give the programmer the opportunity to access the Amiga's user-friendly interface. It's the Intuition routines that allow applications to provide the end user with the familiar environment of multiple windows and menu selections. More than 60 library routines are available. They allow the manipulation of screens, windows, gadgets, requesters, menus, text items, and messages. An interface to the Workbench is also provided.

layers.library

Contained in this library are the low-level routines used in maintaining layers of screen objects.

The Mathematics Libraries

Three separate library files are provided for dealing with floating-point quantities in Motorola and IEEE format. They are as follows:

mathffp.library. This provides routines for dealing with numbers in Motorola Fast Floating Point format.

mathtrans.library. This is a transcendental math library that contains functions for dealing with floating-point numbers in the same Motorola format.

mathieeedoubbas.library. This library file contains routines to deal with double-precision floating-point numbers in IEEE format.

Chapter

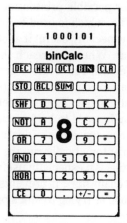

8

The Amiga 68000 Development System

The Amiga Macro Assembler Development System is available as the official Commodore-Amiga tool for assembly-language software developers. Although most material in this chapter is based specifically around that product, the principles involved won't change very much from one development package to another. Some might offer enhancements to the material that is covered here; some might save you money by offering less. Either way, whatever editor/assembler you happen to be using and whichever debugger you have, this chapter will give you an overview of the typical parts in any development system.

The Commodore-Amiga development package consists of a number of interrelated programs. First, you'll be using one of the two Amiga editors—either Ed or Edit—that are available from the Workbench disk. The editor is normally included as part of many assembler packages, but in the Amiga's case it's already available in the c directory. On the Macro Assembler development disk, in addition to the assembler itself, there's a linker, a debugger, a few utilities, a linking library, and those all-important include files. Also from the Workbench disk, the Execute command can be put to good use to automate an entire pass through the assembler, utilities, and linker.

A normal sequence of events is started by entering the source code into the editor. It doesn't matter which one you use as long as it produces ASCII text. The file produced by the editor is then input to the assembler, which produces a relocatable linker file. The linker program, upon reading this file, produces the final application file, linking with other files or libraries if necessary. Theoretically, the application program can then be run; however, this process assumes everything goes perfectly the first time (which it rarely does). Usually, a few typographical errors creep into the source code the first time it is input. Upon sensing these, the assembler gives some error messages; at this point you have to retrace your steps back to the editor stage to correct them.

As well as an object-code file, the assembler can also produce two other files. The first is an optional listing file for possible printout or perusal on the screen. Second, you can request a verification file, which is used to keep a list of any error messages that may be generated. This is especially useful if a lot of errors that would otherwise go flying by on the screen occur. When you reach the stage at which all typos have been weeded out, the assembler will run without producing any error messages.

After the linker produces an executable application, the chances are that something won't work exactly as anticipated. Then the debugger part of the development system—called ROMWack—can be used to help track down the problem. (This is assuming that cold, logical common sense can't identify the problem first.)

The Execute command can automatically run the assembler, linker, and even the application itself from a script file. An especially useful thing about the Execute command is that if one step in the chain fails, it prevents the next from being executed. This prevents wasted efforts, such as trying to link a program that was assembled with errors in it.

The following sections provide a look at each of the main parts of the system in more detail.

THE EDITOR

The editor part of the Amiga development system will be used to produce link control files as well as to process assembly-language source code. The link control files contain instructions that are used by the linker to find out which relocatable files to link together. You will also use the editor if you wish to produce a job control (or script) file. This is read by the Execute command to direct its automatic sequencing of operations on the Amiga.

There are two main editors available on the Amiga; they differ mainly in the way they let you deal with the file being edited. One of the editors, called Edit, only deals with text one line at a time. The other, called Ed, lets you manipulate a whole screenful at a time. Line editors are a throwback to the days when the most common console in use was a teletype terminal. These could only function using a line at a time for input and output, and were thus best served by a line editor. With the advent of video terminals, screen editors became available. Screen editors can take advantage of the fact that a large rectangle of characters is available for viewing. It would seem from these facts that a screen editor is the most natural choice on the Amiga. If you're already used to using a line editor, however, you might want to use Edit—otherwise Ed seems the more natural choice.

Most modern screen editors function in a similar manner. When Ed starts up, you are either looking at a blank screen because you're creating a new file, or you see the beginning screenful of an existing file. Either way, if you start typing printable characters, they are placed on the screen at the position where the cursor is displayed. Certain keys—such as the arrows—move the cursor around the screen, scrolling the file forwards or backwards on the screen if necessary. Other keys perform commands the instant they are pressed; for example, the backspace key immediately deletes the character to the left of the cursor. Other immediate commands that are performed by control keys include inserting and deleting lines, moving to the top and bottom of the screen, and other simple functions.

Many functions are performed by using *extended commands*. These commands usually require more than a single keystroke in order to work. This includes things such as saving the file, inserting files, and manipulating blocks, all of which require multiple keystrokes to define the item being worked on. Extended commands are initiated by pressing the escape key. A command line upon which you type the extended command then appears at the bottom of the screen.

The kinds of text manipulation allowed by the editor include the movement, insertion, and deletion of demarcated blocks of text. Also, a command to find or change a string of characters is included in the extended commands. This will look for the specified string and optionally change it to another. Other features are included to help in formatting text in columns for easy reading. Tab stops can be set at predefined regular points across the page by changing the tab distance (variable tab fields are not supported). The editor also provides an auto-indent facility. This lets you set an automatic left-hand margin that will be taken as the alignment for the first character on each new line after the return key is pressed.

The editor can deal with text files only. Don't try to edit Amiga files containing pictures; the editor simply cannot deal with such nontextual information. Files produced by one editor can, however, be input to another as long as they are saved in ASCII format. Most editors do this normally, but some word-processors don't.

THE ASSEMBLER

The assembler is probably the heart of the whole development system. This is the program that takes the source text files and produces a file containing relocatable object code and the symbol table. None of the output from the assembler is directly executable as a machine-code application. Even an application consisting of a single source-code file has to be dealt with by the linker before a usable application is produced.

The assembler is started up from the command line interface and takes the following form:

```
ASSEM <sfile> <parameters>
```

where <sfile> is the name of the source-code file, and <parameters> specifies information to direct the assembler as follows:

- −o object file
- −l listing file
- −v verification file
- −h header file
- −c options
- −i include directories

The − o switch specifies the object file to be output by the assembler. If this is not given, no object file will be produced. The listing file is also optional and is specified after the −l switch. Any errors detected are normally displayed on the screen unless redirected by the specification of a verification file. The assembler can be forced to include a file at the head of the source code by using the −h flag. Normally, include files are assumed by the assembler to be present in the current directory. You can specify other directories to be scanned by naming them after the −i switch. Finally, the assembler can be passed some options after the −c switch. These options are as follows:

C   ignore case distinction in labels.
D   don't dump local labels as part of the symbol dump.
S   output a symbol dump with the object file.
Wn use a workspace of size n bytes.
X   append a cross-reference table to the listing file.

Only ASCII text files can be input to the assembler. These files consist of lines of text separated by new line characters. They may be assembler directives (pseudo-ops), assembly-language lines, comment lines, or blank lines. The listing file, which can be optionally produced by specifying the −l switch, can subsequently be output to the printer or the serial port by using the regular utilities on the Amiga, such as TYPE or PRINT.

Assembler source-code lines contain four possible fields: a label, an opcode mnemonic, an operand, and a comment. An example looks like this:

```
label1:    MOVE      #3,D0          ;Use two-bit mask
```

Normally the assembler discriminates between upper- and lowercase in labels, taking LoOp and loop as separate symbols. If, however, you use the −c C option, the assembler doesn't make any distinctions between upper- and lowercase—label1 would be exactly the same to the assembler as LaBeL1. Strings within quotes, however, are always used as specified in upper- and lowercase with no case conversion. If a label is indented from the left-hand side, the assembler has no way of knowing if the indentation leads to a label or an unlabeled opcode. Therefore, to identify a label that has been indented, it must be immediately followed by a colon; for example, Label2:. Otherwise, as long as a label starts in the leftmost column, it doesn't have to have a colon appended. *Local labels*, which are labels whose scope is limited to a delimited section of code; are allowed. Local labels are identified by a decimal number up to three digits in length followed by a dollar sign. These local labels are significant to the assembler only within a section of code delimited at both ends by a normal, nonlocal label. They are useful because they can be used over and over again, thus saving space in the assembler's symbol table.

The opcode field has to be preceded by at least one space or tab character. It can be a 68000 opcode mnemonic, an assembler directive, or a macro instruction. The operand, if any, that follows must also be preceded by a space or a tab. The final item on the line—the comment—is often delineated by a semicolon, but this is not mandatory. The Amiga assembler ignores anything following the space or tab after the operand field. The remainder of the line is then bypassed by the assembler. An asterisk in the first column signifies that the whole line is a comment and will be entirely skipped over during the assembly process.

The normal 68000 instruction lengths of byte, word, and long word are signified by the opcode suffixes .B, .W, and .L. Branch instructions are normally assembled in their long form, but .S may be appended to a branch opcode to cause it to be assembled in its short form. In contrast, jump instructions default to the word form unless the address specified is 32 bits long. The assembler does not recognize the .L suffix as specifying the long-word form of a jump.

In numerical expressions, binary, decimal, hexadecimal and octal numbers are all recognized by the assembler. Decimal is the default, and can be overruled by prefixing the number with a symbol. A percent sign specifies a binary number, a dollar sign specifies a hexadecimal number, and an at symbol (@) is used to denote an octal number. Expressions involving any of these number bases may be used wherever an operand requires a number.

Strings are specified by placing single quotes around the characters. A single quote within the string is represented by two successive single quotes.

Symbols used within the assembly may contain the alphanumeric characters (A-Z, a-z, and 0-9), an underline, a period, or a dollar sign. To be distinguished as a symbol, it can only start with an alphabetical character, an underline, or a period. The symbol names used can be up to 30 characters in length. If they are any longer, they will be truncated, and a warning message will be issued. Although the assembler normally distinguishes between upper- and lowercase in labels, it doesn't make any such distinction with opcodes or register names.

Figure 8-1 is a list of assembler directives available. This will give you a good idea of the capabilities available to the macro assembler within the Amiga Development System.

THE LINKER

The linker program produces the final executable version of an application by linking together its constituent object files as produced by the assembler.

The linker uses two kinds of input files: a WITH file that can optionally control the linker, and any number of relocatable object files (including libraries). It produces up to four kinds of output files: the application itself, a map file, a cross-reference file, and a verification file. The verification file lists any errors or warnings that might have been detected during the link process. The linker is invoked from the CLI using the following format:

```
ALINK FROM <ffile> TO <tfile> WITH <wfile> VER <vfile>

     LIBRARY <lfiles> MAP <mfile> XREF <xfile> WIDTH n
```

The files specified are:

<ffile>	the file to link from (output from the assembler).
<tfile>	the file to send link output to (the application).
<wfile>	a parameter file as specified below.
<vfile>	a verification file containing linker error messages.

Assembler Control Directives

CNOP	Conditional no op
END	End of source code
ENDC	End conditional assembly
IFcc	Assembly conditional on cc
IDNT	Name program unit
INCLUDE	Include source file
OFFSET	Define offset table
RORG	Relative origin
SECTION	Program section

Symbol Definition Directives

DC	Define constant
DCB	Define constant block
DS	Define storage
ENDM	End macro definition
EQU	Equate permanent value
EQUR	Equate register
MACRO	Define macro
MEXIT	Exit macro expansion
REG	Define register list
SET	Equate temporary value
XDEF	Symbol defined as external
XREF	Symbol referenced is externally defined

Assembler Listing Control

FAIL	Flag assembler error
LIST	Enable program listing
LLEN	Set listing line length
NOOBJ	Disable object code output
NOLIST	Disable program listing
NOPAGE	Disable listing pagination
PAGE	Eject to top of page
PLEN	Set listing page length
SPC	Space blank lines
TTL	Set program listing title

Fig. 8-1. Assembler directives available to the macro assembler in the Amiga Development System.

<lfiles>	library files to be searched for any unresolved labels.
<mfile>	a link map output file.
<xfile>	a cross-reference output file.

The linker can be directed in its execution by the control file, which is named using the WITH parameter at the CLI command line to ALINK. This file determines which object files and libraries should be linked and, optionally, how the application should be segmented. It can also select the listing width option. Each command in the control file is contained in a separate line and is preceded by any of the command keywords as specified on the CLI command line itself.

Here's the full list of linker commands that can appear in a WITH files:

FROM (or ROOT)	<ffiles>
TO	<tfile>
LIBRARY	<lfiles>
MAP	<mfile>
XREF	<xfile>
OVERLAY	
<tree structure>	
#	
WIDTH	n

The parameters are, for the most part, the same as those specified on the ALINK command line. One additional command can be used, and that involves the sequence OVERLAY <tree structure> #. This permits an application to be split into separate pieces to save memory.

Each program overlay is actually loaded into memory only when a call is made to one of its routines. This is all totally invisible to the program code, which just executes as if it were in one whole piece. The linker provides the workhorse in the form of an overlay supervisor that it links in with the application code. This overlay supervisor then keeps track of which module needs to be in memory at any particular time. The tree structure given with the OVERLAY command tells the linker which module is capable of being called by (and therefore overlaying) another.

THE AMIGA DEBUGGER

The debugging section of any development system is one of its most important parts. Many programmers would argue that it's even more important than the assembler. That's why the assembler was described as *probably* the heart of the development system. The reason for the debugger's eminence is because more development time is often spent in debugging the program than in writing and assembling it.

The Amiga debugger, ROMWack, can be used when the application is loaded to allow some control over its execution. This is taken for granted by programmers of interpreted languages like BASIC, but for a machine-code programmer, such control rarely exists. The most common occurrence involving a bug in a machine-code program is that the system crashes and the offending code is overwritten by garbage. Even if you can recover the operating system, there might be no evidence left to analyze.

ROMWack resides in memory as part of the Amiga ROM software. As with other ROM routines, library calls that enable use of some of the debugger facilities are available. These routines are provided for convenience only; they are not meant to provide the major interface to the debugger.

ROMWack works by communicating at 9600 baud through the serial interface. Thus, to use it, you need another terminal connected to the serial port. By working this way, operation of the debugger doesn't affect anything that appears on the screen. In fact, ROMWack minimizes interference with any of the internal Amiga organization by using a small area of memory and effectively freezing the operating system. Even the Amiga pointer stops tracking when ROMWack is in control. Therefore, you can scan through memory knowing that you're seeing the system exactly as it was when the debugger was invoked.

There are two main ways to use ROMWack. One is to use a utility provided on the system development disk. The utility is itself called ROMWack, and provides a way to enter the ROM debugger. By simply typing ROMWack, the system comes to a dead stop and all the registers are displayed on the external terminal, which now takes control. This method of using the debugger assumes that there is already something in memory that you wish to debug. As you become adept with the Amiga, you can take limited control of the entire operating system from the external terminal.

The easiest way to use ROMWack while debugging an application program is slightly different. You use a special library routine _LVODebug in your code at the point where you want the debugger to take over. Using the debugger like this lets your program execute normally until the _LVODebug call is made. At that point, your program, along with the whole system, stops under control of ROMWack.

When you are in ROMWack, you can step or trace instructions in ROM or RAM, display and change memory or registers, display and set breakpoints, and redirect program execution. Unfortunately, a disassembler that displays opcode mnemonics is not provided, but other Amiga debuggers that provide extra facilities, such as the use of the Amiga console, are available. ROMWack has been kept intentionally simple, and thus small and unobtrusive. When it first gets control, it displays all the 68000's registers and stack frame (memory pointed to by the stack pointer). It then awaits input in the form of one of the commands outlined above. Unfortunately, the buck stops there.

THE UTILITIES

Alongside the assembler and linker, several utilities are provided with the Amiga software development package. Here's a short description of each one:

AbsLoad: This utility loads a relocatable program into an absolute address in memory. All programs output from the linker are relocatable. At run time, they are loaded into whatever memory is available under the control of the executive. Absload lets you specify an absolute address (which may be useful for debugging purposes) and loads it there. Care has to be taken that the memory chosen has not already been allocated to another task.

AddMem: This allows you to manually configure external memory.

ATOM (Alink Temporary Object Modifier): This program allows you to place code and data modules into specific types of the Amiga's memory. For instance, you might want a particular data hunk of a program to be loaded into the Amiga's chip memory area. ATOM specifies this by preprocessing an object module before it is dealt with by the linker. After being modified, it is processed by Alink in the normal way.

Avail: This program lets you list available memory.

Frags: This program allows you to scan memory fragments.

ObjDump: This utility performs a dump of a linked program file. The output is formatted in rows of hexadecimal long words. The constituent code and data chunks are identified as they are encountered in the file.

ROMWack: This program allows you to enter the ROM debugger.

Snoop: This program lets you check on memory usage.

THE INCLUDE FILES

As you will realize by now, the include files are an extremely important part of any software development system. Without them, you're forced to use numerical quantities instead of more easily remembered mnemonics. The include files supplied with the Amiga software development system are so comprehensive that it's difficult to imagine having to program without them.

libraries (dir)		**intuition (dir)**	
diskfont.i	dos.i	intuition.i	
dosextens.i	translator.i		
		resources (dir)	
workbench (dir)		cia.i	ciabase.i
icon.i	startup.i	disk.i	misc.i
workbench.i.		potgo.i	
exec (dir)		**hardware (dir)**	
ables.i	alerts.i	adkbits.i	blit.i
devices.i	errors.i	cia.i	custom.i
exec.i	execbase.i	dmabits.i	intbits.i
execname.i	exec__lib.i		
funcdef.i	initializers.i		
interrupts.i	io.i	**devices (dir)**	
libraries.i	lists.i		
memory.i	nodes.i	audio.i	bootblock.i
ports.i	resident.i	clipboard.i	console.i
strings.i	tasks.i	gameport.i	input.i
types.i		inputevent.i	keyboard.i
		keymap.i	narrator.i
		parallel.i	printer.i
graphics (dir)		serial.i	timer.i
		trackdisk.i	
clip.i	copper.i		
display.i	gels.i		
gfx.i	gfxbase.i		
layers.i	rastport.i		
regions.i	sprite.i		
text.i	view.i		

Fig. 8-2. The layout of the include directory.

It is possible for the include files to be even more accurate than the documentation. This is because the include files are actually used within your program: their contents provide the absolute definition of any quantities or structures used by your program. In fact, while working on the calculator program (see Chapter 13), I came across two mistakes in the preliminary documentation. Each one misdefined a structure, causing the program to malfunction. By scanning the appropriate include file, it was possible to determine the real structures and rectify the program accordingly. In effect, the includes become part of your code; in the case of macros, the includes do actually generate code for you (as in the case of the ALERT macro).

Figure 8-2 shows the layout of the include directory as supplied with the development system. Each file has a descriptive name that gives an idea what software it supports and whether or not it may be worth using in your program.

Chapter

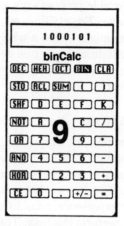

1000101

binCalc

DEC HEH OCT BIN CLR
STO RCL SUM
SHF D E F K
NOT A C /
OR ? 9 *
AND 4 5 6 -
HOR 1 2 3 +
CE 0 . +/- =

9

The Program Design Process

Once you have the programming tools and expertise at your disposal, the temptation to rush in and start writing a program is enormous. The sheer pleasure that can be derived from piecing together the building blocks that comprise a program causes too many programmers to forge ahead regardless of the consequences. The building blocks to build a house can't be put into place until the house has been designed, and exactly the same is true for a program.

Unfortunately, interactive programming languages like BASIC provide such an easy means of writing and debugging programs that many people pick up bad habits. It's so easy to enter a few lines of BASIC code that achieve a small but useful purpose. Then an enhancement is added. Then another. It's not too long before a program of respectable length grows from this process. Then an early routine needs to be changed to deal with a situation that didn't exist when the first few lines were written. More than likely, some of the later routines will use this now-changed routine. Suddenly bugs appear. Things don't work as they did before the change.

Of course, these routines are not at fault, and probably neither is the changed routine. It's just that they don't interface any more—in effect, they don't speak the same language. The results expected from that early routine might have only been changed slightly, but the change affects several other routines. This is a typical design problem. Not only can it be avoided by careful design in the first place, but certain problems can be anticipated and dealt with at the design level.

When you are using assembly language, the testing and debugging stages are much more stringent than when you are using a high-level (especially an interpreted) language. Most often, there are no symbolic names to help identify variables. Comments aren't there in memory along with the code, and a program crash (even from a simple cause) can wipe the program from memory. This is why the debugging phase of assembly language program development nearly always takes longer than the coding. Debugging itself can be an enjoyable process—it's akin to solving logic puzzles—but it can hardly be termed productive. Twenty lines of code sounds like a small amount, and when you consider that you might spend a whole day debugging it, it genuinely is a small amount. Thus, the discipline of program design is of paramount importance in being a productive programmer. A little discipline will reduce development time and result in a higher quality product.

THE PROGRAM SPECIFICATION

The first act of discipline within the overall design of a program is to define the object of the program. Traditionally, in the mainframe world, this task was undertaken by the systems analyst. This person would visit a customer who needed a program. The customer would let the analyst know what was wanted, and the analyst, in the light of considerable computer experience, would form an overall picture of how the computer might be expected to perform this task. The analyst can also cool down some of the more exotic expectations an inexperienced user might expect within the budget and deadline. Finally, a program specification will emerge. This is handed to a programmer, who then turns it into code.

What kinds of things would the analyst need to know? First, results that are required from the program must be determined. Also, the media on which these results are to appear needs to be known. They could be on old-fashioned punched cards or paper tape, or they could be printed out on custom-designed forms. Even the most common output form—printed copy—can be presented in different ways: graphs, numbers, and charts are all possibilities. Another possibility is video output with user-interaction via the keyboard.

The next item in the program specification is the input. To achieve results, some data has to be made available for the computer to work on. Once again, the media can be of many forms; magnetic tape and disk are just two. With small amounts of data, it might be more efficient to have data input directly to the program from the keyboard (or perhaps a mouse). The program will also need to know the input data format. The data might be set up in character blocks of a constant length. The data records might be of varying lengths with delimiters such as carriage returns denoting the ends. Separate items of data, such as numbers and strings, might be in fixed character positions within the record, or might themselves be separated by delimiters such as commas. All these factors will influence the *front end* of a program.

The next concern involves actually processing the data. If memory size is an important constraint, small algorithms will be preferred, even at a cost in processing speed. Conversely, if a real-time application is being designed, the algorithms used will all need to be fine-tuned with an emphasis on speed; sacrifices in memory size will be given a lower priority.

Later, more subtle points arise during a program's specification stage. There might be a requirement for a particularly user-friendly interface between the program and an inexperienced human operator. The program might have to deal with users who range from someone with minimal computer experience to someone who has worked with computers for 20 years. This is the kind of factor that determines the perceived quality of a program, as distinct from its efficiency.

THE PROGRAM DESIGN

Once a specification has been put together, the program must be designed. Unfortunately for impatient programmers, this is not quite yet the time to start writing code.

The design phase may be undertaken by the same person who came up with the specification, or it may be done by the programmer. Obviously, in many—if not most—microcomputing situations, the analyst, designer, programmer, and debugger are all the same person—you.

Program design is often carried out by laying out some kind of graphic representation of the separate parts of a program. The input, output, and error-handling will all be there, as well as a breakdown of the "number crunching" to be performed. Preferably, this should all be represented on a single sheet of paper (or graphics screen), but eventually, most programs will require more. Even so, the basic building blocks should be set out. If any changes are made to the program specification, they can be placed in the block diagram and any possible side effects deduced.

The Flowchart

A block diagram that is more detailed still will often be used. This is the *flowchart*, and is highly recommended at the outset of a programming venture. Sadly, the flowchart has recently taken a few knocks from purists of the structured-programming fraternity. This is because flowcharts tend to encourage thinking in a linear sequence rather than in distinct, separate blocks. For assembly-language programmers, however, there is little choice in how you perceive the workings of the processor. All digital computer processors work in this linear, step-at-a-time fashion with the odd jump to a different sequence. (This is called the *Von Neuman system*.) So, what is anathema to aficionados of structured programming is forced by computer architecture and history on the machine-code programmer. Use flowcharts. They clarify the procedures and possibilities in an algorithm like no other design tool. Once you know the basic shapes used in flowcharts (and most can be drawn with just lines, boxes, and diamonds), you can jot them down in freehand. The time saved in coding and the overall insight gained into any program's workings have even helped build the languages that support structured programming. Figure 9-1 is a list of the more common flowchart symbols, and Fig. 9-2 shows a sample flowchart.

Other useful techniques can be used at the design stage immediately prior to coding. You have a number of options available that are, as much as anything else, an expression of your individual style and preference. These options all involve the structure of your program. As you gain experience in assembly language, you'll be able to build up a library of subroutines. These can be coded in such a way that they become separately usable modules. Even if you don't have such a library available, a program can often be approached in a modular way. The advantage of this is that each module can be written and debugged separately. Thus, instead of having to debug a thousand bytes of a program containing numerous random errors lurking within its code, you can spend 10 sessions working with a hundred bytes at a time. If each module is prop-

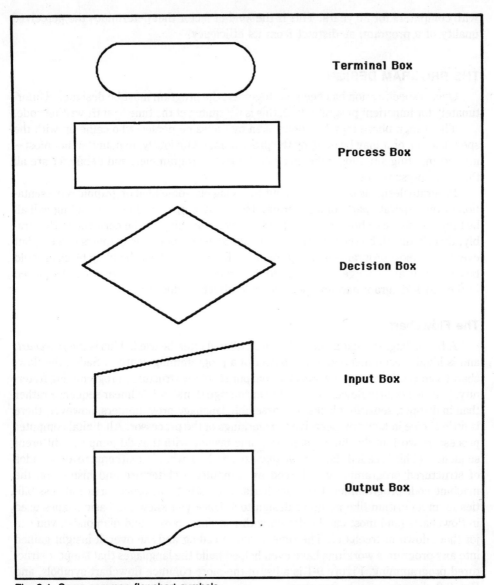

Terminal Box

Process Box

Decision Box

Input Box

Output Box

Fig. 9-1. Some common flowchart symbols.

erly tested and debugged, it can be eliminated from the debugging stage as the whole program is assembled—not only that, but these working modules become candidates for a library.

Structured Programming

Structured programming is another worthwhile tool to explore, even at the machine-code level. This involves breaking the flow of a program into a small number of known constructs. The most important of these are the **do/while** and **if/then/else** constructs. With this pair, it has been proved possible by computer mathematicians to write any program possible on a Von Neuman machine. Keeping your program to these structures simplifies its design and makes it easier to understand.

Coding Discipline

You have one more decision to make before you start coding the program. Two terms are commonly used to describe the overall coding discipline used. One is called *bottom-up* programming, the other, *top-down*. With bottom-up, you start coding at the lower levels first and work your way up. For instance, you would write a routine to read a keyboard before you'd write the routine that used the keyboard's input.

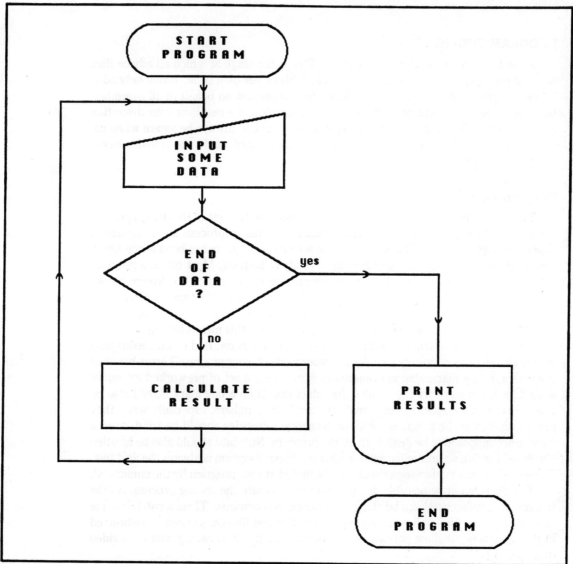

Fig. 9-2. A general flowchart example.

It's the other way around with top-down programming. Here, you program at the upper levels first, to ensure the program handles data as per the specification. Then you fill in the fine details. If you were using this method, the data-handling routines would be written first, with the keyboard data preset somewhere within the program's data area (something like using DATA statements in BASIC). Then, when the program was sufficiently debugged that it was handling data correctly, the keyboard-input routine would be written. When any unwritten routine is called which is to be filled in later, it is called a *stub*.

It's a matter of choice as to whether you use bottom-up or top-down techniques. If you don't have any idea which you'd prefer, try both and see which best suits your style.

PROGRAM CODING

At last, you arrive at the coding phase. This is the stage at which all advice flies out of the window. Each programmer develops his or her own style, which only adds to the enjoyment of this creative art. Apart from a request on behalf of all assembly-language programmers to properly document your code, the rest is at your discretion and experience. It might be useful to point out one caveat: always be aware when using coding tricks that they need extra documentation, and might not transfer easily to another processor.

Program Testing

Program coding is such an enjoyable experience that the rest of the design process becomes forgotten; however, even after coding, the design process has to continue. The next stage is testing. This is the stage at which the program has been successfully passed through the assembly process and is ready to be tried. Most often, a program won't work the first time, so it's always wise to use some kind of breakpoint before it even starts execution. This is covered in further detail under the topic of debugging.

Assuming that a program works well enough that it will even accept data, it's time to make sure that the data is manipulated correctly. First, this means having some data prepared, to test the various building blocks of your program. Bad or erroneous data should always be intentionally included, in order to check your program's error-handling responses. If any manipulation of numbers is involved, a set of preworked examples should be fed in to verify the results. Any data that is on a boundary should also be tried. This would consist of very small or very large numbers, especially when they are anticipated in the program's coding. Negative quantities should be tried, even if they're not supposed to be dealt with by the program. Null data should also be handled correctly. Placing an unfamiliar user in charge of your program is always the acid test. It is incredible what unforeseen events can be hurled at your program by the uninitiated.

Finally, it might be possible in a program to automate the testing process. All the test inputs just described can be placed in a file on the computer. Then, a patch is made to your program, forcing it to accept input from this test file. Output can be redirected in the same way, to allow perusal of results that might otherwise fly past on a video display.

Be hard on your program; if you are not, I can guarantee that somebody else will be—intentionally or otherwise. There's always a temptation to finish a program at all costs, but "all costs" shouldn't include skipping a thorough test. You might be in the middle of writing a section of code and realize that a situation that it hasn't been designed to handle can occur. At the very least, you should write yourself a note to test that situation as soon as possible. Often, you can update the code before a test renders the update mandatory. In the rare case when you have to release "second best" as a working version, ensure that the operator of your program knows of any special cases to avoid. Although this might sound a little unprofessional, the demands of programming in the commercial world sometimes necessitate the release of a flawed program. It still takes thorough testing to reveal these flaws, and a known bug is less likely to cause a catastrophe than a hidden one.

Program Debugging

Debugging is the last phase in which you twist and bend your code with the help of the computer. First, it's useful to become adept at scanning a program that has been dumped to a printer as a list of numbers. These numbers, usually in octal or hexadecimal, can tell you a great deal about where and why your program failed. By getting used to such a dump, or "post mortem," you'll sharpen your skills with an interactive debugger at a keyboard.

Start by identifying the sections of code and data. The operating system or assembler usually provides some indication as to where your program was loaded in memory and where its entry point was. By referring to a printout produced by the assembler, you can pinpoint various opcodes and data areas. Naturally, the dump is just numbers as seen by the processor, but at least you can map it into pieces you recognize. Then, check the data. Often, this will include buffers that contain the last data brought in from an input device or data about to be output. This gives you a good general idea of what the program was dealing with before being dumped. Uninitialized data is an indication of failure in the early stages of a program's execution. Gradually, in the manner of Sherlock Holmes, the evidence provided by the program's data can be connected with the culprit in the form of an errant piece of code.

Happily, these days, interactive debugging is the vogue, but the same techniques can still be applied. Interactive debugging is much less mentally demanding than attempting to digest reams of hexadecimal numbers, and of course, programmers need all the help they can get. If you've become an expert at debugging from a hard-copy dump, you're likely to be a genius with an interactive debugger. These work by allowing you to set breakpoints in your code.

The breakpoint is simply some type of jump or call to the debugger's entry point. When entered, the debugger will display on the screen the current state of the program (i.e., as it was at the breakpoint). You will be able to display registers or memory and, if desired, change the values they contain. There will be some way of setting and removing breakpoints at various places in your program, and a way to jump back to your code. Then, to debug your program, it's a matter of setting the breakpoint as close as possible before the bug occurs. With the program stopped and under control of the debugger, you can spot where a wrong jump was taken or an incorrect value used and take steps to rectify the problem.

Where you place your breakpoints is totally up to you. Use your judgement to suggest a possible trouble spot. If the program still crashes, you simply have to use your judgement again until you get control via the debugger before your program goes awry.

Many debuggers offer spectacular features to aid in the debugging process. Some will allow you to single-step through your code to watch registers and memory being changed. Others allow single-stepping to occur automatically until a preset condition, such as a particular number being placed at a known memory location, is met. *Tracing* is allowed by some debuggers. During a trace, each instruction is printed out as it is executed. The contents of the registers are also displayed. Then it's back to poring over the printout to trace where a fault occurred.

The most sophisticated debuggers allow you to specify a *symbol table* area in memory. This symbol table will consist of addresses and symbols used in your assembly-language source code. Whenever the debugger encounters an address that is stored in the symbol table, it will display the symbol instead of the absolute address. This way, you can disassemble or single step a machine-code program, and the debugger will provide output that closely resembles the original source code. A scan through the features of different debuggers will give you some idea of the kind of options available. Debugging is next in importance to coding in the programmer's art.

DOCUMENTING THE PROGRAM

Finally . . . At last . . . At the very end . . . You have a working program. You can release it to the outside world and feel safe in the knowledge that your hard work and diligence is reflected in a quality program. Unfortunately, there's more yet! You can't just give your program to the user and expect him or her to remember your every step as you demonstrated it. You're going to have to document it first. This is not as easy as it might sound. You're in a unique position as the programmer of a finished project. You know better than anyone else on the planet how your software functions. You know its every intricacy and detail.

Unfortunately, you probably know your program so well you might not do a good job with its documentation. You might take for granted the fact that you hit ENTER at the end of a line or close a disk-drive door before reading a disk—but look out for the neophyte. Alternatively, you might be targeting your program at a highly computer-literate operator, so a minimum of hand-holding is required. But still beware—you have worked on your program for so many weeks, you might easily overlook documenting something that seems to be obvious.

Your documentation should state what the program is supposed to do, with what data. It should specify any error conditions built in and what restart procedures, if any, are available to rescue work already accomplished. Each command in an interactive menu should be thoroughly explained. There should be the name of someone to contact if a serious problem occurs. You should include a section that gives an overview in scant detail of all commands and errors. That way, you have a fact sheet about your program that can be used by a new user of your program who is not yet familiar with your style.

Spend a reasonable amount of time on your documentation. Often, it acts as an ambassador for your work. If it's badly written, terse, or full of grammatical errors, a user will probably suspect the same of your code and the care you put into writing it.

MAINTAINING THE PROGRAM

You could be forgiven for thinking that providing documentation was the end of the program design process; however, there is one last stage that you might hope won't arise, but should be no big surprise if it does. That stage is program maintenance, which includes software upgrades.

If a user decides that a new feature should be added to a program, there's usually no reason why it should not be added. You should be the first "port of call" to accomplish this. As all too often happens, a user may—heaven forbid—find a bug in your program, or an unforeseen change in the data might require the program to be changed in order to handle it. Once again, it's always you who is likely to be the first source for maintaining or upgrading your own work.

By the time the need for maintenance occurs, many months might have passed since you wrote the software. Now is your chance to be the victim of your own coding techniques and documentation. If it's not you who does the maintenance, then the next programmer will be in an even more vulnerable position. The moral is this: very few programs will ever be written and left as they are. Program maintenance is a fact of life. All the foregoing program design processes will manifest themselves in front of your eyes before too long. Previous bad habits in coding and documentation will take their revenge during the debugging stage.

This chapter might have made it seem like programming should be done solely by a monastic order of disciplinarians, but it's only to make a point. All that's really required is a modicum of common sense rather than a severe disciplined approach. That way, you can be as carefree and quality-conscious as a programmer as an artist is in any other artform.

Chapter

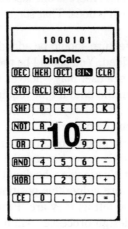

1 0 0 0 1 0 1

binCalc

10

Alternatives to Assembly Language

Since the first chapter, the basics of assembly language through the 68000 microprocessor to the Amiga itself have been covered. What comes after this? First, you have to get an assembler and debugger. Without an assembler, only the most trivial machine-code routines are possible. Without a debugger, correcting errors in programs will be impossible at worst and a nightmare at best. To take advantage of that rich and promising Amiga software interface, to save much work, and to improve source code quality, you should acquire equates files containing the layout of the system structures and their various possible contents. All these constituents come under the heading of an *assembly-language development system*. Any worthwhile system will already contain these parts.

A reference source is required for the library routines available to interface with the Amiga operating system. Because so many library routines are available for use, and the existing routines each have different parameter-passing requirements, it's impossible to use any but the most commonly-used ones. The ROM Kernel Manual published on behalf of Commodore is the bible on this subject.

Once you're comfortable with the instruction set of the 68000 and the system libraries of the Amiga software interface, you're as armed and ready to go as any software developer can be. It's up to your imagination and skill from that point on.

In a book on assembly language, it's difficult to allot a fair amount of space to other programming languages; however, not to do so would be denying their importance, which is considerable, even to an assembly-language programmer. If the effort of programming constantly in assembly language becomes too time-consuming, there are alternatives that are attractive to machine-code programmers. High-level languages can be used in conjunction with assembly language to greatly increase productivity. A Pascal compiler, for example, could be recruited. This would be used to compile Pascal source code into a machine-code program. This might be done via an assembly-language intermediate program or straight from compiler to machine code.

A language such as Pascal gives you the advantage of programming at a high level using structured-programming constructs such as do/while and if/then/else. These constructs are known to encourage logically clear thinking and, thus, more accurate code. The assembly language output rendered by a compiler can then be improved upon to yield source code approaching the quality of a human programmer. Remember, though, that no Pascal or other compiler—no matter how sophisticated—can produce assembly language that runs with anything like the same speed or efficiency as that produced by a human programmer.

The very process of compilation results in the generation of synthetic routines that are built one on top of another. These routines are in complete isolation from each other, often resulting in code that lacks insight and is easily optimized by hand. With a library of routines written in high-level source code, it's possible to manufacture a large volume of assembly-language software that even though not high in efficiency, will work almost as well as a hand-written piece of machine code.

Everything you've just read about Pascal applies to C. Both languages share many similarities and offer you the ability to use structured code to help you write programs that are more likely to work the first time.

Because of its power, C is fast becoming the language of choice for many software professionals. One thing particularly in its favor is the fact that it's easy to visualize the machine code that is being generated by the compiler. C doesn't impose too many rules on programmers and allows for many of the techniques used in assembly language (and many of the abuses). Using C, it is possible to write a program that, when compiled, looks similar to what might have been written directly in assembly language. This fact alone assures its success among many programmers who would otherwise not use a high-level language. In fact, among its advocates are Commodore-Amiga, whose programmers appear to highly favor the use of the C language. Evidently, much of the Amiga operating system was written in C. A C compiler for the Amiga was in use at the same time as the assembler, testifying to its importance as a development tool. All the library routines on the Amiga can be called from C just by using a library routine name followed by its parameters in parentheses. A special interface routine loads these parameters into the correct registers for use by the machine code library routines. Note, however, that even with such a sophisticated language, the ultimate interface is at the machine-code level.

If you want to take advantage of the huge software base of science and engineering programs that already exists, Fortran might be more applicable than either Pascal or C. Business-oriented programmers can use the most widely-used computer language in the world—COBOL. Because they are compiled into machine code, all these languages represent an evolutionary next step after assembly language, but the skills acquired in learning and using assembly language are required before the fullest use can be made of a compiler's output. With these skills, you can rearrange code to make whatever improvements are not possible at the compiler level. Portions can be totally rewritten if necessary, and the compiler will still have done most of the hard work in providing the body of the code. Thus, you can utilize a compiler for the bulk of the code and then use your assembly-language skills in fine-tuning the results. Obviously, this cannot be done without sound knowledge and expertise at the machine-code level.

The use of a higher-level language is entirely at your discretion. You might be quite happy programming away in machine code, but it might be that for a particular project, your productivity will increase as a result of using higher-level software tools, such as compilers and medium-level languages. Unless you become an assembly-language purist (and there are already enough computer elitists), the logical next step is a high-level language, but with your programming roots still firmly embedded in the foundations of assembly language.

A major advantage of using a high-level language is that you can easily build up a large library of modules. This can also be done at the assembly-language level, but the library will contain processor-specific modules. A library of Z-80 routines, for example, has to be completely rewritten for use on a 68000, but the same routines in a C library only have to be recompiled on a different compiler to produce code native to any particular processor.

Here's an example of how low-level code might be generated from some source code written in C:

```
if(x > 1) y=2; else y=3;

        MOVE    x,D0

        CMP     #1,D0

        BLS     .1021

        MOVEQ   #2,y

        BRA     .1022

.1021:  MOVEQ   #3,y

.1022:  ....

        ....
```

This example shows that even though the code was written in C (and looks almost as high-level as BASIC), the assembly language generated by the compiler is just about the same as would have been written by a human programmer.

Using a high-level language, it's almost as if the code were generated from the comments column of the assembly-language source code. This is how, as you achieve familiarity with a compiler, it becomes possible to anticipate the code that will be generated by a compiler. You can then control it by manipulating the high-level code. In effect, you take one step back from the assembler, but still determine what appears as assembly source code. Almost as an added bonus, the high-level language imposes its structure on your thinking, which allows you to see the flow of your logic more clearly. It's as if you were taking a few steps back from a painting while it was still in progress.

None of this high-level language discussion is meant to detract from the art and science of assembly-language programming. Rather, its use should be regarded as a luxury best utilized only by the most competent machine-code programmers. Anyone else programming in a high-level language is totally at the mercy of the compiler. Without an awareness of the final assembly phase, it's almost as if the resultant machine-code program appears by magic.

The step towards a high-level language is by no means mandatory. Many extremely fine pieces of software have been written purely in assembly language, but bear it in mind that if you start feeling frustrated by the rate at which you're producing debugged and working code, it might be time to start thinking about using a compiler. It is hard to imagine how long it would have taken to program the well-known Unix operating system if most of it hadn't been written in C—and this even includes the C compiler running under Unix.

Whatever your next step, take it only after you're fully confident about the language of the computer processor. Although this book focuses on the 68000 chip, any processor will suffice for this first step. It's when you've mastered the low-level techniques that the high-level ones truly open up to you—and you still retain the mystique and respect enjoyed by assembly-language programmers in the upper echelons of programming society.

Chapter

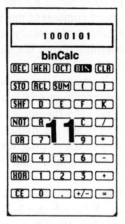

Two Simple
Programming Examples

At long last, the chance to put all that you learned in the preceding chapters into practice has arrived. This chapter describes two simple assembly-language programs written specifically for the Amiga to demonstrate the methods used to interface with the libraries. The following examples assume you are in a CLI window and have ASSEM and ALINK installed in the c directory. The source, object, linked output, and lib/amiga.lib files should also be in the current directory.

THE TEXT PROGRAM

The first program, shown in Fig. 11-1, is just about as simple a program as you can write for the Amiga. It simply checks to see if it has been called from the command line interface and outputs a line of text if it has been. If it was called from the Workbench, the program detects this and exits without doing anything. Because the message is printed using the DOS library call to Write, it can be redirected to a file or device using the standard Amiga method (using the > character followed by a filename). The program ends by returning to the CLI as soon as the message has been output. As long as the stack pointer is not changed from its value at the start of the program, a simple rts opcode is sufficient to ensure a graceful return to the CLI. For simplicity, a call to CloseLibrary has been omitted. This is normally used before ending any program. The second example shows how this call should have been performed.

The source code should only take 10 minutes or so to type in. To try out this example, enter the text into a file, which should be named text.asm. When you've typed it in, you should assemble and link it. The easiest way to do this is to type the follow-

Fig. 11-1. The Text program.

```
;text.asm

**********************************************************************
*
*                    EXTERNAL REFERENCES
*
**********************************************************************

        xref        _AbsExecBase
        xref        _LVOFindTask
        xref        _LVOOpenLibrary
        xref        _LVOOutput
        xref        _LVOWrite


**********************************************************************
*
*                    PROGRAM CODE
*
**********************************************************************

        move.l      _AbsExecBase,a6         ;get Exec library base pointer:
        suba.l      a1,a1                   ;zero register a1
        jsr         _LVOFindTask(a6)        ;get the address of our task
        move.l      d0,a4                   ;move it to a4

        moveq       #20,d0                  ;exit number if not CLI
        tst.l       140(a4)                 ;see if task number = 0
        beq.s       exit                    ;if so, we're not in CLI

        bsr.s       opendos                 ;attempt to open DOS library
        tst.l       d0                      ;got a library pointer?
        beq.s       exit                    ;abort if no DOS

        move.l      d0,a6                   ;DOS Library pointer to a6
        jsr         _LVOOutput(a6)          ;get output handle

        move.l      d0,d1                   ;move output handle to d1
        lea         msg,a0                  ;text-string address to a0
        move.l      a0,d2                   ;text pointer to d2
        moveq       #10,d3                  ;text length to d3
        jsr         _LVOWrite(a6)           ;write to output

        moveq       #0,d0                   ;return code
exit
        rts

opendos
        lea         doslib,a1               ;point a1 at "dos.library"
        move.l      #0,d0                   ;use any dos version
        jsr         _LVOOpenLibrary(a6)     ;open the DOS library
        rts

**********************************************************************
*
*                    PROGRAM DATA
```

```
*
*********************************************************************
msg       dc.b      'Hi there!',$0a
doslib    dc.b      'dos.library',0

          end
```

ing two lines into a file, and save it under the name text.exec:

```
assem text.asm -o text.obj
```

```
alink text.obj to text lib lib/amiga.lib
```

Then type:

```
execute text.exec
```

This will automatically run the assembler and then the linker. If an error occurs in either, check the source code for typos, and ensure that the text.exec file appears as above.

If you wish, you can skip the exec stage by typing each of the above two lines separately; these lines will manually invoke the assembler and then the linker. When writing longer, less trivial programs, it's better to use an execute file to ensure that the assembler and linker are called properly every time you assemble and link. When the process runs to completion, type the word "text" to see the message displayed. If you create an icon for the file, as in the next example, you'll find that the program jumps back to the Workbench if you run it from there. The code to do this appears right after the FindTask call at the start of the source code.

Notice that the linker is instructed to use a library called lib/amiga.lib, which is specified as one of its parameters. This causes the linker to scan that library for any unresolved references. There are five lines declaring references to externally defined objects, so the linker will look for them in lib/amiga.lib. No routines containing any code are loaded from this file—just the numerical values of _AbsExecBase and the _LVO offsets. You can prove that these are no more than numerical values by replacing them with actual numbers and assembling the program without using amiga.lib. This is only recommended as an exercise; you should normally link using the proper method to ensure that the library offsets match those in the executable library.

First, remove the five xref lines that are before the program code. (You can simply insert semicolons at the start of each line; the semicolons cause them to be treated as comments). This saves the linker from having to resolve those references. Now replace _AbsExecBase with 4, _LVOFindTask with −294, _LVOOutput with −60, _LVOWrite with −48, and _LVOOpenLibrary with −552. Assemble the program as before, but when you link, use the command:

```
alink text.obj to text
```

116

The program is now assembled and linked without any external references. It will still run exactly as before, but it's the absolute library offsets you typed into the source code. (This assumes your offsets are the same as those in release 1.2 of the software.)

THE GADGET BOX PROGRAM

The second program shown in Fig. 11-2, is also fairly simple and was designed to be that way. Its only real use is as an example of how to program the Amiga using various library calls at the machine code level. Thus, the code is kept straightforward, with no software tricks in sight. The whole thing has been kept as illustrative as possible.

The program will put up a window on the screen that looks just like an ordinary Amiga window. Included along with the window itself are a close box (which, unsurprisingly, allows the window to be closed) and three gadgets. For no other reason than sheer variety, each gadget is different: the first one is a medium sized square, the second one is a triangle, and the third one is a small square. The program deals with the clicking of any one of these gadgets in a different way for each one. Clicking the large square—which is labeled G0—causes a new title to appear at the head of the gadget window. The second gadget—labeled G1—upon being clicked causes its color to cycle through the current Workbench colors as selected from the Amiga's Preferences utility. The colors cycle from white to black to orange to blue. If you've changed these colors using Preferences, they will cycle through the colors you've set up. Notice that the last color is always the color of the background, so it will be invisible until you press the mouse button over its selectable area. The final control, the small gadget labeled G2, merely causes a short flash to be displayed on the screen of the Amiga.

Fig. 11-2. The Gadget Box program.

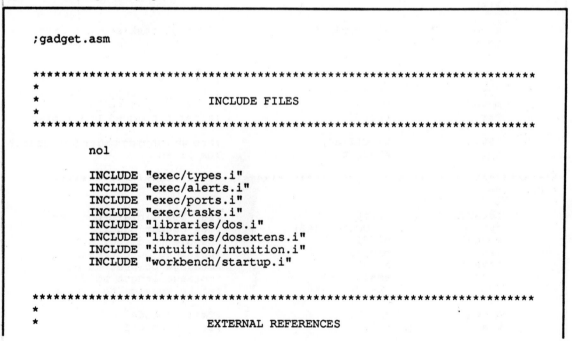

```
;gadget.asm


***********************************************************************
*
*                         INCLUDE FILES
*
***********************************************************************

        no1

        INCLUDE "exec/types.i"
        INCLUDE "exec/alerts.i"
        INCLUDE "exec/ports.i"
        INCLUDE "exec/tasks.i"
        INCLUDE "libraries/dos.i"
        INCLUDE "libraries/dosextens.i"
        INCLUDE "intuition/intuition.i"
        INCLUDE "workbench/startup.i"


***********************************************************************
*
*                      EXTERNAL REFERENCES
```

```
*
**************************************************************************
        xref        _AbsExecBase

        xref        _LVOAlert
        xref        _LVOCloseLibrary
        xref        _LVOCloseWindow
        xref        _LVODebug
        xref        _LVODisplayBeep
        xref        _LVOFindTask
        xref        _LVOForbid
        xref        _LVOGetMsg
        xref        _LVOInput
        xref        _LVOOpen
        xref        _LVOOpenLibrary
        xref        _LVOOpenWindow
        xref        _LVOOutput
        xref        _LVORefreshGadgets
        xref        _LVOReplyMsg
        xref        _LVOSetMenuStrip
        xref        _LVOSetWindowTitles
        xref        _LVOWait
        xref        _LVOWaitPort
        xref        _LVOWrite


**************************************************************************
*
*                         PROGRAM CODE
*
**************************************************************************

        list

        move.l      a7,initialSP          ;initial task stack pointer
        movea.l     _AbsExecBase,a6       ;get exec library base
        move.l      a6,ExecBase           ;save exec lib base

        suba.l      a1,a1                 ;set a1 = 0
        jsr         _LVOFindTask(a6)      ;get the address of this task
        movea.l     d0,a4                 ;task address to a4
        bsr         openDOS               ;attempt to open DOS library

        tst.l       pr_CLI(a4)            ;are we running under Workbench?
        beq         WBStart               ;ok if so

**************************************************************************
* CLI Code

        movea.l     d0,a6                 ;set DOS library pointer
        jsr         _LVOOutput(a6)        ;get output handle
        move.l      d0,d1                 ;handle to d1 for Write
        lea         msg,a0                ;point to output message
        move.l      a0,d2                 ;message pointer to d2
        moveq       #msglen,d3            ;message length to d3
        jsr         _LVOWrite(a6)         ;write message to output

        moveq.l     #10,D0                ;failure code
        bra         exit                  ;return to CLI
```

```
************************************************************************
* Workbench Code

WBStart

        bsr             openInt                 ;open intuition library

        bsr             waitmsg                 ;wait for start message
        move.l          d0,returnMsg            ;save message for later

        movea.l         IntBase,a6              ;use intuition library base
        lea             NewWind,a0              ;address of new window struct
        jsr             _LVOOpenWindow(a6)      ;open the window
        move.l          d0,windptr             ;save ptr to window structure

        movea.l         d0,a0                   ;window structure pointer to a0
        lea             Menu0,a1                ;ptr to menu structure
        jsr             _LVOSetMenuStrip(a6)    ;put up menu

get_event
        movea.l         windptr,a0             ;open window structure ptr
        movea.l         wd_UserPort(a0),a0     ;UserPort addr to a0
        move.l          a0,-(a7)               ;save it for later
        moveq           #0,d1
        move.b          MP_SIGBIT(a0),d1       ;use signal bit allocated
        moveq           #1,d0                   ;set bit 0 in d0
        asl.l           d1,d0                   ;shift to allocated bit
        movea.l         ExecBase,a6            ;use exec library base
        jsr             _LVOWait(a6)            ;wait for signal

        movea.l         (a7)+,a0               ;restore UserPort addr to a0
        jsr             _LVOGetMsg(a6)          ;get IDCMP message
        movea.l         d0,a1                   ;message pointer to a1
        move.l          im_Class(a1),d4        ;class
        move.w          im_Code(a1),d5         ;code
        movea.l         im_IAddress(a1),a2     ;address in case gadget
        jsr             _LVOReplyMsg(a6)        ;tell exec we got message

        movea.l         IntBase,a6             ;Ready to use intuition lib
        cmpi.l          #CLOSEWINDOW,d4         ;request to close window?
        beq             bye                     ;exit if so

        cmpi.l          #MENUPICK,d4            ;picked menu?
        bne.s           chkgadg                 ;check gadgets if not
        cmpi.w          #MENUNULL,d5           ;no menu item chosen?
        beq.s           get event               ;next event if not
        andi.w          #$7ff,d5               ;extract item/menu #

        cmpi.w          #%100000,d5            ;item 1/menu 0?
        beq.s           bye                     ;quit if so

;Only menu item left is #0 (reset)

        lea             wtitle,a1              ;point to original title
        bsr.s           setttl                  ;set title
        lea             Gadget1,a0             ;point to gadget 1
        movea.l         gg_GadgetRender(a0),a2 ;border ptr to a2
        moveq           #1,d0                   ;original gadget 1 color
        bra.s           setcol                  ;replace old color
```

```
chkgadg
        cmpi.l              #GADGETUP,d4             ;has a gadget been picked?
        bne.s               get_event               ;if not, it's an unknown message
        move.w              gg_GadgetID(a2),d0       ;get id of gadget
        beq.s               chgttl                   ;if zero, change title
        cmpi.w              #1,d0                    ;gadget id = 1?
        beq.s               chgcol                   ;change color if so

;only gadget left is id 2

        suba.l              a0,a0                    ;set a0 = 0
        jsr                 _LVODisplayBeep(a6)      ;flash the screen
        bra                 get_event               ;loop around for next event

chgcol
        movea.l             a2,a0                    ;gadget ptr to a0
        movea.l             gg_GadgetRender(a0),a2   ;border ptr to a2
        move.b              bd_FrontPen(a2),d0       ;get current gadget color
        addq                #1,d0                    ;increment color register #
        andi.b              #3,d0                    ;mask out color bits
setcol
        move.b              d0,bd_FrontPen(a2)       ;replace new color
        movea.l             windptr,a1               ;setup window ptr
        suba.l              a2,a2                    ;set a2 = 0
        jsr                 _LVORefreshGadgets(a6)   ;redisplay all gadgets
        bra                 get_event               ;get next event

chgttl
        lea                 newtitle,a1              ;ptr to new title
        bsr.s               setttl                   ;set title
        bra                 get_event               ;loop to get next event

setttl
        movea.l             windptr,a0               ;ptr to window
        movea.l             #-1,a2                   ;don't change screen title
        jmp                 _LVOSetWindowTitles(a6)  ;change title

;close down
bye
        movea.l             IntBase,a6               ;use intuition library base
        movea.l             windptr,a0               ;pointer to open window
        jsr                 _LVOCloseWindow(a6)      ;close window
        moveq.l             #0,d0                    ;Successful return code

exit
        movea.l             initialSP,a7             ;restore stack pointer
        move.l              d0,-(a7)                 ;save return code

;close libraries
        movea.l             ExecBase,a6              ;use exec libraries
        move.l              DOSBase,d0               ;DOS library loaded?
        beq.s               1$                       ;skip close if DOS not open
        movea.l             d0,a1                    ;lib base into a1
        jsr                 _LVOCloseLibrary(a6)     ;close DOS
1$
        move.l              IntBase,d0               ;intuition library loaded?
        beq.s               2$                       ;skip if intuition not open
        movea.l             d0,a1                    ;lib base into a1
        jsr                 _LVOCloseLibrary(a6)     ;close intuition
2$
```

```
            move.l          returnMsg,d0            ;started from workbench?
            beq.s           3$                      ;skip if from CLI

;return startup message to parent

            jsr             _LVOForbid(a6)          ;so workbench won't UnLoadSeg
            movea.l         returnMsg,a1            ;startup message pointer
            jsr             _LVOReplyMsg(a6)        ;reply to initial message
3$
            move.l          (a7)+,d0                ;restore success code
            rts                                     ;back to operating system

****************************************************************************
noDOS
            ALERT           (AG_OpenLib!AO_DOSLib)  ;display alert box
            moveq.l         #100,d0                 ;error exit code
            bra.s           exit                    ;exit program


****************************************************************************
* Get the message that workbench sends to start us off.
* Called with task id in a4.

waitmsg
            lea             pr_MsgPort(a4),a0       ;our process base
            jsr             _LVOWaitPort(a6)        ;await message
            lea             pr_MsgPort(a4),a0       ;our process base
            jsr             _LVOGetMsg(a6)          ;pick up message
            rts

****************************************************************************
*   Open the DOS library.

openDOS
            lea             DOSName,a1              ;point to DOS library name
            move.l          #LIBRARY_VERSION,d0     ;use included library version
            jsr             _LVOOpenLibrary(a6)     ;open DOS library
            move.l          d0,DOSBase              ;save DOS library base
            beq             noDOS
            rts

****************************************************************************
*   Open the intuition library.

openInt
            lea             IntName,a1              ;point to intuition lib name
            move.l          #0,d0                   ;use any version
            jsr             _LVOOpenLibrary(a6)     ;open intuition library
            move.l          d0,IntBase              ;save library base
            rts

****************************************************************************

                               DATA

****************************************************************************

ExecBase        dc.l    0                           ;space for exec library base
DOSBase         dc.l    0                           ;space for DOS library base
IntBase         dc.l    0                           ;space for intuition lib base
```

```
initialSP        dc.l    0                                    ;saved initial stack pointer
returnMsg        dc.l    0                                    ;saved startup message pointer

windptr          dc.l    0                                    ;space for opened window ptr

NewWind          equ     *                                    ;NewWind = structure address
LeftEdge         dc.w    100                                  ;window initial coordinates
TopEdge          dc.w    50
Width            dc.w    200
Height           dc.w    60
DetailPen        dc.b    -1                                   ;default pen
BlockPen         dc.b    -1                                   ;default pen
IDCMPFlags       dc.l    CLOSEWINDOW!GADGETUP!MENUPICK
Flags            dc.l    WINDOWCLOSE!SMART_REFRESH!ACTIVATE!WINDOWDRAG
FirstGadget      dc.l    Gadget0                              ;pointer to first gadget
CheckMark        dc.l    0
Title            dc.l    wtitle                               ;pointer to window title
Scren            dc.l    0
BitMp            dc.l    0
MinWidth         dc.w    0
MinHeight        dc.w    0
MaxWidth         dc.w    0
MaxHeight        dc.w    0
Type             dc.w    WBENCHSCREEN

Gadget0
                 dc.l    Gadget1                              ;pointer to next gadget
                 dc.w    20                                   ;left edge
                 dc.w    20                                   ;top edge
                 dc.w    40                                   ;width
                 dc.w    20                                   ;height
                 dc.w    GADGHCOMP                            ;flags
                 dc.w    RELVERIFY                            ;activation flags
                 dc.w    BOOLGADGET                           ;gadget type
                 dc.l    border0                              ;ptr to border structure
                 dc.l    0
                 dc.l    g0itxt                               ;ptr to text structure
                 dc.l    0
                 dc.l    0
                 dc.w    0                                    ;id
                 dc.l    0

border0
                 dc.w    0                                    ;left edge
                 dc.w    0                                    ;top edge
                 dc.b    2                                    ;front pen
                 dc.b    0                                    ;back pen
                 dc.b    RP_JAM1                              ;draw mode
                 dc.b    5                                    ;# of coords
                 dc.l    g0xy                                 ;pointer to 1st coord
                 dc.l    0                                    ;pointer to next border

g0xy
                 dc.w    0,0                                  ;gadget coordinate list
                 dc.w    0,19
                 dc.w    39,19
                 dc.w    39,0
                 dc.w    0,0

g0itxt
```

```
                dc.b    2                       ;front pen
                dc.b    0                       ;back pen
                dc.b    RP JAM1                 ;draw mode
                dc.w    10                      ;left edge
                dc.w    7                       ;top edge
                dc.l    0                       ;font ptr (dflt)
                dc.l    g0txt                   ;text pointer
                dc.l    0                       ;ptr to nxt txt structure

Gadget1

                dc.l    Gadget2                 ;pointer to next gadget
                dc.w    70                      ;left edge
                dc.w    20                      ;top edge
                dc.w    40                      ;width
                dc.w    20                      ;height
                dc.w    GADGHCOMP               ;flags
                dc.w    RELVERIFY               ;activation flags
                dc.w    BOOLGADGET              ;gadget type
                dc.l    border1                 ;ptr to border structure
                dc.l    0
                dc.l    g1itxt                  ;ptr to text structure
                dc.l    0
                dc.l    0
                dc.w    1                       ;id
                dc.l    0

border1

                dc.w    0                       ;left edge
                dc.w    0                       ;top edge
                dc.b    1                       ;front pen
                dc.b    0                       ;back pen
                dc.b    RP_JAM1                 ;draw mode
                dc.b    4                       ;# of coords
                dc.l    g1xy                    ;pointer to 1st coord
                dc.l    0                       ;pointer to next border

g1xy

                dc.w    0,19                    ;gadget coordinate list
                dc.w    39,19
                dc.w    20,0
                dc.w    0,19

g1itxt

                dc.b    1                       ;front pen
                dc.b    0                       ;back pen
                dc.b    RP_JAM1                 ;draw mode
                dc.w    10                      ;left edge
                dc.w    21                      ;top edge
                dc.l    0                       ;font ptr (dflt)
                dc.l    g1txt                   ;text pointer
                dc.l    0                       ;ptr to nxt txt structure

Gadget2

                dc.l    0                       ;pointer to next gadget
                dc.w    120                     ;left edge
                dc.w    30                      ;top edge
                dc.w    24                      ;width
                dc.w    10                      ;height
                dc.w    GADGHCOMP               ;flags
                dc.w    RELVERIFY               ;activation flags
```

```
                dc.w    BOOLGADGET              ;gadget type
                dc.l    border2                 ;ptr to border structure
                dc.l    0
                dc.l    g2itxt                  ;ptr to text structure
                dc.l    0
                dc.l    0
                dc.w    2                       ;id
                dc.l    0

border2
                dc.w    0                       ;left edge
                dc.w    0                       ;top edge
                dc.b    3                       ;front pen
                dc.b    0                       ;back pen
                dc.b    RP_JAM1                 ;draw mode
                dc.b    5                       ;# of coords
                dc.l    g2xy                    ;pointer to 1st coord
                dc.l    0                       ;pointer to next border

g2xy
                dc.w    0,0                     ;gadget coordinate list
                dc.w    0,9
                dc.w    23,9
                dc.w    23,0
                dc.w    0,0

g2itxt
                dc.b    3                       ;front pen
                dc.b    0                       ;back pen
                dc.b    RP_JAM1                 ;draw mode
                dc.w    2                       ;left edge
                dc.w    2                       ;top edge
                dc.l    0                       ;font ptr (dflt)
                dc.l    g2txt                   ;text pointer
                dc.l    0                       ;ptr to nxt txt structure

Menu0
                dc.l    0                       ;ptr to next menu structure
                dc.w    50                      ;Left edge
                dc.w    0                       ;Top edge
                dc.w    60                      ;Width
                dc.w    0                       ;Height
                dc.w    MENUENABLED             ;Flags
                dc.l    MenuName                ;Pointer to menu name
                dc.l    Menuitm0                ;Pointer to first item
                dc.w    0,0,0,0                 ;internal use

Menuitm0
                dc.l    Menuitm1                ;ptr to next menu item
                dc.w    0                       ;Left edge
                dc.w    0                       ;Top edge
                dc.w    95                      ;Width
                dc.w    11                      ;Height
                dc.w    ITEMTEXT!COMMSEQ!ITEMENABLED!HIGHCOMP ;Flags
                dc.l    0                       ;Mutual Exclude
                dc.l    itemname0               ;Item Fill
                dc.l    0                       ;Select Fill
                dc.b    'r'                     ;Command
                dc.l    0                       ;Sub Item
                dc.w    0                       ;Next Select
```

```
itemname0
                dc.b        2                               ;front pen
                dc.b        0                               ;back pen
                dc.b        RP_JAM1                         ;draw mode
                dc.w        2                               ;left edge
                dc.w        2                               ;top edge
                dc.l        0                               ;font ptr (dflt)
                dc.l        i0txt                           ;text pointer
                dc.l        0                               ;ptr to nxt txt structure

Menuitm1
                dc.l        0                               ;ptr to next menu item
                dc.w        0                               ;Left edge
                dc.w        12                              ;Top edge
                dc.w        95                              ;Width
                dc.w        11                              ;Height
                dc.w        ITEMTEXT!COMMSEQ!ITEMENABLED!HIGHCOMP ;Flags
                dc.l        0                               ;Mutual Exclude
                dc.l        itemname1                       ;Item Fill
                dc.l        0                               ;Select Fill
                dc.b        'q'                             ;Command
                dc.l        0                               ;Sub Item
                dc.w        0                               ;Next Select

itemname1
                dc.b        2                               ;front pen
                dc.b        0                               ;back pen
                dc.b        RP_JAM1                         ;draw mode
                dc.w        2                               ;left edge
                dc.w        2                               ;top edge
                dc.l        0                               ;font ptr (dflt)
                dc.l        i1txt                           ;text pointer
                dc.l        0                               ;ptr to nxt txt structure

MenuName        dc.b        'Menu',0                        ;Menu title
i0txt           dc.b        'Reset',0                       ;first item text
i1txt           dc.b        'Quit ',0                       ;second item text
g0txt           dc.b        'G0',0                          ;first gadget name
g1txt           dc.b        'G1',0                          ;second gadget name
g2txt           dc.b        'G2',0                          ;third gadget name

wtitle          dc.b        'Some Gadgets',0                ;initial window title
newtitle        dc.b        'New Title',0                   ;alternative window title

IntName         dc.b        'intuition.library',0           ;intuition library name
DOSName         DOSNAME                                     ;DOS library name macro

msg             dc.b        'This program must be run from the Workbench.',$0a
msglen          equ         *-msg

        end
```

To keep the assembly source code simple, all the structures for the window, the gadgets, and the text have been defined using the assembler dc directive,which is used to define a constant. Normally, structures such as these would have been defined using the type macros defined in the types.i include file. For the purposes of illustration, the regular assembler directives were used so no ambiguity would arise as to the length or purpose of each constant defined within a structure.

A large proportion of this program (and the calculator program in Chapter 13) is comprised of data structures. If you have an editor that allows it, you can save time and increase accuracy if you enter a template of each structure just once and then duplicate it each time it is needed in the source code. When all structures are in place, step through each constant definition and set each constant to its proper values. This is a time consuming process, but it is less so than entering each structure one at a time.

The menu that is available is very simple. It contains only two items, reset and quit, either of which can be selected using the ALT/r and ALT/q key combinations respectively. The reset option puts the window back the way it was at the start of the program (original title and color of second gadget). The quit option follows the same path that is taken if the pointer is clicked in the window's close box—namely back to the Amiga Workbench. The sequence of steps you should follow when assembling the gadget program is the same as in the first example. The gadget.asm file (the source code) is submitted to the assembler and the resultant gadget.obj file is submitted to the linker, which produces an executable gadget file. Instead of going through this sequence one step at a time, you can automate it by creating a file called gadget.exec containing the following lines and then inputting it to the execute application:

```
assem gadget.asm -c W160000 -i include -o gadget.obj

alink gadget.obj to gadget lib lib/amiga.lib
```

These lines tell execute to invoke the assembler with the gadget.asm source file and then pass control to the linker if no errors occur. If there are no errors, the linker will be fired up to produce the final gadget program from the output of the assembler. The assembler has two extra parameters specified in this example: the −c W160000 option, which tells the assembler to use a workspace of 160,000 bytes, and the −i include parameter, which tells it to look for included files in the directory called include. The extra workspace is required because all the included equates use up a great deal of room in memory. Note that the directory specifying the include files is assumed to be relative to the current working directory.

When the program is running, each event of interest to it is detected by picking up a message from the executive. To do this, the program informs exec which signal it is interested in and then goes to sleep by doing a call to the Wait routine. The program has nothing to do until such a signal arrives, so this action is appropriate, it frees the Amiga to execute other tasks within its memory.

When the mouse is pressed, causing an event related to the program, exec sends a signal to wake it up. The program can then fetch the message that Intuition will have sent. This message is in the form of a structure containing items of information pertaining to the event that just occurred. On return from the call to GetMsg, register d0 will contain a pointer to this message structure. The program can then extract the information it needs from the structure and return the memory area containing the message for further use by the operating system. This is achieved with the ReplyMsg call. Note that a similar message is sent from the Workbench, before the program can start executing. This is the first thing the program waits for after opening the Intuition library.

Three items from within the message are all that is needed to find out which event caused a signal to be sent to the program. First, the class of the message is required, the class determines whether a menu, gadget, or close window has been selected. Second, if a menu was chosen, the code field within the message will contain the item and menu number picked. Third, the address field of the message will point to the structure of any gadget that might have been selected. Thus, if a gadget event occurs, the program can check to see which gadget was selected and take action accordingly.

The program is easily modified, and you are encouraged to do just that. Modifying programs is an excellent way to gain confidence in manipulating the Amiga environment. For instance, a new gadget could be added, or perhaps one of the existing ones moved somewhere else. Try adding a new menu item and after that works, add some code to deal with it.

When the program is successfully assembled, you'll need to assign an icon to it, because you have to start it from the Workbench. To do this, use the program IconEd on the Workbench disk. You'll need at least one icon to be already available for this to work. These are stored in files with an extension of .info. Thus, the icon for the gadget program will be stored in gadget.info.

When IconEd has started and has at least one icon loaded into a display frame, you can graphically alter it as desired. When your icon is designed, select the menu option to save it to disk. A window will appear asking for more details. First, select the icon name box and enter the name "gadget." (If the gadget program is on the external drive, you should specify "df1:gadget.") Then click the mouse on the gadget entitled "Frame and Save." This allows you to draw a frame around your icon, which determines its size. You can then save the icon, after which it will appear when you open the window containing the gadget program. Opening this icon will start the gadget program.

When viewing a "finished" program such as this, the tendency is to think it was created in its entirety out of thin air and worked the first time. Unfortunately, that's not how programming goes—there were numerous crashes between the first version and the version published here. So don't feel too bad when you witness your first program crash—it's just part of the programming process.

While writing this program, extensive use was made of the __LVODebug routine to help in pinpointing bugs. I placed the debug call immediately in front of any errant routine, if I knew which routine was causing a crash. Alternatively, if all else failed and I didn't have a clue as to what was going on, I would place the call at the very beginning of the program. This allowed me to single-step the program until the problem occurred. Then I knew that it was the last encountered routine that was at fault. I could then either restart the program and set a breakpoint prior to the offending code, or reassemble the program with the __LVODebug routine just ahead of the problem. A check of all the parameters in the registers would follow, until one that didn't make sense was found. Once or twice this involved trial and error attempts.

As was pointed out previously, assembly-language program development is certain to incur a few crashes before a finished result is produced. Some of the functions in the ROM Kernel Manual are described more clearly than others. It's almost a certainty that any function that is misunderstood and is called with the resulting incorrect parameter setup will cause a crash. This kind of bug can be frustrating because it's not the logic of the program that's wrong—it's the understanding of the Amiga library routine that's in error. Usually one or two experiments are needed with the setup of the parameters until the right one is hit upon.

The advantage of using a debugger in this way is that it's possible to change the parameters used in a library call from the debugger itself. Thus it was possible, in a couple of instances, to change a parameter and try the call; if it didn't work, I changed the parameter and tried the call again until the routine worked. At that stage, it would be back to the editor to change the source code, remove the __LVODebug call, and check that the reassembled program now functioned. This is one of the many kinds of situation where a debugger is absolutely invaluable. It's no exaggeration to say that the debugger was indispensible in the development of even this simple program.

Use the program and experiment with the source code. Often a good way to start your own programming project is to start with a skeletal program such as the one printed here and build around it. From small beginnings. . .

Chapter

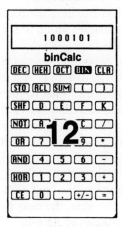

Number-Crunching

The intent of this chapter is to give an introduction to number-crunching and a closer look at the binary number system as used on digital computers. *Number-crunching* is a term that's generally used to describe the actions of the computer when it manipulates numbers. On large mainframe computers, this term invokes images of thousands of numbers being mashed together. In certain scientific and mathematical applications, this is almost true, as literally millions of equations might be solved to arrive at an answer. Numbers come as close as they ever will to being crunched together in these types of circumstances. For lesser mortals using microcomputers, number-crunching takes on the lesser role of solving such things as equations in a spreadsheet or calculating the memory space required to store a certain amount of data. You will be better able to perform numeric manipulations on a computer if you have a good overall understanding of the methods available. This chapter will elucidate some of these methods.

The two program examples in Chapter 11—the one to write text on the CLI screen and the other to draw a gadget window—needed no number-crunching activity at all. It is possible to write programs that simply don't need to manipulate numbers to any great degree. For instance, if you wrote a program that was an editor or word-processor, you'd hardly need any numeric manipulation (except maybe a tiny amount in counting words or calculating margins and the like).

Number-crunching on a computer can really be broken up into a specific few actions. A computer is normally called upon to add, subtract, multiply, and divide numbers, and also to perform logical operations such as AND, OR, and XOR. This chapter will discuss how these are accomplished on the Amiga and also give a sample program that allows you to take a look at some results for yourself.

THE BINARY NUMBERING SYSTEM

First of all, a more thorough look needs to be taken at something that was touched upon in an early chapter: the binary number system. All modern digital computers use the binary numbering system when handling numbers. It's worthwhile to get a good grasp of this system because it provides an understanding of the most fundamental level of digital computer operation.

When we use numbers in everyday life, we use a number system called the *decimal* system. We use the symbols 1, 2, 3, 4, 5, 6, 7, 8, and 9, and the symbol 0 to mean a null quantity. There are 10 digits in all. What happens when we get past the number nine? We're still talking about quantities that need to be represented using some kind of symbols, but in the decimal system a decision has evolved that dictates we don't use another symbol after nine. What we do is to start over with symbols we already have and start a new column to the left. Instead of having an entirely new symbol after 9, the number ten is represented by the digits 10. Thus, a system has been implemented to carry over digits to the left every time the limit of the number base of ten is reached. When a digit in any column reaches nine, the next time that digit is increased it will cause a one to be added to the column to its left.

All number systems—no matter what base they count in—employ this method of carrying across. Otherwise, an infinite number of number symbols, each one representing the next higher numerical quantity, would be needed. Obviously, this is impractical, and the decimal numbering system demonstrates a realization of that fact. The actual reason why we count using a number base of ten has never been convincingly explained. It's often assumed to have something to do with the simple fact that we have ten fingers upon which to count. It's ironic that, if binary rather than decimal had emerged as our normal number system, we'd be able to count to 1,023 on our fingers! Apparently, if we'd have been made with four fingers on each hand instead of five, the chances are we'd have counted in *octal*. (Octal will be covered in a short while, after investigating binary in greater detail.)

When a lot of people think of binary, they think of it as a complicated, alien numbering system and are intimidated by the sight of it. There's no need to be, however; it's the simplest possible numbering system there is. It's much simpler than the decimal numbering system we use all the time without giving any thought to it. It's simple because, instead of 10 digits, only two digits are needed. The two digits are 0 and 1, as was pointed out in Chapter 1. The same basic rules apply as in the decimal system: whenever a digit in any column reaches the limit imposed by its number base, the next column to the left is incremented by a carry. If that column has reached its limit, then the next digit receives a carry, and so on until a digit can represent the carried quantity. This is the same as when one is added to the decimal number 999. The one causes the first column to flip to zero, and a carry to be added to the second column, which also flips to a zero, generating another carry, and so on until finally the fourth column shows the carry as a one and the number 1000 is produced. The same thing happens in binary with the number 111. If one is added to that, then column one (which has reached the limit of the number base) flips to a zero and a carry is added to column two. In exactly the same way as with 999 in decimal, the excess digit is carried across until it can be accommodated. Thus, the 111 in binary becomes 1000 when one is added to it. Don't be confused by the number 1000 though; in this case it's binary, and not 1000 as we normally think of it. You are looking at the number 1, 0, 0, 0 in binary. If you're an absolute newcomer to binary, you'll soon see that these numbers make absolute sense.

You can learn an awful lot about binary by analyzing what you do, without thinking much about it, in decimal. One thing that is absolutely taken for granted when looking at a decimal number is the weighting of each column in a string of digits. For example, look at the number 999. Just from regular habit, you know that it consists of three digits and is a quantity that is the number 9 from the right-hand column added to the number 90 from the middle column added to the number 900 from the left. To understand the number, you don't even have to mentally add these numbers together—it becomes intuitive after the use of numbers has been learned. This, unfortunately, is not the case in binary or any other number base. In these cases it is necessary to think about the quantity that's being represented; however, the same principle, applies as in decimal.

The decimal system multiplies each column by 10 times the value of the preceding column. Therefore, the first column represents units or ones; the next column represents tens; the next, hundreds, then thousands, and so on up to infinity. In binary, the first column represents one; column two represents two; column three represents four, the next, eight, then sixteen, and so on up to infinity. Figure 12-1 shows the weighting of the first few columns in binary—this can be a help in converting numbers from binary to decimal. In both decimal and binary (and in fact any number base), each column represents the previous column multiplied by the number base. Therefore, in binary, every column to the left represents the column to the right multiplied by two. For instance, 10 in binary is no ones and one two—or the number 2 in decimal. Notice that the binary 10 is binary 1 shifted left one place. Any number shifted left one place in binary is multiplied by two, so 10 is double 1. This is akin to the decimal system, in which any number shifted left is multiplied by ten, so 10 is ten times 1. This is another property common to all number bases: shift a number left and it is multiplied by the number base. This is one of those tricks that can be useful to remember when you are using number bases other than 10.

Take a close look at a couple of binary numbers and see if they make sense following what you've learned so far. First, look at that number 111 that was used earlier. In binary, this is a one in the first column, a two in the second column, and a four in the third column. To understand the quantity being expressed, the numbers are added together, as was 900, 90, and 9 in the decimal number 999. Thus, binary 111 is four plus two plus one—yielding the result of seven in decimal. Therefore, the number 111 in binary is the number 7 in decimal. Both 111 and 7 represent the same quantity, but each is a different way of expressing the same number. Because of the ease with which zeros and ones can be represented electronically, binary has become the favored number system used in computers.

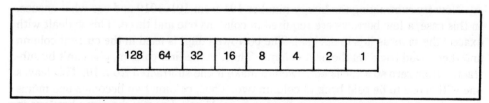

| 128 | 64 | 32 | 16 | 8 | 4 | 2 | 1 |

Fig. 12-1. The weighting of the first eight columns in the binary numbering system.

```
0   0   1    1
0   1   0    1
──  ──  ──  ──
0   1   1    10
```

Fig. 12-2. The binary addition table.

Consider the addition of one to that binary 111 to see if things add up. The result—after carrying across—was 1000. Analyzing that number reveals that there are no ones, no twos, and no fours, but there is one eight in the leftmost column. This binary number is the number eight. Happily, the number seven (binary 111) with a one added to it becomes eight (binary 1000), just as we'd expect.

To gain a little more confidence with this strange number system, imagine the number 101. Using the same method, we see that there is a one in the right column, nothing in the middle (twos) column, and a one in the fours column on the left. This number is therefore four plus one, or five. Now we can shift it left one place and get 1010. Breaking this number down, there are no ones on the right, one two, no fours, and one eight at the extreme left. In other words, this is the number 10, and as promised, shifting a number left in binary has multiplied it by two.

Let's look at some more binary numbers using the knowledge we've gleaned so far and make sure that everything makes sense. A good review would be to take a couple of binary bytes of eight bits each in length and convert them to decimal. Take the number 10101010 and see what happens when it is added to the number 00000011. Notice there's no problem in column one. Adding a one to a zero gives a one as shown in the binary addition table in Fig. 12-2.

In the next column, a one is added to another one, resulting in a zero with a one carried over in a similar fashion to a carry in decimal arithmetic. This one that is carried over is then added to the zeros in column three, and the result is the number 10101101. This is how the addition looks:

```
     10101010
 +   00000011
     10101101
```

When this is converted to decimal, you can see that everything does indeed make sense. The first number, 10101010, has ones in the columns representing 128, 32, 8, and 2; when these are added, the result is 170. The second number has ones in the columns for 2 and 1; thus this is 3. The result has ones in the columns for 128, 32, 8, 4, and 1; this is 173 in decimal. It should be no surprise to see you've added the number 170 to 3 and have a total of 173.

Now try subtracting the binary number 101 from 10101010 and see what ensues. In this case, a few borrows are required in columns one and three. This is dealt with exactly the same as it is in decimal. The borrowed digit is used in the current column and then "paid back" in the next column. Thus, in the first column, one can't be subtracted from zero so a one is borrowed to make it one subtracted from 10. This leaves one with a one to be paid back to column two. Thus, column two becomes one minus one rather than one minus zero as the one is paid back. Exactly the same happens in columns three and four to give the result as follows:

```
  10101010
-  00000101
  10100101
```

It would be wise to check to ensure it looks right in decimal. From the previous example, you know 10101010 is 170. 101 is a four and a one—or five. 10100101 is 128, 32, 4, and 1—or 165. Perfect; five has been subtracted from 170 to get 165.

At this point, it starts becoming apparent that dealing with binary—although it's starting to look simple and easy to understand—is rather cumbersome. Binary requires so many digits that they threaten to sprawl off the edge of the page. If you think about it, the higher the number base, the more digits that are available to represent numbers, and therefore the fewer columns that are needed to express a quantity. This means that binary, with its meager two symbols, requires more columns than any other number base.

SHORTHAND METHODS OF REPRESENTING BINARY NUMBERS

A shorthand method of representing binary numbers would be helpful. This would allow the manipulation of the same quantities—still in binary—but using fewer digits. There are a couple of systems that are commonly used to do this. Before being perturbed by the sound of them, just remember that all they represent are the binary digits you've seen so far, in a slightly different way. One of these is the *hexadecimal numbering system* and the other one is the *octal numbering system*. Despite their ominous-sounding names, these numbering systems are only different ways of manipulating simple binary numbers. A computer knows nothing about octal or hexadecimal—they are just conveniences for human programmers.

First, take a look at that number 10101010. In decimal, it is the number 170. Three digits are all we're used to seeing for the number 170, and this seems convenient enough; however, its binary representation, required by the computer, takes eight digits, which becomes somewhat cumbersome for humans. This is even more true when we start dealing in 16 and 32-bit quantities. A computer couldn't care either way, but we humans need all the breaks we can get.

The Octal Numbering System

First of all, let's try splitting those eight binary digits, or bits, into sections that can be represented by the more familiar symbols of zero to nine. If the eight bits are split into three bits on the right hand side and then three bits to the left, that leaves two bits on the far left, like so: 10 101 010. All eight bits are taken into account, but they are now split up as shown. The three bits at the right-hand side are the bits 010. This three-bit quantity represents the number 2 in decimal—that's no ones, one two, and no fours. The three bits to the immediate left are 101. This, taken on its own as a binary number, is decimal 5—one one, no twos, and one four. The remaining two digits at the far left represent the number two—no ones and one two. Put together, these decimal-type symbols—252—provide us with a convenient shorthand for 10101010. You have to bear in mind, though, that each of the three digits 2, 5, and 2 are not decimal digits, but simply represent three bits apiece. This would seem to leave nine bits, but because we're dealing with eight-bit bytes, it is assumed that the ninth bit is always zero. In other words, 252 converts back to 010 101 010, and the leftmost bit is ignored in an eight-bit byte.

Without consciously thinking about it, what you've done is taken a leap into the octal numbering system. We're still talking about binary numbers, but they are being split into groups of three. These groups of three bits are used to arrive at digits that can be written and read in a more familiar fashion. If you look at any three-bit group, you'll see that they can't hold a number higher than 7. The maximum number that can be held in three bits is 111, which imposes that upper limit. Therefore, you'll never see a digit higher than seven in any column of an octal number. This is just as it ought to be—remember in the decimal numbering system you can't go higher than nine in any column before having to carry over.

Let's see if this works on its own using a carry-over. Take the number 17 in octal, add a one to it, and see if it makes any sense in binary and decimal. Because the number 7 is as high as you can go in octal, adding one to it makes it flip to a zero and a one has to be carried over to the next column; so the result is 20. On the face of it, adding one to 17 to result in 20 seems strange, but because we're manipulating octal rather than decimal, everything makes perfect sense. Split these octal digits into groups of three and see if that makes any sense. In binary, octal 20 is 010 000. Counting from the right, the single one bit is in the 16's column, so 010 000 is decimal 16. The original octal number, before it was added to, was 17. In binary, this looks like 001 111. The four bits here stand for a one, a two, a four and an eight, respectively. This leaves decimal 15. And so you've added one to 15 (octal 17) to arrive at 16 (octal 20). So far everything is perfect.

Now let's see if there's any way of converting directly from octal to decimal without recourse to binary. Remember that octal is being used here as a shorthand for binary, so it would be nice not to have to use binary as the key to octal. All you have to do is *weight* the columns in octal in a similar manner to weighting the columns in binary. In the octal numbering system, the column on the right represent ones, the next column to the left is eights, the next column is eight times eight (or 64s), the next column is eight times 64 (or 512s) and so on. See Fig. 12-3, which shows the first few columns of octal weighting. Now look at that octal number 17 and convert directly to decimal. This is seven ones (or 7), and one eight (or eight). It couldn't be simpler—seven and eight is 15, so octal 17 converts to decimal 15—and you didn't look at a binary quantity.

Decimal numbers in computer programming are not very often converted to and from octal by hand. The main reason for octal is just as a shorthand for dealing with binary numbers, so don't be put off by all these number-base conversions; most program-

| 2,097,152 | 262,144 | 32,768 | 4096 | 512 | 64 | 8 | 1 |

Fig. 12-3 The weighting of the first eight columns in the octal numbering system.

268,435,456	16,777,216	1,048,576	65,536	4096	512	16	1

Fig. 12-4. The weighting of the first eight columns in the hexadecimal numbering system.

mers who need to use octal in any numeric manipulations use a special calculator that converts from one number base to another.

The Hexadecimal Numbering System

What happens if you split the eight bits of a byte more sensibly into two groups of four? Intuitively, this seems tidier than splitting them into groups of three, which would be more appropriate if the byte was a multiple of three bits. With two groups of four bits, you don't have any bits that don't quite fit, as with the example above. Now, each group of four can represent from 0000 to 1111 (or in decimal, zero to 15). Using this method, a byte could be written as two digits, each one standing for four bits. The number 55, for instance, could represent the binary number 0101 0101.

What should be done if a number greater than 1001 (decimal 9) is needed in one of the groups? Adding one to a column containing 1001 gives a number for which there is no single symbol. For example, with 99, if you add one to the right-hand column (in binary), you get the number 1001 1010. There is no symbol to substitute for the group 1010 (which is decimal 10). You can't write 1001 1010 as 9 followed by 10 (or 910) because that gives three digits. Using each digit to represent four bits, 910 would be expected to stand for 1001 0001 0000. This is a twelve-bit binary number, and not the binary 1010 1010 that is intended. To get past this problem, some new number symbols must be invented. Six of them are needed, to represent 1010, 1011, 1100, 1101, 1110, and 1111. The number 1010 is therefore represented by the letter A, the number 1011 by B, the number 1100 by C, and so on up to F for 1111.

Whereas in the octal numbering system, the highest you could count was seven in each three-bit column, the highest you can count with four bits is 15. This indicates the maximum before needing to carry over. With decimal (tens), you carry over after reaching nine, with octal (eights) you carry over after reaching seven. Because you are currently carrying over after 15, it can be deduced that the number base is now 16. Thus, you're now dealing with the hexadecimal numbering system.

This means that the number 99 in hexadecimal (or hex for short) represents 9 ones on the right, and nine sixteens on the left. In hex, the columns are split up from the left into ones, 16s, 256s, 2048s and so on. See Fig. 12-4, which shows the weighting of the first few columns. Adding one to hexadecimal 99 yields the result 9A by the rules set so far. Counting onwards from here would give 9B, 9C, 9D, 9E, 9F, and (after carrying over) A0, A1, A2, and so on.

Try adding one to hex 99 in all the numbering systems you know, to convince yourself that you are dealing with the same quantities in every different number base. First of all, the hexadecimal number 99: this is nine ones (decimal 9) plus nine 16s (decimal

144) to give decimal 153. In binary this is 10011001, which is one one, one 8, one 16, and one 128, which happily add to give decimal 153. How about octal? Split the binary into groups of three, like so: 010 011 001. Octally stated, these are the digits 2, 3, and 1. Using the octal column weightings on each digit gives one one, three 8s, and two 64s. That's 1, 24, and 128, which once again totals to 153. Thus, in all three number bases (four counting decimal), the quantity is the same.

Finally, let's make sure that adding one to hex 99 indeed gave the truth when it yielded 9A. In hex, (remembering that A is decimal 10) 9A is ten ones (decimal 10) and nine 16s (decimal 144), which gives 154. In binary 9A splits into two groups of four bits: 1001 1010. That's one two, one eight, one 16, and one 128 (See how binary can never be more than one of anything?)—154 again. Octal splits the bits into 010 011 010 or 232; that's two ones, three eights, and two 64s, which, not surprisingly by now, gives 154. So, 153 plus one in any number base always gives 154.

Choosing a Number System

Which numbering system you decide to use as a programmer is entirely at your own discretion. Not too many people flit back and forth between number bases—at least not without the help of a calculator. If you feel uncomfortable with either octal or hex, you could be pedantic and stick to binary just like the computer, but once the binary system is understood, the use of octal and/or hexadecimal is almost inevitable as a convenient shorthand. In the professional world, programmers seem to use the system they used on their last job; however, it makes more sense to use hexadecimal on a computer whose word length is a multiple of four, and octal on one with a multiple of three. You have a choice on 12 and 24-bit machines. On the Amiga, with object lengths of 8, 16, and 32 bits, hexadecimal is the most appropriate system. Remember that the computer knows nothing of all this—binary is all it works with. When you are using hex, two digits conveniently represent eight bits, four represent 16 bits, and eight digits represent 32 bits. Writing eight digits saves considerable effort compared to grappling with 32 binary digits.

Binary-Coded Decimal

You've looked at splitting the binary number into groups of three (which gives octal) and four (which gives hexadecimal). There's another method of splitting into groups of four that is useful to look at, although it's not as common as hexadecimal. Its main use is for arithmetic manipulation within the computer, rather than as a shorthand for binary. This is a method whereby you don't need to go beyond the familiar digits zero to nine. Instead of using those digits A to F in hex, the normal decimal rules are adhered to. Thus, when one of the groups of four digits goes past the number 9, a carry is generated into the next column. By using four digits per column, if you stick to a range of 0000 to 1001, you can elect to have those four bits stand for the numbers zero to nine as in decimal. For that reason, this method is called *binary-coded decimal* (BCD). It can be used with special instructions within a computer on the understanding that, if any group of four binary digits contains a 1001, a carry will be generated if it is incremented. Thus, adding two to 89 in BCD looks like this:

	1000 1001	BCD 89
BCD add	0000 0010	BCD 02
	1001 0001	BCD 91

If this were done using a pure binary addition instead of a binary-coded decimal one, the result would have looked like this:

	1000 1001	BCD 89
binary add	0000 0010	BCD 02
	1000 1011	BCD garbage

Notice that in BCD, you're still using bits zero and one to represent quantities (albeit in groups of four bits), but now you're using the numbers zero to nine in the same way as if you were dealing in decimal. Apart from the ease of arithmetic manipulation, it's easy to convert these groups of four bits into their correct ASCII characters for printing. The drawback is that in BCD, a byte can only hold up to 99, whereas in binary it can hold up to 255.

USING NEGATIVE QUANTITIES IN BINARY

Now, back to binary: let's look at some quantities and see how they behave under certain conditions. This will give some extra interesting insights into how to deal with negative numbers. You've already seen binary addition and subtraction, but let's see a different example using subtraction that yields ambiguous results. If the number one is subtracted from zero in binary, you end up having to borrow for every digit of the eight-bit quantity. The result is all ones (from the constant borrows), and a borrow will fall off the left hand side of the result into the carry flag of the computer. Ignore the carry flag for the time being and concentrate on the result, which looks like this:

	0000 0000	binary 0
binary subtraction	0000 0001	binary 1
	1111 1111	

The resultant number, 11111111, would seem to be 255 if it's converted to decimal. It looks as if the calculation has gone awry. One has been subtracted from zero and the result is 255, which is obviously wrong; however, that's only because no decision has been made as to how to represent negative quantities using the binary number system. Up to now, only positive numbers have been dealt with. In the zeros and ones that the computer uses, there appears to be no way of specifying a minus or plus sign, but the concept of a plus or a minus can itself be represented as a zero or a one. What is done is to use the most significant bit (at the extreme left), of any binary number as a sign. If this bit is a zero, you're dealing with a *positive number*, and if it's a one, you're looking at a *negative number*. This doesn't have to be so in every number in the computer—only where a signed quantity has to be manipulated.

Even though the top bit gives a simple way of storing a sign, +1 is not actually stored as 00000001, nor −1 as 10000001. (If you really wanted to, however, your program could do this.) Instead, a more convenient system called *two's complement* is used. Two's complement provides a "magic" way of converting a positive to a negative number. It also allows you to perform the fascinating trick of being able to subtract one quantity from another using addition.

To arrive at the two's complement of any binary number, you simply invert all the bits and add one. Let's try this with the number three to demonstrate how to subtract three from a number using addition. Three, as a binary byte, is 00000011. Using the two's complement, invert all the bits to 11111100 and add one to give 11111101. Now add this number to the number four, which is 00000100 in binary. The addition looks like this:

	0000 0100	binary 4
binary add	**1111 1101**	2's comp 3
	0000 0001	binary 1

Follow the addition from the right hand side. Zero and one gives one; then zero and zero gives zero. One and one gives zero carry one, and finally the carry is added all the way out of the end of the result byte. Magically, you end up with the number one, so it seems that four minus three works using the addition of the two's complement of three. In fact, deep inside the electronics in any digital microprocessor, all arithmetic computations are performed using addition only. At its innermost arithmetic heart, that's all a microprocessor knows how to do. As you've seen, by taking a two's complement and then adding, the processor can do a subtraction. Later in this chapter, the same additions are used to perform a multiplication and even a division.

Before doing that, consider the number one that was subtracted from zero to apparently produce 255. Remembering that two's complement is being used to give negative numbers, try negating the number one. Eight bits of binary number one is 00000001; take the inverse of all the bits (this is called the *one's complement*), to get 11111110. Get the two's complement by adding one to this, which gives 11111111. The negative of one in eight bits is 11111111, which is exactly what was produced when one was subtracted from zero earlier. What you ended up with wasn't 255 at all—it was in fact −1, in two's complement form.

So now you have a convenient method of representing both positive and negative integers in the computer. Bear in mind that it's the programmer who decides which way to interpret the number 11111111. It can be viewed either as an unsigned quantity, in which case it really is 255, or it can be used as a signed quantity, in which case it's −1. For example, if monetary amounts are being manipulated, it's quite likely that signed quantities will be used. If you're counting objects, on the other hand, you'll probably use an unsigned quantity because you expect to count from zero to some positive quantity. Note that the number zero is taken to be a positive quantity, which is the normal way it's viewed in computing. It isn't negative, so it's regarded as a positive number.

This gives two ways of looking at an eight-bit number. It can be a positive number from zero to 255, or it can be a signed number from −128 to +127. It could also store zero to 99 if you decide to regard and use it as a binary-coded decimal number. This underlines the fact that numbers in a computer mean only what you want them to mean in a particular program. It shows three possible ways of storing a number in eight bits: signed binary, unsigned binary, and BCD.

Remember that only eight-bit quantities are being used here to keep the demonstrations simple. The 68000 works happily in either 8, 16, or 32-bit quantities. If desired, you can work with even larger numbers of bits if the numerical precision of computations needs to be increased. To do this, the carry and overflow flags in the processor are used. As you've already seen in some examples, the carry flag is set whenever a number is added to a quantity that results in a carry being generated out of the leftmost bit of a binary number. Because this bit is outside of the binary number, it can be tested by the programmer and continued into another number if desired. Often, if the carry-out bit is important, it will be added to or subtracted from a binary number to the left of the number that produced the carry. This gives a way of extending the digits out from the left-hand side of a number.

The carry is all well and good when used with unsigned numbers, but what happens when a byte of 11111111, representing −1, has a one added to it? Because the one is just added in, it will generate a carry, having flipped the number to zero. This is fine; the sign of the number has been changed and flagged with a carry. Now look at the case of +127 with a one added to it (assuming that the 127 is being used as a signed binary number). The addition will look like this:

```
               0111 1111    signed 127
binary add     000 00001    signed 1
               ─────────
               1000 0000
```

Here, the most significant bit has become set; because of signed quantities, the number looks like −128. This is incorrect; one has been added to 127 and, in the representation of binary numbers the sign has been changed. Notice also that, in doing this, a carry has not been generated from the left-hand side, so there seems to be no warning of what's happened. This is where the overflow flag comes in. In this instance, the overflow flag would have been set to let the programmer know that a number has gone above or below the limits that apply to signed quantities. That's the main difference between the carry and the overflow flags.

FIXED-POINT AND FLOATING-POINT NUMBERS

Up to this point, only integers have been dealt with. What happens when you want to represent a number that contains a decimal point? There are two main ways of accomplishing this. One is called *fixed-point*; the other, *floating-point*. First, let's look at fixed-point. With this method, the point is assumed to be in a particular place within the binary digits. Because binary is being discussed, this point (more familiarly known as a decimal point) is now referred to as a binary point. In looking at integers up to now, we've really been talking about fixed-point, because it has always been assumed that the binary point is at the right hand side of all the bits being manipulated. Integers have been used, so it has also been taken as a given that there's no fractional part to the number.

To deal with a fractional part of a number, look at what weightings are given to the binary digits to the right of this imagined binary point. There's no big surprise here, because, just as bits increase in significance by powers of two for each shift to the left, they decrease in significance by powers of two for each shift to the right. In other words, each bit to the right represents half the bit to its left. Therefore, the bit to the right of the binary point (and to the right of the one's bit) represents the quantity 0.5. The next rightwards bit is half of that (or 0.25), the next is half of that (or 0.125), and so on. Figure 12-1 showed the binary weighting given to each column to the left of the binary point. Thus, it's possible to store a fair amount of fractional precision in as few as eight bits because the least significant bit of this fractional part represents .00390625.

Adding and subtracting these fixed-point numbers is exactly the same as adding and subtracting integers. The binary point is in the same place in each quantity, so you can simply add the fixed-point numbers together and be assured that you'll end up with the binary point in the same place. As an example of that, the number 1.5 is added to 1.25 in binary, using eight bits each for the integer and fractional parts:

```
00000001.10000000    (1.5)
00000001.01000000    (1.25)
```
_____
```
00000010.11000000    (2.75)
```

The binary point is only shown here for illustration. In the computer, the 16 bits just run together as if they were a 16-bit integer. As you can see, there's no difference between this example and ordinary integer addition. All that has been done is to decide to weight each binary digit from .00390625 on the extreme right up in powers of two to 128 on the extreme left. If you wished, you could assume signed numbers using the same two's complement system previously discussed.

Note that in fixed-point notation, it is assumed that both numbers have the binary point in the same place (in the above example, it is after the eighth bit). This is very important. If one number was set up with a binary point after the seventh bit, for example, the numbers couldn't be added until the points lined up.

The last method of storing numbers to be looked at here is floating-point. This is a method in which the binary point is allowed to *float* within the digits being represented, enabling you to use the maximum number of significant bits in the representation of a number. As a result, a greater degree of accuracy can be achieved in computations involving very large or very small numbers. This can be seen by looking again at the fixed-point binary representation of 1.5. This number used only two set bits out of the 16 in the fixed-point word. If a greater degree of precision in the fractional part (past the least significant bit) was needed, there would be no way to do it. There was no room in the number to store beyond the rightmost .00390625 bit. In floating-point, however, it would be possible.

You can learn something by looking at that fixed-point number. It was decided that the binary point was located at bit position eight from the right-hand side within the 16-bit quantity. That position is implicit within the example, but when 1.5 is used, all seven bits to the left of the leftmost one are wasted. If, somehow, the whole number could be moved to the left, still keeping track of the binary point, there would be extra room at the right-hand side for more fractional digits.

Similarly, large numbers with few or no fractional bits could make good use of the wasted bits to the right of the point. Moving the binary point in this way would allow freedom to maximize the number of bits used, thereby giving greater precision.

Floating-point enables you to do this by having an extra number alongside the current digits. This number is used to keep track of the floating binary point. In the example with 1.5, you could make room for another seven bits by shifting the whole number seven bits to the left. Minus seven would then be stored in the new, extra byte of data—this byte is used to keep a tally of how far the point was moved. This is how the 1.5 would look, assuming eight bits for the point tally and 16 bits for the number part:

Fixed point 1.5

00000000   00000001   10000000

Floating point 1.5

11111001   11000000   00000000

The point tally in the second of these is two's complement of seven; it shows that the point is displaced seven bits to the left. All that has been done is to shift and keep track of the two ones in the number, allowing room for more digits to their right. You could, if you wished, store digits rather than these zeros to enhance the overall precision of the stored fractional part.

This example has been kept intentionally small. In normal computing, there are at least four bytes used to store what is known as *single precision*, eight bytes are used for *double precision*, and ten bytes for *extended precision* floating-point. One byte is usually used to keep track of the floating binary point. This part is called the *exponent*, and the numerical part is called the *mantissa*. Let's look at a real single-precision floating-point number and work out what it represents:

11111110   0110000   00000000   00000000

First, it's necessary to know that floating-point numbers are stored with the binary point to the left of the numerical part (mantissa). The number on the left (the exponent) is −6. Work this out by taking the one's complement to get 00000101, and then taking the two's complement by adding one to get 00000110, or decimal 6. This means you have to locate the binary point three places to the right of its current position. Its current position is to the left of the mantissa, which starts immediately after the eight-bit exponent. Thus, after placing the point, the number would look like this:

11.110000   00000000   00000000

It consists of an integer part of three (two plus one) followed by a fractional part of .75 (.5 + .25). This number is, in fact, a floating-point representation of 3.75.

So far, it has been assumed that the numbers are positive. As with fixed-point integers, floating-point can also represent negative numbers. Not only can the exponent contain a positive or negative displacement of the binary point, but the mantissa itself can be negative. This is accomplished in exactly the same way as with normal integer arithmetic; a two's complement system can be used for signed numbers with the most significant bit standing for a minus sign. In floating-point, however, this minus sign can be somewhat bothersome, and is dealt with in a slightly different way. To understand why, you need to look at how a floating-point number is set up and aligned by the computer. (Incidentally, this process is automatic on floating-point hardware but has to be done by a program otherwise.) Take another look at the number 1.5 to see the steps in converting it from a fixed- to a floating-point number.

A subroutine to do this would take the number and just keep shifting it consecutively one bit left until the most significant bit had become a one. (Thus, only insignificant zeros are shifted out at the left.) Each left shift that the routine did would decrement the tally in a byte that would finally end up becoming the exponent. Once the most significant bit has been set, the process comes to a halt; otherwise meaningful bits would be lost from the left of the mantissa. This important alignment process is called *normalization*. It ensures that the binary point is accounted for and that the maximum amount of bits can be packed into the mantissa. This is the way all floating-point numbers are stored within the computer while not being used in a calculation.

Once you understand that this process is always carried out before a floating-point number is stored, you know for certain that any nonzero floating-point number will always have its most significant bit set as a result of the normalization. (A quantity of zero is treated as a special case.) Because you are aware that this topmost bit is always set, you can now put it to good use. In fact, with a little ingenuity, it can be used as a minus sign. Usually, the way this is done is to leave the bit set on only if the mantissa is negative; otherwise the bit is artificially coerced to a zero. The fact that it is really a one means that it has to be reset as such before the number can be used. It can be allowed to remain as a one if the number is negative (assuming the mantissa is a two's complement negative number), or it can be replaced with a zero if it's positive. Following this, the number can be stored in memory with full confidence that the sign can be reinstated.

When the quantity is recovered from memory for use in a calculation or conversion, the most significant bit will first be tested to see if the mantissa is positive or negative. The result of this test is temporarily saved somewhere, and that bit is set back to a one. At that point the program has a reinstated floating-point number and a knowledge of the sign of the mantissa.

The exponent is a normal two's complement eight-bit number, so it doesn't have to be aligned, and there's no special treatment of its sign bit. Some systems, however, store a floating-point zero as a special case by setting the exponent to zero and ignoring any bits in the mantissa. If this method is used (and it often is), there will be a special check to ensure that the exponent can never be zero in any other case. Many computers use a method whereby 128 is added to the exponent to prevent it from accidentally being a zero. This 128 is later subtracted to find the real exponent.

Using this information, you can now see that the number 1.5 would have been stored in memory in a different manner than it would be manipulated in a calculation. The example above showed the mantissa with all bits present as it would be during a calculation. When stored in memory, however, it would look like this:

11111110   0110000   00000000   00000000

Notice that it's exactly the same, except for the high bit of the mantissa being switched off.

This concludes the overview of how numbers can be stored in a machine to facilitate their use in calculations. In looking at other people's programs, you might find slight departures from the above, but the principles behind each type will always be the same.

PERFORMING CALCULATIONS USING BINARY NUMBERS

Earlier it was mentioned that all manipulations are performed on a digital computer using addition within the processor itself. You saw how subtraction can be accomplished by using the two's complement and adding it to the number being subtracted from. But how are multiplication and division performed?

Multiplying Binary Numbers

The way multiplication is performed is refreshingly simple. It relies on the fact that shifting a number left in binary has the same effect as multiplying it by two. Shifting a number left by a zero amount is the same as multiplying by one. Because every number that exists is some multiple of two and one, it's possible to accomplish multiplication by any amount using a combination of shifts and adds with the number being multiplied. For instance, to multiply a number by two, it is shifted left one bit; to multiply by one, the number is not shifted at all. To multiply by three, the number is shifted left one (to multiply it by two) and then added to itself in its unshifted state. Any number multiplied by two and added to the original number has been multiplied by three.

Let's look at a slightly more complicated example to show that this process works with any number. For instance, multiply the number five by eleven. In binary, five is 101, and eleven is 1011. The numbers line up like this:

00000101
00001011

Look at the bits in the eleven. They dictate how to shift that number five. Starting on the right at the least significant bit, the one says to shift the five left by none. The next bit says to shift the five by one, which multiplies it by two. The next bit is not set, so skip to the next. This bit is set, and tells you to shift the five by three places, which multiplies it by eight. Each bit in the multiplier simply says to shift the multiplicand by one more byte. The three quantities resulting from that shifted five look like this:

```
00000101        shifted 0 (X 1)
00001010        shifted 1 (X 2)
00101000        shifted 3 (X 8)
--------
00110111            (X 11)
```

The result when the numbers are added together is 00110111. If you convert the byte to decimal, you end up with the splendid number of 55—exactly what you want from five multiplied by eleven.

Bear in mind that with binary multiplication the result can occupy twice as many bits as each of the original two numbers. This means that multiplying two eight-bit quantities together could produce a 16-bit result. For example 11111111 multiplied by 11111111 results in 1111111000000001 ($255 \times 255 = 65025$).

Dividing Binary Numbers

Division can be accomplished in a similar manner to multiplication, except that the number of times one number is contained in another is determined, by subtracting it. You could simply keep subtracting the divisor from the dividend, keeping a count of how many times it was subtracted. This would give a result, but it is a little tedious.

There is a more elegant method of division that works in the reverse way to the multiplication method shown earlier. To use this method, you need to know how many bits are in the dividend. Remember that with multiplication, the answer is always twice the number of bits in the integers being multiplied. In division, the reverse is true: the divisor and resultant quotient will always be half the number of bits in the dividend. This makes sense, as these two numbers multiplied together should yield the original dividend. Using this knowledge, you can see how many times a divisor goes into a dividend by subtracting it after it has been multiplied by subsequent powers of two.

Just as multiplication works by adding the original number shifted left, division works by subtracting the divisor shifted right. It's a little less intuitive than multiplication, but a couple of examples should help. Let's try dividing eleven by three. To keep the example short, the answer (the quotient) will have to be assumed to be two bits—this is because the dividend will be shown in four bits. The divisor has to be the same length as the quotient, so it is also two bits in this example.

The four-bit byte of eleven is 1011, and the two-bit divisor is 11. Before the first subtraction, the divisor is shifted left by its own length. It is then sequentially subtracted and shifted right until it becomes the original divisor again. At that point, the last subtraction is performed to see if it goes into what's left of the dividend. Every time the divisor goes into the dividend, the divisor is subtracted from the dividend to produce a new dividend. The quotient is then incremented to show this. Every time the divisor is shifted right, the quotient is shifted left to reflect the fact that the previous subtraction was twice the value of the current one. Eleven divided by three looks like this:

```
1011      4-bit 11
1100      2-bit 3, left 2
----
          quotient = 00
```

This first subtraction gives a negative result, so the quotient is not incremented and you go to the next step. The divisor is shifted right one place, and the quotient is shifted left. Because the quotient is zero, it stays the same.

```
1011      4-bit 11
0110      2-bit 3, left 1
——        quotient = 00
0101
          quotient = 01
```

The result of this subtraction is positive, so the quotient is incremented. The dividend is now replaced by the result of the subtraction—0101 in this case. The divisor is shifted right one last time (it now becomes the original divisor of three), and the quotient is shifted left. The next step looks like this:

```
0101      new dividend
0011      2-bit 3, left 0
——        quotient = 10
0010
          quotient = 11
```

The result of this last subtraction was also positive, so the quotient is incremented again. The calculation is now complete. The answer of binary 11 is in the quotient and the remaining dividend is, in fact, the remainder of binary 10. Thus, eleven divided by three is three remainder two. That took two shifts, which was the number of bits in the divisor.

As a last example of division, let's see if the eight-bit representation of decimal 55 can be correctly divided by the four-bit eleven. Here's the sequence of steps. Remember that the subtractions would be performed using two's complement addition.

```
00110111      8-bit 55
10110000      4-bit 11, left 4
————          quotient = 0000
```

(negative result, do next step)

```
00110111      8-bit 55
01011000      4-bit 11, left 3
————          quotient = 000
```

(negative result, do next step)

```
00110111      8-bit 55
00101100      4-bit 11, left 2
————          quotient = 0000
00001011
              quotient = 0001
```

```
00001011        8-bit divisor from above
00010110        4-bit 11, left 1
————            quotient = 0010
```

(negative result, do last step)

```
00001011        8-bit divisor
00001011        4-bit 11, left 0
————            quotient = 0100
00000000
                quotient = 0101
```

The last step has given the result: a quotient of five with a remainder of zero.

LOGICAL FUNCTIONS

Logical functions are very useful because of the bit-manipulation capabilities they offer. For instance, you'd use the OR function to set bits on in a number, regardless of their previous state. As an example, if you OR 100 with 011, the result is 111. This is used whenever a bit needs to be forced on (like a flag or control bit). The AND function is used to mask bits off in a number. For example, if you start with the number 110 and then AND it with 011, the result would be 010; the operation switched off the leftmost bit.

The XOR operation is primarily used to reverse the state of any particular bit. For example, if you have a number with a bit set and XOR it with another number with the same bit set, the bit in the result will be changed to a zero. If this same operation were then repeated, it would set that bit back on. This property of the XOR operation is interesting. It means that if you XOR a number twice with a mask contained in another number, the original number returns. This is often used as a simple encoding method in which XOR is used to provide characters with a mask, which are later decoded by using XOR with the same mask.

The NOT operation is used whenever a mirror-image of the zeros and ones in a binary number is required. This is the first step in changing the sign of a number using its twos' complement (by performing a NOT and then adding one). On most processors, such as the 68000, a complement instruction does this automatically.

The bit tables for these four logical functions are shown in Fig. 12-5.

```
        OR          AND          XOR          NOT
      0 0 1 1      0 0 1 1      0 0 1 1
      0 1 0 1      0 1 0 1      0 1 0 1      0 1
      ———————      ———————      ———————      ———
      0 1 1 1      0 0 0 1      0 1 1 0      1 0
```

Fig. 12-5. The bit tables for the OR, AND, XOR, and NOT logical operators.

MATHEMATICAL ROUTINES ON THE AMIGA

The 68000 provides the ability to do certain operations, such as add and subtract, on integers. The MULU, MULS and DIVU, DIVS instructions allow multiplication and division of integers. As far as fixed-point quantities are concerned, addition and subtraction operations on them can be performed using the 68000's instructions ADD and SUB, with a note being kept of the position of the binary point. You will have to write subroutines to do multiplication and division of fixed-point numbers, but fixed-point numbers tend to be used somewhat infrequently, so you'll probably be better off using floating-point routines.

The floating-point environment has its own set of software library within the Amiga. It is available in the libraries called mathffp.library, mathieeedoubbas.library, and mathtrans.library. These libraries contain all the routines likely to be required for dealing with floating-point numbers of single or double precision, and include routines to perform square roots as well as other transcendental functions. The documentation for these libraries is included in the ROM Kernel Manual.

Chapter

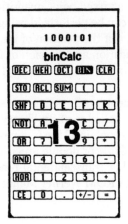

13

An Assembly-Language
Calculator Program

The calculator program found in Fig. 13-1 at the end of this chapter shows how assembly language can be used to produce a complex, multifunctional program. Rather than provide a line-by-line description of the program, a full set of comments has been provided in the source code. The comments detail the full operation of the program. There are, however, a few things worth pointing out to help you understand how the program works.

The object of the program is to emulate, as closely as possible, the integer operation of a Texas Instruments programmer's calculator. Apart from the operation of the decimal point key, this program closely models the functioning of that calculator.

The following points are intended both to illustrate how the calculator works and to highlight some salient points about the program. First, the TI calculator lets you use parentheses to determine the order of operations. For instance, normally, the sequence 2 * 3 − 1 is performed in the same sequence that it's typed in. Without parentheses, this would be performed as two times three, yielding six, minus one, yielding five. With parentheses, it's possible to change the order of these operations so that it becomes 2 * (3 − 1), which is two multiplied by the result of three minus one, giving the answer four. Note that in the latter example, the number two has to be saved while the calculation three minus one is performed.

With multiple levels of parentheses like this, it's necessary to save pending operations so that higher priority ones are done first. This is, undoubtedly, the hardest part of the program to code. It is accomplished by having an internal register area where the pending numbers are stacked. This is done in a way similar to the way the 68000 handles the stack, except that these numbers are saved in ascending rather than descending order. It's not so much the direction that they're saved in that determines the area's definition as a stack; rather, it's the fact that the last number into the stack becomes the first one removed from it as calculations are performed. (This is called a *first-in-first-out*, or *FIFO* stack.)

There's a room on this stack for four numbers of 32 bits apiece. This is a totally arbitrary number and was chosen to emulate the TI calculator, which also has room for four numbers. It would be very easy to change the program to deal with more numbers by reserving more space where the variable numstk is defined in the program's data area. As it is, it's set up as:

```
numstk          dcb.l       5,0
```

This defines a constant block of memory consisting of five long words initialized to zero. The extra word is used to store pending operations along with the pending numbers. Each operation only needs one byte, so one extra long word of four bytes is added to the four needed for the number stack.

The calculator's display is always kept in data register d7; this allows for easy manipulation of the display number (which is naturally the most often used number). Thus, the calculator can deal with five numbers in total: one in the display and four on its stack. There is one additional number that can be used in the calculator: the *store*. This is easy to emulate in a program by allotting another long word—called *calcstore*.

The store allows you to save the display in a temporary location for retrieval with the recall key. Also, it's possible to add the display to the store with the sum key. Errors can occur if you try to place numbers in the store that can't be displayed in the current number base. Whenever any such error occurs, the word "Error" is displayed, and the program will prevent any further key entry until clear has been pressed.

A constant, or K feature, is also provided. This allows the number in the display and the last entered operation to be saved as a constant and performed every time the equals button is pressed. The constant number and operation are thus performed on the number in the display whenever equals is pressed with a K operator set up. You can escape from this mode by pressing a new operator key, by pressing a close parenthesis, or by using the clear button. For example, entering + 2 K saves the number two and the operation (addition) in the constant register. Then, every time equals is hit, two is added to the number in the display. The K operator and constant number are, in reality, simply saved on the calculator's register stack like any other number. They are differentiated from ordinary numbers by having bit 3 set in the operation code. This is how a pending K operator is detected and cleared within the program.

Normally, the four saved numbers in the internal stack are pointed to by register a4. This defines the start of the register save area. Because each register is four bytes long and there are four numbers, this area is 16 bytes in length. This is followed by four bytes containing an operation code and the parenthesis level to which it applies—this is where the K bit is also squeezed in. As register a4 points to the beginning of the saved numbers, 16 plus a4 points to the start of the saved operators.

The lower half of register d6 is used as an index to point to the next position available on the stack.This is initially zero, and can contain valid values up to three. Thus, the next pending number to be saved to the internal register stack will be saved at 0(a4,d6.W). The next operator to be saved along with this number will be stored at 16(a4,d6.W). Note that this means that the last saved operator is to be found at 15(a4,d6.W), or one less than the location of the next available position.

A maximum of 15 parentheses can precede any number, and an error message is generated if this level is exceeded. An error message is also displayed if overflow occurs in any calculations. Note that this is true overflow—not carry. Subtracting one from zero is permitted; however, subtracting one from the largest negative number in any number base is not. Subtracting one from negative 128 in binary will, therefore, generate an error message.

The calculator treats all numbers as signed, but the allowable magnitude of numbers is determined by the number base in current use. This is selected by the DEC, HEX, OCT, and BIN keys. Pressing one of these keys will generate an error if the number won't fit in the selected base.

Note that the gadget structures that comprise the calculator keys have numbers within their id fields that were judiciously chosen to make it easier to program this calculator model. For instance, the number keys 0 to 9 and A to F all have consecutive id numbers. This makes it simple to decode the gadget selected by the mouse into a number button on the calculator. The same technique is also used to decode the operator and some function keys. These keys return gadget id numbers that are used as offsets within the program to point to the routine dealing with that key's operation.

Note that the operator keys are split into two groups: arithmetic operators and logical operators. This is necessary because logical operators are not allowed on decimal numbers. Once again, this follows the TI calculator's lead, is completely arbitrary, and could be changed if desired. In the program, these operations have been labeled binary operations not because they operate on binary numbers, but because each one operates on two numbers.

As in the gadget program in Chapter 11, you can elect to automatically assemble and link the program. Assuming that the source-code file is called calc.asm, enter these two lines into a script file called calc.exec for the Execute utility:

```
assem calc.asm -c W160000 -i include -o calc.obj

alink calc.obj to calc lib lib/amiga.lib
```

Then type:

```
Execute calc.exec
```

You should do this until all typos have been weeded out of the source code; at that point you'll end up with an executable tool called calc. You'll also need to create an icon in a file called calc.info as described in Chapter 11.

If you decide to become adventurous, there are some modifications that could improve the usefulness of this program. One, of course, is the inclusion of the algorithms to deal with the decimal point. You could also implement an addressable calculator store with multiple locations. These could even be saved in a file, and restored each time the calculator is fired up. Without too much bother, it is possible to add some code to force the use of a particular text size. As it stands, the program uses the current font size as set up from the Preferences utility. The calculator will work properly with font sizes of both 60 and 80 without modifications. The only reason you might want to force a particular font width to be used is to prevent the user changing it after the calculator has started execution.

You can see the effects of this if you start the calculator, change the font size from the Preferences window, and then return to the calculator and use it. The two font sizes can then be seen, one on top of the other, in the same application. A user is unlikely to change font sizes in mid-program, but the result is not something that is particularly desirable.

Apart from the lack of a decimal point, this program provides a fair emulation of a programmer's calculator. It allows you to perform many useful functions and conversions that are helpful when you are programming a computer, especially in assembly language. It also gives you a perfect feel for how numbers are crunched for a purpose in the 68000.

Fig. 13-1. The Calculator program.

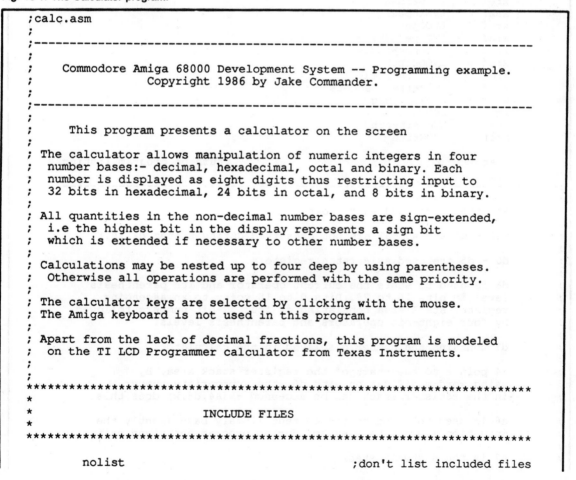

```
;calc.asm
;
;----------------------------------------------------------------------
;
;       Commodore Amiga 68000 Development System -- Programming example.
;                 Copyright 1986 by Jake Commander.
;
;----------------------------------------------------------------------
;
;       This program presents a calculator on the screen
;
; The calculator allows manipulation of numeric integers in four
;  number bases:- decimal, hexadecimal, octal and binary. Each
;  number is displayed as eight digits thus restricting input to
;  32 bits in hexadecimal, 24 bits in octal, and 8 bits in binary.
;
; All quantities in the non-decimal number bases are sign-extended,
;  i.e the highest bit in the display represents a sign bit
;  which is extended if necessary to other number bases.
;
; Calculations may be nested up to four deep by using parentheses.
;  Otherwise all operations are performed with the same priority.
;
; The calculator keys are selected by clicking with the mouse.
; The Amiga keyboard is not used in this program.
;
; Apart from the lack of decimal fractions, this program is modeled
;  on the TI LCD Programmer calculator from Texas Instruments.
;
;
**********************************************************************
*
*                         INCLUDE FILES
*
**********************************************************************

         nolist                              ;don't list included files
```

```
        INCLUDE  "exec/types.i"                 ;for following includes
        INCLUDE  "exec/alerts.i"                ;to access ALERT macro
        INCLUDE  "exec/ports.i"                 ;to access message structure
        INCLUDE  "libraries/dosextens.i"        ;to access process structure
        INCLUDE  "intuition/intuition.i"        ;to access intuition structures


**************************************************************************
*
*                       EXTERNAL REFERENCES
*
**************************************************************************

        xref     _AbsExecBase

        xref     _LVOAlert
        xref     _LVOCloseLibrary
        xref     _LVOCloseWindow
        xref     _LVODebug
        xref     _LVODisplayBeep
        xref     _LVOFindTask
        xref     _LVOForbid
        xref     _LVOGetMsg
        xref     _LVOInput
        xref     _LVOOpen
        xref     _LVOOpenLibrary
        xref     _LVOOpenWindow
        xref     _LVOOutput
        xref     _LVOPrintIText
        xref     _LVORefreshGadgets
        xref     _LVOReplyMsg
        xref     _LVOWait
        xref     _LVOWaitPort
        xref     _LVOWrite

        list                                    ;turn on program listing

;------------------------------------------------------------------------
;
;       Registers are used as follows:
;
;       (d0 - d1 and a0 -a1 are not preserved during system calls.)
;
;       d0 - d5 are used as scratch registers.
;
;       d6 is used to store the current operator and its parenthesis
;       level in bits 16 to 23. Bits 0 to 15 point to an ascending
;       register stack area consisting of four 32-bit numbers followed
;       by four eight-bit operators and parenthesis levels.
;
;       d7 contains the number displayed in the calculator.
;
;       a4 points to the start of the register stack area. By
;       using word-modification with d6, the appropriate number
;       in the register stack can be accessed - (a4,d6.w) does this.
;
;       a6 is used to point to the current library base (mostly the
;       intuition library base except during program entry and exit.)
;
;       a7 is the system's stack pointer.
```

```
;
**********************************************************************
*
*                    PROGRAM STARTUP CODE
*
**********************************************************************

Begin
        move.l          a7,initialSP            ;initial task stack pointer
        movea.l         _AbsExecBase,a6         ;get exec library base
        move.l          a6,ExecBase             ;save exec lib base

        suba.l          a1,a1                   ;set a0 = 0
        jsr             _LVOFindTask(a6)        ;get the address of this task
        movea.l         d0,a4                   ;task address to a4

        bsr             openDOS                 ;attempt to open DOS library

        tst.l           pr_CLI(a4)              ;are we running under Workbench?
        beq             WBStart                 ;ok if so

;
;       If in CLI, send a message and abort
;
        movea.l         d0,a6                   ;set DOS library pointer
        jsr             _LVOOutput(a6)          ;get output handle
        move.l          d0,d1                   ;handle to d1 for Write
        lea             msg,a0                  ;point to output message
        move.l          a0,d2                   ;message pointer to d2
        moveq           #msglen,d3              ;message length to d3
        jsr             _LVOWrite(a6)           ;write message to output

        moveq.l         #10,D0                  ;failure code
        bra             exit                    ;return to CLI

**********************************************************************
*
*                    WORKBENCH STARTUP CODE
*
**********************************************************************

WBStart

        bsr             openINT                 ;open intuition library

        bsr             waitmsg                 ;wait for start message
        move.l          d0,returnMsg            ;save message for later

**********************************************************************
*
*                    MAIN PROGRAM
*
**********************************************************************

        bsr             DrawWind                ;draw calc window to screen
        lea             numstk,a4               ;point to number stack

;
; Perform a reset as per the CLR button
;
```

```
rstcalc
        moveq           #0,d7                       ;reset calculator display
        moveq           #0,d6                       ;reset calc reg stack pointer
        clr.b           crntkey                     ;reset current key
        clr.b           errflg                      ;reset error flag
        clr.b           newparen                    ;reset new parenthesis flag


;
; Start numeric character entry
;
newchrs
        clr.b           chrcnt                      ;reset numeric chr count
prdisp
        bsr             disp                        ;print calculator display
        move.b          crntkey,prevkey             ;save previous key
getkey
        bsr             getbutton                   ;get a calculator button


;
; Find out which key has been selected
;
        move.b          d0,crntkey                  ;hold current key
        cmpi.b          #40,d0                      ;CLR key?
        beq.s           rstcalc                     ;reset calculator if so
        tst.b           errflg                      ;displaying 'error'?
        bne.s           getkey                      ;ignore other keys if so

        cmpi.b          #15,d0                      ;decimal point?
        beq.s           getkey                      ;ignore it if so
        cmpi.b          #14,d0                      ;+/- key?
        bne.s           tryops                      ;no
        bsr             chsign                      ;else change sign
        bra.s           prdisp                      ;and print display

tryops
        pea             newchrs                     ;place return address on stack

        cmpi.b          #32,d0                      ;operation key?
        bcc             operate                     ;do it if so
        cmpi.b          #16,d0                      ;number key?
        bcs             keys                        ;if not, deal with others


;
; A number has been selected.
; Use it if it's legal for this number base
;
        lea             4(a7),a7                    ;numbers don't need rts addr

        cmpi.b          #8,chrcnt                   ;already got 8 characters?
        beq.s           getkey                      ;ignore number if so

        tst.b           chrcnt                      ;in mid number?
        beq.s           1$                          ;if not, don't check minus

        cmpi.b          #10,base                    ;in decimal mode?
        beq.s           1$                          ;no minus check if so
        tst.l           d7                          ;display negative?
        bmi.s           getkey                      ;ignore keys if so
1$
```

```
        andi.w          #$0F,d0                 ;extract number from key
        cmpi.b          #2,d0                   ;number greater than 1?
        bcs.s           numok                   ;always accept 0 or 1
        cmpi.b          #2,base                 ;in binary mode?
        beq.s           getkey                  ;if so, ignore number > 1

        cmpi.b          #8,d0                   ;number greater than 7?
        bcs.s           numok                   ;up to 7 ok if not binary
        cmpi.b          #8,base                 ;in octal mode?
        beq             getkey                  ;if so, ignore number > 7

        cmpi.b          #10,d0                  ;number greater than 9?
        bcs.s           numok                   ;up to 9 ok if not octal
        cmpi.b          #10,base                ;in decimal mode?
        beq             getkey                  ;if so, ignore number > 9
numok
        tst.b           chrcnt                  ;first digit of number?
        bne.s           notchr1                 ;no
        cmpi.b          #10,prevkey             ;previous key = '(' ?
        beq.s           1$                      ;don't push op if so

        bsr             pushop                  ;else push op on reg stack
1$
        moveq           #0,d7                   ;initialize display = 0
        tst.b           d0                      ;leading zero?
        beq             prdisp                  ;if so, don't shift display

notchr1
        move.w          d0,-(a7)                ;save current digit
        moveq           #0,d0                   ;reset high byte in low word
        move.b          base,d0                 ;get num base to low word

;
; Multiply display by the number base
;

        bsr             multop                  ;do multiply
        clr.b           errflg                  ;in case high bit on in hex

        cmpi.b          #10,base                ;in decimal mode?
        bne.s           1$                      ;add in digit if not
        tst.l           d7                      ;negative decimal # in display
        bpl.s           1$                      ;no, add new digit
        sub.w           (a7)+,d7                ;else subtract new digit
        bra.s           3$                      ;skip add
1$
        add.w           (a7)+,d7                ;add in keyed number

;
; Sign-extend binary and octal to 32 bits after number is entered
;

3$
        cmpi.b          #2,base                 ;binary mode?
        bne.s           4$                      ;no, see if octal
        ext.w           d7                      ;sign-extend to 16 bits
        ext.l           d7                      ;sign-extend to 32 bits
        bra.s           5$                      ;number all ready
4$
```

```
             cmpi.b          #8,base                  ;octal mode?
             bne.s           5$                       ;no, use number as is
             swap            d7                       ;prepare to sign-extend
             ext.w           d7                       ;sign-extend to last byte
             swap            d7                       ;put right way round
5$
             addq.b          #1,chrcnt                ;increment chr count
             bra             prdisp                   ;show calculator display

;
; Function keys not dealt with previously are now used
; as pointers to the address performing their function
;

keys
             subq            #1,d0                    ;align to jump-table start
             add.w           d0,d0                    ;*2 bytes per jump index
             move.w          dotable(d0),d0           ;get index for key's address
             jmp             dotable(d0)              ;jump to key handler

dotable
             dc.w            decimal-dotable
             dc.w            hexdec-dotable
             dc.w            octal-dotable
             dc.w            binary-dotable
             dc.w            equals-dotable
             dc.w            clentry-dotable
             dc.w            store-dotable
             dc.w            recall-dotable
             dc.w            sum-dotable
             dc.w            openp-dotable
             dc.w            closep-dotable
             dc.w            notop-dotable
             dc.w            Kop-dotable


;
; +/- key
;
chsign
             tst.l           d7                       ;display = 0?
             beq.s           1$                       ;don't bother if so
             neg.l           d7                       ;else 2's complement display
             svs             errflg                   ;set error flag if overflow
             bsr             disp                     ;do display
             move.b          dispcnt,chrcnt           ;update display chr count
1$
             rts
;
; HEX key
;
hexdec
             moveq           #16,d0                   ;set hexadecimal radix
             bra.s           setbase
;
; DEC key
;
decimal
             moveq           #10,d0                   ;set decimal radix
             bra.s           setbase
;
```

```
;  OCT key
;
octal
        moveq           #8,d0                   ;set octal radix
        bra.s           setbase
;
;  BIN key
;
binary
        moveq           #2,d0                   ;set binary radix
setbase
        move.b          d0,base                 ;store number base

*  After either HEX, DEC, OCT, or BIN has been
*  selected, the gadget address in a2 is used to
*  highlight the selected button by setting the
*  gadget's text to white. Before doing this, the
*  previously selected button's text is set orange.

        move.l          base_gadget,a0          ;previous current-base gadget
        move.l          a2,base_gadget          ;reset current-base gadget
        move.l          gg_GadgetText(a0),a1    ;previous gadget text address
        move.b          #1,it_FrontPen(a1)      ;previous gadget text to white
        move.l          gg_GadgetText(a2),a1    ;selected gadget text address
        move.b          #3,it_FrontPen(a1)      ;selected gadget text to orange

;
;  refresh all button gadgets
;
        lea             Gadget1,a0              ;1st gadget to refresh
        movea.l         windptr,a1              ;point to our window
        suba.l          a2,a2                   ;set a2 = 0
        jsr             _LVORefreshGadgets(a6)  ;redisplay gadgets

        rts


;
;  = key
;
equals
        tst.w           d6                      ;register stack empty?
        beq.s           1$                      ;all done if so
        bsr.s           closep1                 ;else do binary operation
        btst.b          #3,15(a4,d6.w)          ;got a K operator?
        bne.s           2$                      ;if so, exit after K op
        bra.s           equals                  ;do until reg stack empty
1$
        moveq           #0,d6                   ;reset crnt op and reg stk
2$
        rts
;
;  CE key
;
clentry
        tst.l           d6                      ;operator awaiting stack?
        bmi.s           clout                   ;yes, leave display alone
        moveq           #0,d7                   ;else clear display number
clout
        rts
```

```
;
; STO key
;
store
        move.l          d7,calcstore            ;display register to store
        rts


;
; RCL key
;
recall
        move.l          calcstore,d7            ;store to display register
        bra             pushop                  ;pending op to stack


;
; SUM key
;
sum
        add.l           d7,calcstore            ;store = disp + store
        svs             errflg                  ;error if overflow
        rts


;
; ( key
;
openp
        cmpi.b          #10,prevkey             ;previous key = '(' ?
        beq.s           1$                      ;don't push op if so

        bsr             pushop                  ;crnt op to register stack
        st              newparen                ;flag new parentheses open
        andi.l          #$FF0FFFFF,d6           ;reset parenthesis level
1$
        move.l          d6,d0                   ;parenthesis count to d0
        andi.l          #$F00000,d0             ;extract paren count
        cmpi.l          #$F00000,d0             ;paren count at max (15)?
        bne.s           2$                      ;no, all ok

        st              errflg                  ;else set error flag
2$
        addi.l          #$100000,d6             ;increment paren count
        rts


;
; ) key
;
closep
        bsr.s           tstresK                 ;test and reset K if set
        tst.b           d6                      ;register stack empty?
        beq.s           closout                 ;nothing to do if so
closep1
        move.b          15(a4,d6.w),d0          ;get previous paren count
        andi.l          #$F0,d0                 ;extract paren count
        swap            d0                      ;move paren count up

        andi.l          #$FFFFF,d6              ;mask out old paren count
        or.l            d0,d6                   ;or in new paren count
```

```
        bsr             binop                   ;do binary operation
        move.l          d6,d0                   ;paren count to d0
        andi.l          #$F00000,d0             ;extract paren count
        beq.s           closout                 ;if already at zero

        tst.w           d6                      ;at stack bottom?
        bne.s           1$                      ;if not, decrement paren cnt
        move.l          #$100000,d6             ;else ensure paren cnt = 0
1$
        subi.l          #$100000,d6             ;decrement paren count
closout
        rts


;
; NOT key
;
notop
        cmpi.b          #10,base                ;in decimal mode?
        beq.s           nout                    ;no NOT if so
        not.l           d7                      ;1's complement of display
nout
        rts


;
; K key
;
Kop
        btst.b          #3,15(a4,d6.w)          ;already got K operator?
        bne.s           Kout                    ;if so, do nothing

        bsr             pushop                  ;any pending op to stack
        tst.b           d6                      ;op on stack?
        beq.s           Kout                    ;out if no op on stack

        lsl.w           #2,d6                   ;d6 * 4 to align long words
        move.l          -4(a4,d6.w),d0          ;hold register from stack
        move.l          d7,-4(a4,d6.w)          ;display to register stack
        lsr.w           #2,d6                   ;realign d6

        move.l          d0,d7                   ;replace display
        andi.b          #7,15(a4,d6.w)          ;reset paren count
        bset.b          #3,15(a4,d6.w)          ;set K flag
        clr.b           newparen                ;reset new paren flag
Kout
        rts


tstresK
        btst.b          #3,15(a4,d6.w)          ;in Konstant mode?
        beq.s           1$                      ;no
                                                ;else...
        bclr.b          #3,15(a4,d6.w)          ;reset K flag
        clr.w           d6                      ;reset register stk ptr
1$
        rts
operate
        cmp.b           #$24,d0                 ;is it a logic op?
        bcc.s           1$                      ;no
```

159

```
            cmpi.b          #10,base                    ;in decimal mode?
            beq.s           operout                     ;no logic ops on decimal
1$
            bsr.s           tstresK                     ;test and reset K op if set
            bsr.s           binop                       ;do pending binary operation

            lsl.w           #2,d6                       ;d6 * 4 to align long words
            move.l          d7,0(a4,d6.w)               ;save display on reg stack
            lsr.w           #2,d6                       ;realign d6

            move.b          crntkey,d0                  ;current calculator key
            andi.l          #7,d0                       ;extract op from key
            swap            d6                          ;current op to lower half
            andi.b          #$F0,d6                     ;remove old op
            or.b            d0,d6                       ;put current op in place
            swap            d6                          ;realign d6
            bset            #31,d6                      ;flag op awaiting stack
operout
            rts


binop
            tst.b           newparen                    ;just opened new parens?
            beq.s           1$                          ;no
            clr.b           newparen                    ;else reset flag
            rts                                         ;and do nothing
1$
            tst.b           d6                          ;register stack empty?
            beq.s           binout                      ;yes, no op to do

            move.l          d6,d0                       ;use d0 for paren info
            swap            d0                          ;align paren count to lower
            andi.b          #$F0,d0                     ;extract current paren count
            move.b          15(a4,d6.w),d1              ;get stacked operation
            andi.b          #$F0,d1                     ;get its parenthesis level
            cmp.b           d0,d1                       ;correct parenthesis level?
            bne.s           binout                      ;no, don't do op yet

            move.l          d6,-(a7)                    ;save d6 on user stack
            bsr.s           opdo                        ;do operation on stack
            move.l          (a7)+,d6                    ;restore d6
            btst.b          #3,15(a4,d6.w)              ;K flag set?
            bne.s           binout                      ;don't pop op if so

            subq            #1,d6                       ;decrement register stk ptr
binout
            rts

;*********************************************************************************
;
; This is where the actual number-crunching is performed
; The key selected is used as an offset to a table of
; operations which perform the actual work
;
;*********************************************************************************


opdo
            move.b          15(a4,d6.w),d0              ;get stacked op
            andi.w          #7,d0                       ;extract op
```

```
            cmp.w           #4,d0                   ;is it a logic op?
            bcc.s           opdo1                   ;no
            cmpi.b          #10,base                ;in decimal mode?
            bne.s           opdo1                   ;no, so ok
            st              errflg                  ;no can do
            rts
opdo1
            add.w           d0,d0                   ;*2 (use op as word index)
            move.w          optable(d0),d1          ;get index for op jump
            subq            #1,d6                   ;align d6 to crnt stk reg
            lsl.w           #2,d6                   ;*4 to align with long words
            move.l          0(a4,d6.w),d0           ;ready previous number in d0
            lsr.w           #2,d6                   ;realign d6
            jmp             optable(d1)             ;jump to op

optable
            dc.w            shfop-optable
            dc.w            orop-optable
            dc.w            andop-optable
            dc.w            xorop-optable
            dc.w            divop-optable
            dc.w            multop-optable
            dc.w            subop-optable
            dc.w            addop-optable


;
; SHF key
;
shfop
            bsr             ckkop                   ;chk number order for K ops

            tst.l           d7                      ;shift count negative?
            bpl.s           shf1                    ;if left shift
            neg.l           d7                      ;convert to pos right shift
            lsr.l           d7,d0                   ;do shift op
            bra.s           shf2
shf1
            lsl.l           d7,d0                   ;do shift op
shf2
            move.l          d0,d7                   ;result to display register
            rts


;
; OR key
;
orop
            or.l            d0,d7                   ;do or op
            rts


;
; AND key
;
andop
            and.l           d0,d7                   ;do and op
            rts

;
```

```
; XOR key
;
xorop
        eor.l           d0,d7                   ;do xor op
        rts


;
; / key
;
divop
        bsr             ckkop                   ;chk number order for K ops

        tst.l           d7                      ;divisor = 0 ?
        seq             errflg                  ;divide by zero error if so
        beq.s           divout                  ;out if error

        bsr             dosigns                 ;change numbers to positive

        cmp.l           d0,d7                   ;divisor = dividend ?
        bne.s           1$                      ;no, not special case
        moveq           #1,d2                   ;else result is 1
        bra.s           divout                  ;see about sign
1$
        cmp.l           d0,d7                   ;dividend > divisor?
        bcs.s           2$                      ;yes, result is > 0
        moveq           #0,d7                   ;else result is zero
        rts                                     ;sign doesn't matter
2$
        moveq           #0,d3                   ;initialize iteration count
3$
        addq            #1,d3                   ;increment iteration count
        asl.l           #1,d7                   ;see if d7 goes > d0
        bmi.s           4$                      ;it did if now negative
        cmp.l           d7,d0                   ;d7 > d0 ?
        bcc.s           3$                      ;no, try again
4$
        lsr.l           #1,d7                   ;readjust divisor
        moveq           #0,d2                   ;initialize quotient
5$
        sub.l           d7,d0                   ;divisor goes in?
        bmi.s           6$                      ;no
        addq            #1,d2                   ;else record it
        bra.s           7$
6$
        add.l           d7,d0                   ;restore dividend
7$
        subq            #1,d3                   ;done all bits?
        beq.s           divout                  ;yes
        asl.l           #1,d2                   ;quotient * 2
        asr.l           #1,d7                   ;divisor / 2
        bra.s           5$                      ;next round

divout
        move.l          d2,d7                   ;move quotient to result

        tst.b           sgnflg                  ;should result be negative?
        beq.s           1$                      ;no, exit
        neg.l           d7                      ;else change sign of result
1$
        rts
```

```
;
; * key
;
multop
        bsr.s           dosigns                 ;make both numbers positive
        move.w          d7,d2                   ;for lower half multiply
        move.w          d0,d3                   ;ditto
        swap            d7                      ;upper to lower
        swap            d0                      ;ditto
        mulu            d2,d0                   ;do long multiply...
        mulu            d3,d7
        mulu            d3,d2
        add.w           d0,d7                   ;add products
        swap            d7                      ;lower to upper
        clr.w           d7                      ;clear lower
        add.l           d2,d7                   ;final product
        tst.l           d7                      ;did it overflow?
        smi             errflg                  ;set error if so

        tst.b           sgnflg                  ;should result be negative?
        beq.s           1$                      ;no, exit
        neg.l           d7                      ;else change sign of result
1$
        rts


;
; - key
;
subop
        bsr.s           ckkop                   ;chk number order for K ops

        sub.l           d7,d0                   ;do subtract op
        svs             errflg                  ;error if overflow
        move.l          d0,d7                   ;put result in place
        rts


;
; + key
;
addop
        add.l           d0,d7                   ;do addition op
        svs             errflg                  ;error if overflow
        rts


;
; This routine changes both numbers in D0 and D7 to positive quantities.
; The sign of a resultant multiplication or division of these two
; numbers is recorded in sgnflg for use by the multiply/divide routines.
;
dosigns
        clr.b           sgnflg                  ;default sign = positive
        move.l          d0,d1                   ;move d0 to a work register
        move.l          d7,d2                   ;move d7 to a work register
        andi.l          #$80000000,d1           ;extract sign bit
        andi.l          #$80000000,d2           ;extract sign bit
        eor.l           d1,d2                   ;see if signs are different
        rol.l           #1,d2                   ;get difference bit to bit 0
```

```
        move.b          d2,sgnflg               ;set if result negative

        tst.l           d0                      ;d0 positive?
        bpl.s           1$                      ;yes
        neg.l           d0                      ;else make it positive
1$
        tst.l           d7                      ;d7 positive?
        bpl.s           2$                      ;yes
        neg.l           d7                      ;else make it positive
2$
        rts


;
; This routine reverses the operands if a K operation
; is being performed.
;
ckkop
        btst            #3,16(a4,d6.w)          ;is this a K operation?
        beq.s           1$                      ;no
        exg             d7,d0                   ;else numbers are reversed
1$
        rts


;
; Save the current calculator operation on the stack immediately after
; the four registers, i.e. 16 bytes after.
;
pushop
        cmpi.b          #4,d6                   ;reg stk ptr at max (4)?
        bcs.s           pushok                  ;ok if less
        st              errflg                  ;too many numbers
        rts
pushok
        tst.l           d6                      ;op awaiting stack?
        bpl.s           pushout                 ;out if no pending op

        move.l          d6,d5                   ;save op from d5
        swap            d5                      ;move current op down
        move.b          d5,16(a4,d6.w)          ;save current level and op

        addq            #1,d6                   ;increment register stk ptr
        andi.l          #$F0FFFF,d6             ;reset op and pending bit
pushout
        rts


;
; Display register D7 in the current number base.
; An error message is generated if this is not possible.
;
disp
        tst.b           errflg                  ;error flag set?
        bne.s           disperr                 ;display 'error' if so

        move.l          d7,d0                   ;use d0 as temp test reg
        clr.b           sgnflg                  ;reset sign flag
        tst.l           d0                      ;negative number?
```

```
        bpl.s       1$                      ;no
        neg.1       d0                      ;convert to pos for tests
        st          sgnflg                  ;and set sign flag
1$
        cmpi.b      #2,base                 ;in binary mode?
        bne.s       disp1                   ;no, try octal

        cmpi.l      #128,d0                 ;outside binary num range?
        bhi         seterr                  ;error if so
        bne.s       2$                      ;ok if lower
        tst.b       sgnflg                  ;if at max, must be negative
        bpl.s       seterr                  ;else error
2$
        bsr         binstr                  ;convert d7 to binary string
        bra.s       printstr                ;print it in calc display

disp1
        cmpi.b      #8,base                 ;in octal mode?
        bne.s       disp2                   ;no, try decimal
        cmpi.l      #800000,d0              ;outside octal num range?
        bhi         seterr                  ;error if so
        bne.s       3$                      ;ok if lower
        tst.b       sgnflg                  ;if at max, must be negative
        bpl.s       seterr                  ;else error
3$
        bsr.s       octstr                  ;convert d7 to octal string
        bra.s       printstr                ;print it in calc display

disp2
        cmpi.b      #10,base                ;in decimal mode?
        bne.s       hexd7                   ;no, must be hex

        cmpi.l      #100000000,d0           ;num beyond decimal range?
        bcc.s       seterr                  ;error if so

        bsr         decstr                  ;cnvrt d7 to decimal string
        bra.s       printstr                ;print it in calc display
hexd7
        bsr.s       hexstr                  ;convert d7 to hex string
        bra.s       printstr                ;print hex in calc display

seterr
        st          errflg                  ;set error flag
disperr
        lea         errstr+9,a1             ;point past error string end
        bra.s       printst1                ;print it

printstr
        lea         numstr+9,a1             ;point past number string end
printst1
        lea         dispstr+18,a2           ;point past display string end
        moveq       #8,d4                   ;pad nine characters
pad
        move.b      #' ',-(a2)              ;pad string with space
        move.b      -(a1),-(a2)             ;put character into string
        dbra        d4,pad                  ;do all nine characters

;
; register a2 now points to dispstr
;
```

```
                lea         g0itxt,a1               ;intuition text structure ptr
                move.l      a2,it_IText(a1)         ;emplace text pointer
                movea.l     windptr,a0              ;opened window structure ptr
                movea.l     wd_RPort(a0),a0         ;pointer to window's rastport
                moveq       #0,d0                   ;left offset
                moveq       #0,d1                   ;right offset
                jsr         _LVOPrintIText(a6)      ;print display string
                rts


binstr
                moveq       #1,d1                   ;# bits per digit in binary
                moveq       #1,d2                   ;mask for each binary digit
                bra.s       strchrs                 ;convert digits to ascii

octstr
                moveq       #3,d1                   ;# bits per digit in octal
                moveq       #7,d2                   ;mask for each octal digit
                bra.s       strchrs                 ;convert digits to ascii

hexstr
                moveq       #4,d1                   ;# bits per digit in hex
                moveq       #$F,d2                  ;mask for each hex digit

strchrs
                lea         numstr+9,a2             ;point to string end + 1
                moveq       #7,d0                   ;convert 8 digits
                move.l      d7,-(a7)                ;hold display on stack
                bra.s       norot                   ;don't rotate first time
disprot
                lsr.l       d1,d7                   ;rotate display register
norot
                move.b      d7,d3                   ;form ascii character in d3
                and.b       d2,d3                   ;extract necessary bits
                ori.b       #$30,d3                 ;make an ascii digit
                cmpi.b      #$3A,d3                 ;digit greater than 9 ?
                bcs.s       noltr                   ;no, digit is ok
                addi.b      #7,d3                   ;else make it A to F
noltr
                move.b      d3,-(a2)                ;store character in string
                dbra        d0,disprot              ;do all characters
                bra.s       leadzer                 ;now remove leading zeros

decstr
                move.l      d7,-(a7)                ;save display reg on stack
                tst.b       sgnflg                  ;negative decimal number?
                beq.s       1$                      ;no
                neg.l       d7                      ;else make positive
1$
                moveq       #7,d0                   ;convert 8 decimal digits
                lea         numstr+1,a2             ;point past sign
                lea         pwrs10,a1               ;point to powers of ten
nxtpwr
                moveq       #'0',d2                 ;initialize d2 to ascii '0'
decpowr
                addq        #1,d2                   ;increment ascii digit
                sub.l       (a1),d7                 ;display contains this # ?
                bcc.s       decpowr                 ;again if not overstepped
                subq        #1,d2                   ;else readjust ascii digit
                add.l       (a1),d7                 ;readjust display remainder
```

```
        move.b          d2,(a2)+                ;ascii digit to string
        lea             4(a1),a1                ;next power of ten
        dbra            d0,nxtpwr               ;do all 8 digits this way

leadzer
        lea             numstr,a2               ;point to string start
        move.b          #' ',(a2)+              ;replace any previous minus
        moveq           #6,d0                   ;remove up to 7 zeros
testzer
        cmpi.b          #'0',(a2)+              ;leading zero?
        bne.s           donelz                  ;no, all done
        move.b          #' ',-1(a2)             ;else replace it with space
        dbra            d0,testzer              ;try next digit
        lea             1(a2),a2                ;make way for possible sign
donelz
        addq.b          #2,d0                   ;get # chars in display
        move.b          d0,dispcnt              ;save result

        cmpi.b          #10,base                ;in decimal mode?
        bne.s           donestr                 ;no, string finished

        tst.b           sgnflg                  ;negative decimal number?
        beq.s           donestr                 ;no, string finished

        move.b          #'-',-2(a2)             ;else implant minus sign
donestr
        move.l          (a7)+,d7                ;restore display register
        rts


***********************************************************************
*
*                       EVENT HANDLING
*
***********************************************************************

; This routine only returns when a calculator button has been
; selected. The number of the selected button (a gadget id)
; is returned in register d0.

getbutton
        movea.l         windptr,a0
        movea.l         wd_UserPort(a0),a0      ;UserPort addr to a0
        move.l          a0,-(a7)
        moveq           #0,d1
        move.b          MP_SIGBIT(a0),d1
        moveq           #1,d0
        asl.l           d1,d0
        movea.l         ExecBase,a6
        jsr             _LVOWait(a6)

        movea.l         (a7)+,a0                ;UserPort addr to a0
        jsr             _LVOGetMsg(a6)
        movea.l         d0,a1                   ;message ptr to a1
        move.l          im_Class(a1),d4         ;class
        move.w          im_Code(a1),d5   ;code
        movea.l         im_IAddress(a1),a2      ;address if gadget
        jsr             _LVOReplyMsg(a6)

        movea.l         IntBase,a6              ;Ready to use intuition lib
        cmpi.l          #CLOSEWINDOW,d4
```

```
        beq             bye

        cmpi.l          #GADGETUP,d4
        bne.s           getbutton               ;unknown message
        move.w          gg_GadgetID(a2),d0      ;get id of gadget
        rts
;*******************************************************************
;
;                SETUP AND DRAW CALCULATOR WINDOW
;
;*******************************************************************************

DrawWind
        movea.l         IntBase,a6
        lea             NewWind,a0
        jsr             _LVOOpenWindow(a6)
        move.l          d0,windptr

        rts
;
;close down
;
bye
        movea.l         IntBase,a6              ;use intuition library base
        movea.l         windptr,a0              ;pointer to open window
        jsr             _LVOCloseWindow(a6)     ;close window
        moveq.l         #0,d0                   ;Successful return code

exit
        movea.l         initialSP,a7            ;restore stack pointer
        move.l          d0,-(a7)                ;save return code


;
;close libraries
;
        movea.l         ExecBase,a6            ;use exec libraries
        move.l          DOSBase,d0            ;DOS library loaded?
        beq.s           1$                   ;skip close if DOS not open
        movea.l         d0,a1                ;lib base into a1
        jsr             _LVOCloseLibrary(a6) ;close DOS
1$
        move.l          IntBase,d0           ;intuition library loaded?
        beq.s           2$                   ;skip if intuition not open
        movea.l         d0,a1                ;lib base into a1
        jsr             _LVOCloseLibrary(a6) ;close intuition
2$
        move.l          returnMsg,d0         ;started from workbench?
        beq.s           3$                   ;skip if from CLI

;
;return startup message to parent
jsr     _LVFord(a6)            ;so workbench won't UnLoadSeg
        movea.l         returnMsg,a1         ;startup message pointer
        jsr             _LVOReplyMsg(a6)     ;reply to initial message
3$
        move.l          (a7)+,d0             ;restore success code
        rts                                  ;back to operating system

;********************************************************************************
```

```
noDOS
        ALERT              (AG_OpenLib!AO_DOSLib)
        moveq.l            #100,d0
        bra.s              exit


;*******************************************************************************
; This routine gets the message that workbench will send to us
; called with task id in A4

waitmsg
        lea                pr_MsgPort(a4),a0        ;our process base
        jsr                _LVOWaitPort(a6)
        lea                pr_MsgPort(a4),a0        ;our process base
        jsr                _LVOGetMsg(a6)
        rts

;*******************************************************************************
;  Open the DOS library and save its base pointer

openDOS
        lea                DOS_Lib,a1
        move.l             #LIBRARY_VERSION,d0
        jsr                _LVOOpenLibrary(a6)
        move.l             d0,DOSBase              ;save DOS library base
        beq                noDOS
        rts

;*******************************************************************************
;  Open the intuition library and save its base pointer

openINT
        lea                INT_Lib,a1
        move.l             #0,d0
        jsr                _LVOOpenLibrary(a6)
        move.l             d0,IntBase
        rts


;*******************************************************************************
;
;                         PROGRAM'S DATA AREA
;
;*******************************************************************************


                cnop       0,2                      ;must be on word boundary

crntkey         dc.b       0                         ;current calculator key
prevkey         dc.b       0                         ;previous calculator key
chrcnt          dc.b       0                         ;# characters entered
dispcnt         dc.b       0                         ;# characters in display
errflg          dc.b       0                         ;set non-zero if error
sgnflg          dc.b       0                         ;non-zero if decimal minus
newparen        dc.b       0                         ;non-zero if opened paren
base            dc.b       16                        ;current number base
base_gadget     dc.l       Gadget2                   ;number-base gadget address
calcstore       dc.l       0                         ;place for calculator store


numstk          dcb.l      5,0                       ;calc's number & ops stack
```

```
pwrs10          dc.l    10000000
                dc.l    1000000
                dc.l    100000
                dc.l    10000
                dc.l    1000
                dc.l    100
                dc.l    10
                dc.l    1


****************************************************************************

ExecBase        dc.l    0
DOSBase         dc.l    0
IntBase         dc.l    0

initialSP       dc.l    0
returnMsg       dc.l    0

winptr          dc.l    0

NewWind         equ     *
LeftEdge        dc.w    40
TopEdge         dc.w    20
Width           dc.w    221
Height          dc.w    155
DetailPen       dc.b    -1
BlockPen        dc.b    -1
IDCMPFlags      dc.l    CLOSEWINDOW!GADGETUP
Flags           dc.l    WINDOWCLOSE!SMART_REFRESH!ACTIVATE!WINDOWDRAG
FirstGadget     dc.l    Gadget0
CheckMark       dc.l    0
Title           dc.l    wtitle
Scren           dc.l    0
BitMp           dc.l    0
MinWidth        dc.w    0
MinHeight       dc.w    0
MaxWidth        dc.w    0
MaxHeight       dc.w    0
Type            dc.w    WBENCHSCREEN

;
; The following equates set the position and spacing of
; the gadgets representing the calculator buttons.
;
GWIDE           equ     32                      ;width of calculator buttons
GHIGH           equ     9                       ;height of calculator buttons
GMINLEFT        equ     20                      ;left-hand button margin
HGAP            equ     5                       ;horizontal button spacing
VGAP            equ     5                       ;vertical button spacing
GLEFT           set     GMINLEFT                ;initial button left coordinate
GTOP            set     40                      ;initial button top coordinate
KEYCOL          equ     1                       ;color of each key's text

Gadget0
                dc.l    Gadget1                 ;pointer to next gadget
                dc.w    GLEFT                   ;left edge
                dc.w    15                      ;top edge
                dc.w    180                     ;width
                dc.w    15                      ;height
```

```
                dc.w    GADGHNONE               ;flags
                dc.w    0                       ;activation flags
                dc.w    BOOLGADGET              ;gadget type
                dc.l    border0                 ;ptr to border structure
                dc.l    0
                dc.l    0                       ;ptr to text structure
                dc.l    0
                dc.l    0
                dc.w    0                       ;id
                dc.l    0

border0
                dc.w    0                       ;left edge
                dc.w    0                       ;top edge
                dc.b    1                       ;front pen
                dc.b    0                       ;back pen
                dc.b    RP_JAM1                 ;draw mode
                dc.b    5                       ;# of coords
                dc.l    g0xy                    ;pointer to 1st coord
                dc.l    0                       ;pointer to next border

g0xy
                dc.w    -1,-1
                dc.w    -1,20
                dc.w    180,20
                dc.w    180,-1
                dc.w    -1,-1

g0itxt
                dc.b    1                       ;front pen
                dc.b    0                       ;back pen
                dc.b    RP_JAM2                 ;draw mode
                dc.w    20                      ;left edge
                dc.w    23                      ;top edge
                dc.l    0                       ;font ptr (dflt)
                dc.l    dispstr                 ;text pointer
                dc.l    0                       ;ptr to nxt txt structure

Gadget1
                dc.l    Gadget2                 ;pointer to next gadget
                dc.w    GLEFT                   ;left edge
                dc.w    GTOP                    ;top edge
                dc.w    GWIDE                   ;width
                dc.w    GHIGH                   ;height
                dc.w    GADGHCOMP               ;flags
                dc.w    RELVERIFY               ;activation flags
                dc.w    BOOLGADGET              ;gadget type
                dc.l    border1                 ;ptr to border structure
                dc.l    0
                dc.l    g1itxt                  ;ptr to text structure
                dc.l    0
                dc.l    0
                dc.w    1                       ;id
                dc.l    0

border1
                dc.w    0                       ;left edge
                dc.w    0                       ;top edge
                dc.b    1                       ;front pen
                dc.b    0                       ;back pen
```

```
                dc.b    RP_JAM1              ;draw mode
                dc.b    5                    ;# of coords
                dc.l    g1xy                 ;pointer to 1st coord
                dc.l    0                    ;pointer to next border

g1xy
                dc.w    -1,-1
                dc.w    -1,GHIGH
                dc.w    GWIDE,GHIGH
                dc.w    GWIDE,-1
                dc.w    -1,-1

g1itxt
                dc.b    KEYCOL               ;front pen
                dc.b    0                    ;back pen
                dc.b    RP_JAM1              ;draw mode
                dc.w    1                    ;left edge
                dc.w    1                    ;top edge
                dc.l    0                    ;font ptr (dflt)
                dc.l    g1txt                ;text pointer
                dc.l    0                    ;ptr to nxt txt structure

GLEFT           set     GLEFT+GWIDE+HGAP     ;set next gadget rightward

Gadget2
                dc.l    Gadget3              ;pointer to next gadget
                dc.w    GLEFT                ;left edge
                dc.w    GTOP                 ;top edge
                dc.w    GWIDE                ;width
                dc.w    GHIGH                ;height
                dc.w    GADGHCOMP            ;flags
                dc.w    RELVERIFY            ;activation flags
                dc.w    BOOLGADGET           ;gadget type
                dc.l    border1              ;ptr to border structure
                dc.l    0
                dc.l    g2itxt               ;ptr to text structure
                dc.l    0
                dc.l    0
                dc.w    2                    ;id
                dc.l    0

g2itxt
                dc.b    3                    ;front pen
                dc.b    0                    ;back pen
                dc.b    RP_JAM1              ;draw mode
                dc.w    1                    ;left edge
                dc.w    1                    ;top edge
                dc.l    0                    ;font ptr (dflt)
                dc.l    g2txt                ;text pointer
                dc.l    0                    ;ptr to nxt txt structure

GLEFT           set     GLEFT+GWIDE+HGAP     ;set next gadget rightward

Gadget3
                dc.l    Gadget4              ;pointer to next gadget
                dc.w    GLEFT                ;left edge
                dc.w    GTOP                 ;top edge
                dc.w    GWIDE                ;width
                dc.w    GHIGH                ;height
                dc.w    GADGHCOMP            ;flags
```

```
                dc.w    RELVERIFY               ;activation flags
                dc.w    BOOLGADGET              ;gadget type
                dc.l    border1                 ;ptr to border structure
                dc.l    0
                dc.l    g3itxt                  ;ptr to text structure
                dc.l    0
                dc.l    0
                dc.w    3                       ;id
                dc.l    0

g3itxt
                dc.b    KEYCOL                  ;front pen
                dc.b    0                       ;back pen
                dc.b    RP_JAM1                 ;draw mode
                dc.w    1                       ;left edge
                dc.w    1                       ;top edge
                dc.l    0                       ;font ptr (dflt)
                dc.l    g3txt                   ;text pointer
                dc.l    0                       ;ptr to nxt txt structure

GLEFT           set     GLEFT+GWIDE+HGAP        ;set next gadget rightward

Gadget4
                dc.l    Gadget5                 ;pointer to next gadget
                dc.w    GLEFT                   ;left edge
                dc.w    GTOP                    ;top edge
                dc.w    GWIDE                   ;width
                dc.w    GHIGH                   ;height
                dc.w    GADGHCOMP               ;flags
                dc.w    RELVERIFY               ;activation flags
                dc.w    BOOLGADGET              ;gadget type
                dc.l    border1                 ;ptr to border structure
                dc.l    0
                dc.l    g4itxt                  ;ptr to text structure
                dc.l    0
                dc.l    0
                dc.w    4                       ;id
                dc.l    0

g4itxt
                dc.b    KEYCOL                  ;front pen
                dc.b    0                       ;back pen
                dc.b    RP_JAM1                 ;draw mode
                dc.w    1                       ;left edge
                dc.w    1                       ;top edge
                dc.l    0                       ;font ptr (dflt)
                dc.l    g4txt                   ;text pointer
                dc.l    0                       ;ptr to nxt txt structure


GLEFT           set     GLEFT+GWIDE+HGAP        ;set next gadget rightward

Gadget5
                dc.l    Gadget6                 ;pointer to next gadget
                dc.w    GLEFT                   ;left edge
                dc.w    GTOP                    ;top edge
                dc.w    GWIDE                   ;width
                dc.w    GHIGH                   ;height
                dc.w    GADGHCOMP               ;flags
                dc.w    RELVERIFY               ;activation flags
```

```
                dc.w    BOOLGADGET              ;gadget type
                dc.l    border1                 ;ptr to border structure
                dc.l    0
                dc.l    g5itxt                  ;ptr to text structure
                dc.l    0
                dc.l    0
                dc.w    40                      ;id
                dc.l    0

g5itxt
                dc.b    KEYCOL                  ;front pen
                dc.b    0                       ;back pen
                dc.b    RP_JAM1                 ;draw mode
                dc.w    1                       ;left edge
                dc.w    1                       ;top edge
                dc.l    0                       ;font ptr (dflt)
                dc.l    g5txt                   ;text pointer
                dc.l    0                       ;ptr to nxt txt structure

GTOP            set     GTOP+GHIGH+VGAP         ;set next gadget lower
GLEFT           set     GMINLEFT               ;initialize gadget left coord

Gadget6
                dc.l    Gadget7                 ;pointer to next gadget
                dc.w    GLEFT                   ;left edge
                dc.w    GTOP                    ;top edge
                dc.w    GWIDE                   ;width
                dc.w    GHIGH                   ;height
                dc.w    GADGHCOMP               ;flags
                dc.w    RELVERIFY               ;activation flags
                dc.w    BOOLGADGET              ;gadget type
                dc.l    border1                 ;ptr to border structure
                dc.l    0
                dc.l    g6itxt                  ;ptr to text structure
                dc.l    0
                dc.l    0
                dc.w    7                       ;id
                dc.l    0

g6itxt
                dc.b    KEYCOL                  ;front pen
                dc.b    0                       ;back pen
                dc.b    RP_JAM1                 ;draw mode
                dc.w    1                       ;left edge
                dc.w    1                       ;top edge
                dc.l    0                       ;font ptr (dflt)
                dc.l    g6txt                   ;text pointer
                dc.l    0                       ;ptr to nxt txt structure

GLEFT           set     GLEFT+GWIDE+HGAP        ;set next gadget rightward

Gadget7
                dc.l    Gadget8                 ;pointer to next gadget
                dc.w    GLEFT                   ;left edge
                dc.w    GTOP                    ;top edge
                dc.w    GWIDE                   ;width
                dc.w    GHIGH                   ;height
                dc.w    GADGHCOMP               ;flags
                dc.w    RELVERIFY               ;activation flags
                dc.w    BOOLGADGET              ;gadget type
```

```
               dc.l    border1                 ;ptr to border structure
               dc.l    0
               dc.l    g7itxt                  ;ptr to text structure
               dc.l    0
               dc.l    0
               dc.w    8                       ;id
               dc.l    0

g7itxt
               dc.b    KEYCOL                  ;front pen
               dc.b    0                       ;back pen
               dc.b    RP_JAM1                 ;draw mode
               dc.w    1                       ;left edge
               dc.w    1                       ;top edge
               dc.l    0                       ;font ptr (dflt)
               dc.l    g7txt                   ;text pointer
               dc.l    0                       ;ptr to nxt txt structure

GLEFT          set     GLEFT+GWIDE+HGAP        ;set next gadget rightward

Gadget8
               dc.l    Gadget9                 ;pointer to next gadget
               dc.w    GLEFT                   ;left edge
               dc.w    GTOP                    ;top edge
               dc.w    GWIDE                   ;width
               dc.w    GHIGH                   ;height
               dc.w    GADGHCOMP               ;flags
               dc.w    RELVERIFY               ;activation flags
               dc.w    BOOLGADGET              ;gadget type
               dc.l    border1                 ;ptr to border structure
               dc.l    0
               dc.l    g8itxt                  ;ptr to text structure
               dc.l    0
               dc.l    0
               dc.w    9                       ;id
               dc.l    0

g8itxt
               dc.b    KEYCOL                  ;front pen
               dc.b    0                       ;back pen
               dc.b    RP_JAM1                 ;draw mode
               dc.w    1                       ;left edge
               dc.w    1                       ;top edge
               dc.l    0                       ;font ptr (dflt)
               dc.l    g8txt                   ;text pointer
               dc.l    0                       ;ptr to nxt txt structure

GLEFT          set     GLEFT+GWIDE+HGAP        ;set next gadget rightward

Gadget9
               dc.l    Gadget10                ;pointer to next gadget
               dc.w    GLEFT                   ;left edge
               dc.w    GTOP                    ;top edge
               dc.w    GWIDE                   ;width
               dc.w    GHIGH                   ;height
               dc.w    GADGHCOMP               ;flags
               dc.w    RELVERIFY               ;activation flags
               dc.w    BOOLGADGET              ;gadget type
               dc.l    border1                 ;ptr to border structure
               dc.l    0
```

```
                    dc.l    g9itxt                  ;ptr to text structure
                    dc.l    0
                    dc.l    0
                    dc.w    10                      ;id
                    dc.l    0

g9itxt
                    dc.b    KEYCOL                  ;front pen
                    dc.b    0                       ;back pen
                    dc.b    RP_JAM1                 ;draw mode
                    dc.w    1                       ;left edge
                    dc.w    1                       ;top edge
                    dc.l    0                       ;font ptr (dflt)
                    dc.l    g9txt                   ;text pointer
                    dc.l    0                       ;ptr to nxt txt structure

GLEFT       set     GLEFT+GWIDE+HGAP                ;set next gadget rightward
Gadget10
                    dc.l    Gadget11                ;pointer to next gadget
                    dc.w    GLEFT                   ;left edge
                    dc.w    GTOP                    ;top edge
                    dc.w    GWIDE                   ;width
                    dc.w    GHIGH                   ;height
                    dc.w    GADGHCOMP               ;flags
                    dc.w    RELVERIFY               ;activation flags
                    dc.w    BOOLGADGET              ;gadget type
                    dc.l    border1                 ;ptr to border structure
                    dc.l    0
                    dc.l    g10itxt                 ;ptr to text structure
                    dc.l    0
                    dc.l    0
                    dc.w    11                      ;id
                    dc.l    0

g10itxt
                    dc.b    KEYCOL                  ;front pen
                    dc.b    0                       ;back pen
                    dc.b    RP_JAM1                 ;draw mode
                    dc.w    1                       ;left edge
                    dc.w    1                       ;top edge
                    dc.l    0                       ;font ptr (dflt)
                    dc.l    g10txt                  ;text pointer
                    dc.l    0                       ;ptr to nxt txt structure

GTOP        set     GTOP+GHIGH+VGAP                 ;set next gadget lower
GLEFT       set     GMINLEFT                        ;initialize gadget left coord

Gadget11
                    dc.l    Gadget12                ;pointer to next gadget
                    dc.w    GLEFT                   ;left edge
                    dc.w    GTOP                    ;top edge
                    dc.w    GWIDE                   ;width
                    dc.w    GHIGH                   ;height
                    dc.w    GADGHCOMP               ;flags
                    dc.w    RELVERIFY               ;activation flags
                    dc.w    BOOLGADGET              ;gadget type
                    dc.l    border1                 ;ptr to border structure
                    dc.l    0
                    dc.l    g11itxt                 ;ptr to text structure
```

```
                dc.l    0
                dc.l    0
                dc.w    32                      ;id
                dc.l    0

g11itxt
                dc.b    KEYCOL                  ;front pen
                dc.b    0                       ;back pen
                dc.b    RP_JAM1                 ;draw mode
                dc.w    1                       ;left edge
                dc.w    1                       ;top edge
                dc.l    0                       ;font ptr (dflt)
                dc.l    g11txt                  ;text pointer
                dc.l    0                       ;ptr to nxt txt structure

GLEFT           set     GLEFT+GWIDE+HGAP        ;set next gadget rightward

Gadget12
                dc.l    Gadget13                ;pointer to next gadget
                dc.w    GLEFT                   ;left edge
                dc.w    GTOP                    ;top edge
                dc.w    GWIDE                   ;width
                dc.w    GHIGH                   ;height
                dc.w    GADGHCOMP               ;flags
                dc.w    RELVERIFY               ;activation flags
                dc.w    BOOLGADGET              ;gadget type
                dc.l    border1                 ;ptr to border structure
                dc.l    0
                dc.l    g12itxt                 ;ptr to text structure
                dc.l    0
                dc.l    0
                dc.w    29                      ;id
                dc.l    0

g12itxt
                dc.b    KEYCOL                  ;front pen
                dc.b    0                       ;back pen
                dc.b    RP_JAM1                 ;draw mode
                dc.w    1                       ;left edge
                dc.w    1                       ;top edge
                dc.l    0                       ;font ptr (dflt)
                dc.l    g12txt                  ;text pointer
                dc.l    0                       ;ptr to nxt txt structure

GLEFT           set     GLEFT+GWIDE+HGAP        ;set next gadget rightward

Gadget13
                dc.l    Gadget14                ;pointer to next gadget
                dc.w    GLEFT                   ;left edge
                dc.w    GTOP                    ;top edge
                dc.w    GWIDE                   ;width
                dc.w    GHIGH                   ;height
                dc.w    GADGHCOMP               ;flags
                dc.w    RELVERIFY               ;activation flags
                dc.w    BOOLGADGET              ;gadget type
                dc.l    border1                 ;ptr to border structure
                dc.l    0
                dc.l    g13itxt                 ;ptr to text structure
                dc.l    0
                dc.l    0
```

```
                dc.w    30                      ;id
                dc.1    0

g13itxt
                dc.b    KEYCOL                  ;front pen
                dc.b    0                       ;back pen
                dc.b    RP_JAM1                 ;draw mode
                dc.w    1                       ;left edge
                dc.w    1                       ;top edge
                dc.1    0                       ;font ptr (dflt)
                dc.1    g13txt                  ;text pointer
                dc.1    0                       ;ptr to nxt txt structure

GLEFT           set     GLEFT+GWIDE+HGAP        ;set next gadget rightward

Gadget14
                dc.1    Gadget15                ;pointer to next gadget
                dc.w    GLEFT                   ;left edge
                dc.w    GTOP                    ;top edge
                dc.w    GWIDE                   ;width
                dc.w    GHIGH                   ;height
                dc.w    GADGHCOMP               ;flags
                dc.w    RELVERIFY               ;activation flags
                dc.w    BOOLGADGET              ;gadget type
                dc.1    border1                 ;ptr to border structure
                dc.1    0
                dc.1    g14itxt                 ;ptr to text structure
                dc.1    0
                dc.1    0
                dc.w    31                      ;id
                dc.1    0

g14itxt
                dc.b    KEYCOL                  ;front pen
                dc.b    0                       ;back pen
                dc.b    RP_JAM1                 ;draw mode
                dc.w    1                       ;left edge
                dc.w    1                       ;top edge
                dc.1    0                       ;font ptr (dflt)
                dc.1    g14txt                  ;text pointer
                dc.1    0                       ;ptr to nxt txt structure

GLEFT           set     GLEFT+GWIDE+HGAP        ;set next gadget rightward

Gadget15
                dc.1    Gadget16                ;pointer to next gadget
                dc.w    GLEFT                   ;left edge
                dc.w    GTOP                    ;top edge
                dc.w    GWIDE                   ;width
                dc.w    GHIGH                   ;height
                dc.w    GADGHCOMP               ;flags
                dc.w    RELVERIFY               ;activation flags
                dc.w    BOOLGADGET              ;gadget type
                dc.1    border1                 ;ptr to border structure
                dc.1    0
                dc.1    g15itxt                 ;ptr to text structure
                dc.1    0
                dc.1    0
                dc.w    13                      ;id
                dc.1    0
```

```
g15itxt
                dc.b      KEYCOL                    ;front pen
                dc.b      0                         ;back pen
                dc.b      RP_JAM1                   ;draw mode
                dc.w      1                         ;left edge
                dc.w      1                         ;top edge
                dc.l      0                         ;font ptr (dflt)
                dc.l      g15txt                    ;text pointer
                dc.l      0                         ;ptr to nxt txt structure

GTOP            set       GTOP+GHIGH+VGAP           ;set next gadget lower
GLEFT           set       GMINLEFT                  ;initialize gadget left coord

Gadget16
                dc.l      Gadget17                  ;pointer to next gadget
                dc.w      GLEFT                     ;left edge
                dc.w      GTOP                      ;top edge
                dc.w      GWIDE                     ;width
                dc.w      GHIGH                     ;height
                dc.w      GADGHCOMP                 ;flags
                dc.w      RELVERIFY                 ;activation flags
                dc.w      BOOLGADGET                ;gadget type
                dc.l      border1                   ;ptr to border structure
                dc.l      0
                dc.l      g16itxt                   ;ptr to text structure
                dc.l      0
                dc.l      0
                dc.w      12                        ;id
                dc.l      0

g16itxt
                dc.b      KEYCOL                    ;front pen
                dc.b      0                         ;back pen
                dc.b      RP_JAM1                   ;draw mode
                dc.w      1                         ;left edge
                dc.w      1                         ;top edge
                dc.l      0                         ;font ptr (dflt)
                dc.l      g16txt                    ;text pointer
                dc.l      0                         ;ptr to nxt txt structure

GLEFT           set       GLEFT+GWIDE+HGAP          ;set next gadget rightward

Gadget17
                dc.l      Gadget18                  ;pointer to next gadget
                dc.w      GLEFT                     ;left edge
                dc.w      GTOP                      ;top edge
                dc.w      GWIDE                     ;width
                dc.w      GHIGH                     ;height
                dc.w      GADGHCOMP                 ;flags
                dc.w      RELVERIFY                 ;activation flags
                dc.w      BOOLGADGET                ;gadget type
                dc.l      border1                   ;ptr to border structure
                dc.l      0
                dc.l      g17itxt                   ;ptr to text structure
                dc.l      0
                dc.l      0
                dc.w      26                        ;id
                dc.l      0

g17itxt
```

```
                dc.b    KEYCOL                  ;front pen
                dc.b    0                       ;back pen
                dc.b    RP_JAM1                 ;draw mode
                dc.w    1                       ;left edge
                dc.w    1                       ;top edge
                dc.l    0                       ;font ptr (dflt)
                dc.l    g17txt                  ;text pointer
                dc.l    0                       ;ptr to nxt txt structure

GLEFT           set     GLEFT+GWIDE+HGAP        ;set next gadget rightward

Gadget18
                dc.l    Gadget19                ;point to next gadget
                dc.w    GLEFT                   ;left edge
                dc.w    GTOP                    ;top edge
                dc.w    GWIDE                   ;width
                dc.w    GHIGH                   ;height
                dc.w    GADGHCOMP               ;flags
                dc.w    RELVERIFY               ;activation flags
                dc.w    BOOLGADGET              ;gadget type
                dc.l    border1                 ;ptr to border structure
                dc.l    0
                dc.l    g18itxt                 ;ptr to text structure
                dc.l    0
                dc.l    0
                dc.w    27                      ;id
                dc.l    0

g18itxt
                dc.b    KEYCOL                  ;front pen
                dc.b    0                       ;back pen
                dc.b    RP_JAM1                 ;draw mode
                dc.w    1                       ;left edge
                dc.w    1                       ;top edge
                dc.l    0                       ;font ptr (dflt)
                dc.l    g18txt                  ;text pointer
                dc.l    0                       ;ptr to nxt txt structure

GLEFT           set     GLEFT+GWIDE+HGAP        ;set next gadget rightward

Gadget19
                dc.l    Gadget20                ;pointer to next gadget
                dc.w    GLEFT                   ;left edge
                dc.w    GTOP                    ;top edge
                dc.w    GWIDE                   ;width
                dc.w    GHIGH                   ;height
                dc.w    GADGHCOMP               ;flags
                dc.w    RELVERIFY               ;activation flags
                dc.w    BOOLGADGET              ;gadget type
                dc.l    border1                 ;ptr to border structure
                dc.l    0
                dc.l    g19itxt                 ;ptr to text structure
                dc.l    0
                dc.l    0
                dc.w    28                      ;id
                dc.l    0

g19itxt
                dc.b    KEYCOL                  ;front pen
                dc.b    0                       ;back pen
```

```
                    dc.b    RP_JAM1                     ;draw mode
                    dc.w    1                           ;left edge
                    dc.w    1                           ;top edge
                    dc.l    0                           ;font ptr (dflt)
                    dc.l    g19txt                      ;text pointer
                    dc.l    0                           ;ptr to nxt txt structure

GLEFT               set     GLEFT+GWIDE+HGAP            ;set next gadget rightward

Gadget20
                    dc.l    Gadget21                    ;pointer to next gadget
                    dc.w    GLEFT                       ;left edge
                    dc.w    GTOP                        ;top edge
                    dc.w    GWIDE                       ;width
                    dc.w    GHIGH                       ;height
                    dc.w    GADGHCOMP                   ;flags
                    dc.w    RELVERIFY                   ;activation flags
                    dc.w    BOOLGADGET                  ;gadget type
                    dc.l    border1                     ;ptr to border structure
                    dc.l    0
                    dc.l    g20itxt                     ;ptr to text structure
                    dc.l    0
                    dc.l    0
                    dc.w    36                          ;id
                    dc.l    0

g20itxt
                    dc.b    KEYCOL                      ;front pen
                    dc.b    0                           ;back pen
                    dc.b    RP_JAM1                     ;draw mode
                    dc.w    1                           ;left edge
                    dc.w    1                           ;top edge
                    dc.l    0                           ;font ptr (dflt)
                    dc.l    g20txt                      ;text pointer
                    dc.l    0                           ;ptr to nxt txt structure

GTOP                set     GTOP+GHIGH+VGAP            ;set next gadget lower
GLEFT               set     GMINLEFT                    ;initialize gadget left coord

Gadget21
                    dc.l    Gadget22                    ;pointer to next gadget
                    dc.w    GLEFT                       ;left edge
                    dc.w    GTOP                        ;top edge
                    dc.w    GWIDE                       ;width
                    dc.w    GHIGH                       ;height
                    dc.w    GADGHCOMP                   ;flags
                    dc.w    RELVERIFY                   ;activation flags
                    dc.w    BOOLGADGET                  ;gadget type
                    dc.l    border1                     ;ptr to border structure
                    dc.l    0
                    dc.l    g21itxt                     ;ptr to text structure
                    dc.l    0
                    dc.l    0
                    dc.w    33                          ;id
                    dc.l    0

g21itxt
                    dc.b    KEYCOL                      ;front pen
                    dc.b    0                           ;back pen
                    dc.b    RP_JAM1                     ;draw mode
```

181

```
                    dc.w    1                       ;left edge
                    dc.w    1                       ;top edge
                    dc.l    0                       ;font ptr (dflt)
                    dc.l    g21txt                  ;text pointer
                    dc.l    0                       ;ptr to nxt txt structure

        GLEFT       set     GLEFT+GWIDE+HGAP        ;set next gadget rightward

Gadget22
                    dc.l    Gadget23                ;pointer to next gadget
                    dc.w    GLEFT                   ;left edge
                    dc.w    GTOP                    ;top edge
                    dc.w    GWIDE                   ;width
                    dc.w    GHIGH                   ;height
                    dc.w    GADGHCOMP               ;flags
                    dc.w    RELVERIFY               ;activation flags
                    dc.w    BOOLGADGET              ;gadget type
                    dc.l    border1                 ;ptr to border structure
                    dc.l    0
                    dc.l    g22itxt                 ;ptr to text structure
                    dc.l    0
                    dc.l    0
                    dc.w    23                      ;id
                    dc.l    0

g22itxt
                    dc.b    KEYCOL                  ;front pen
                    dc.b    0                       ;back pen
                    dc.b    RP_JAM1                 ;draw mode
                    dc.w    1                       ;left edge
                    dc.w    1                       ;top edge
                    dc.l    0                       ;font ptr (dflt)
                    dc.l    g22txt                  ;text pointer
                    dc.l    0                       ;ptr to nxt txt structure

        GLEFT       set     GLEFT+GWIDE+HGAP        ;set next gadget rightward

Gadget23
                    dc.l    Gadget24                ;pointer to next gadget
                    dc.w    GLEFT                   ;left edge
                    dc.w    GTOP                    ;top edge
                    dc.w    GWIDE                   ;width
                    dc.w    GHIGH                   ;height
                    dc.w    GADGHCOMP               ;flags
                    dc.w    RELVERIFY               ;activation flags
                    dc.w    BOOLGADGET              ;gadget type
                    dc.l    border1                 ;ptr to border structure
                    dc.l    0
                    dc.l    g23itxt                 ;ptr to text structure
                    dc.l    0
                    dc.l    0
                    dc.w    24                      ;id
                    dc.l    0

g23itxt
                    dc.b    KEYCOL                  ;front pen
                    dc.b    0                       ;back pen
                    dc.b    RP_JAM1                 ;draw mode
                    dc.w    1                       ;left edge
                    dc.w    1                       ;top edge
```

```
                    dc.l    0                       ;font ptr (dflt)
                    dc.l    g23txt                  ;text pointer
                    dc.l    0                       ;ptr to nxt txt structure

        GLEFT       set     GLEFT+GWIDE+HGAP        ;set next gadget rightward

Gadget24
                    dc.l    Gadget25                ;pointer to next gadget
                    dc.w    GLEFT                   ;left edge
                    dc.w    GTOP                    ;top edge
                    dc.w    GWIDE                   ;width
                    dc.w    GHIGH                   ;height
                    dc.w    GADGHCOMP               ;flags
                    dc.w    RELVERIFY               ;activation flags
                    dc.w    BOOLGADGET              ;gadget type
                    dc.l    border1                 ;ptr to border structure
                    dc.l    0
                    dc.l    g24itxt                 ;ptr to text structure
                    dc.l    0
                    dc.l    0
                    dc.w    25                      ;id
                    dc.l    0

g24itxt
                    dc.b    KEYCOL                  ;front pen
                    dc.b    0                       ;back pen
                    dc.b    RP_JAM1                 ;draw mode
                    dc.w    1                       ;left edge
                    dc.w    1                       ;top edge
                    dc.l    0                       ;font ptr (dflt)
                    dc.l    g24txt                  ;text pointer
                    dc.l    0                       ;ptr to nxt txt structure

        GLEFT       set     GLEFT+GWIDE+HGAP        ;set next gadget rightward

Gadget25
                    dc.l    Gadget26                ;pointer to next gadget
                    dc.w    GLEFT                   ;left edge
                    dc.w    GTOP                    ;top edge
                    dc.w    GWIDE                   ;width
                    dc.w    GHIGH                   ;height
                    dc.w    GADGHCOMP               ;flags
                    dc.w    RELVERIFY               ;activation flags
                    dc.w    BOOLGADGET              ;gadget type
                    dc.l    border1                 ;ptr to border structure
                    dc.l    0
                    dc.l    g25itxt                 ;ptr to text structure
                    dc.l    0
                    dc.l    0
                    dc.w    37                      ;id
                    dc.l    0

g25itxt
                    dc.b    KEYCOL                  ;front pen
                    dc.b    0                       ;back pen
                    dc.b    RP_JAM1                 ;draw mode
                    dc.w    1                       ;left edge
                    dc.w    1                       ;top edge
                    dc.l    0                       ;font ptr (dflt)
                    dc.l    g25txt                  ;text pointer
```

```
                    dc.l    0                           ;ptr to nxt txt structure
GTOP                set     GTOP+GHIGH+VGAP             ;set next gadget lower
GLEFT               set     GMINLEFT                   ;initialize gadget left coord
Gadget26
                    dc.l    Gadget27                   ;pointer to next gadget
                    dc.w    GLEFT                      ;left edge
                    dc.w    GTOP                       ;top edge
                    dc.w    GWIDE                      ;width
                    dc.w    GHIGH                      ;height
                    dc.w    GADGHCOMP                  ;flags
                    dc.w    RELVERIFY                  ;activation flags
                    dc.w    BOOLGADGET                 ;gadget type
                    dc.l    border1                    ;ptr to border structure
                    dc.l    0
                    dc.l    g26itxt                    ;ptr to text structure
                    dc.l    0
                    dc.l    0
                    dc.w    34                         ;id
                    dc.l    0

g26itxt
                    dc.b    KEYCOL                     ;front pen
                    dc.b    0                          ;back pen
                    dc.b    RP_JAM1                    ;draw mode
                    dc.w    1                          ;left edge
                    dc.w    1                          ;top edge
                    dc.l    0                          ;font ptr (dflt)
                    dc.l    g26txt                     ;text pointer
                    dc.l    0                          ;ptr to nxt txt structure

GLEFT               set     GLEFT+GWIDE+HGAP           ;set next gadget rightward
Gadget27
                    dc.l    Gadget28                   ;pointer to next gadget
                    dc.w    GLEFT                      ;left edge
                    dc.w    GTOP                       ;top edge
                    dc.w    GWIDE                      ;width
                    dc.w    GHIGH                      ;height
                    dc.w    GADGHCOMP                  ;flags
                    dc.w    RELVERIFY                  ;activation flags
                    dc.w    BOOLGADGET                 ;gadget type
                    dc.l    border1                    ;ptr to border structure
                    dc.l    0
                    dc.l    g27itxt                    ;ptr to text structure
                    dc.l    0
                    dc.l    0
                    dc.w    20                         ;id
                    dc.l    0

g27itxt
                    dc.b    KEYCOL                     ;front pen
                    dc.b    0                          ;back pen
                    dc.b    RP_JAM1                    ;draw mode
                    dc.w    1                          ;left edge
                    dc.w    1                          ;top edge
                    dc.l    0                          ;font ptr (dflt)
                    dc.l    g27txt                     ;text pointer
                    dc.l    0                          ;ptr to nxt txt structure
```

```
GLEFT         set     GLEFT+GWIDE+HGAP          ;set next gadget rightward

Gadget28
              dc.l    Gadget29                  ;pointer to next gadget
              dc.w    GLEFT                     ;left edge
              dc.w    GTOP                      ;top edge
              dc.w    GWIDE                     ;width
              dc.w    GHIGH                     ;height
              dc.w    GADGHCOMP                 ;flags
              dc.w    RELVERIFY                 ;activation flags
              dc.w    BOOLGADGET                ;gadget type
              dc.l    border1                   ;ptr to border structure
              dc.l    0
              dc.l    g28itxt                   ;ptr to text structure
              dc.l    0
              dc.l    0
              dc.w    21                        ;id
              dc.l    0

g28itxt
              dc.b    KEYCOL                    ;front pen
              dc.b    0                         ;back pen
              dc.b    RP_JAM1                   ;draw mode
              dc.w    1                         ;left edge
              dc.w    1                         ;top edge
              dc.l    0                         ;font ptr (dflt)
              dc.l    g28txt                    ;text pointer
              dc.l    0                         ;ptr to nxt txt structure

GLEFT         set     GLEFT+GWIDE+HGAP          ;set next gadget rightward

Gadget29
              dc.l    Gadget30                  ;pointer to next gadget
              dc.w    GLEFT                     ;left edge
              dc.w    GTOP                      ;top edge
              dc.w    GWIDE                     ;width
              dc.w    GHIGH                     ;height
              dc.w    GADGHCOMP                 ;flags
              dc.w    RELVERIFY                 ;activation flags
              dc.w    BOOLGADGET                ;gadget type
              dc.l    border1                   ;ptr to border structure
              dc.l    0
              dc.l    g29itxt                   ;ptr to text structure
              dc.l    0
              dc.l    0
              dc.w    22                        ;id
              dc.l    0

g29itxt
              dc.b    KEYCOL                    ;front pen
              dc.b    0                         ;back pen
              dc.b    RP_JAM1                   ;draw mode
              dc.w    1                         ;left edge
              dc.w    1                         ;top edge
              dc.l    0                         ;font ptr (dflt)
              dc.l    g29txt                    ;text pointer
              dc.l    0                         ;ptr to nxt txt structure

GLEFT         set     GLEFT+GWIDE+HGAP          ;set next gadget rightward
```

```
Gadget30
                dc.l    Gadget31            ;pointer to next gadget
                dc.w    GLEFT               ;left edge
                dc.w    GTOP                ;top edge
                dc.w    GWIDE               ;width
                dc.w    GHIGH               ;height
                dc.w    GADGHCOMP           ;flags
                dc.w    RELVERIFY           ;activation flags
                dc.w    BOOLGADGET          ;gadget type
                dc.l    border1             ;ptr to border structure
                dc.l    0
                dc.l    g30itxt             ;ptr to text structure
                dc.l    0
                dc.l    0
                dc.w    38                  ;id
                dc.l    0

g30itxt
                dc.b    KEYCOL              ;front pen
                dc.b    0                   ;back pen
                dc.b    RP_JAM1             ;draw mode
                dc.w    1                   ;left edge
                dc.w    1                   ;top edge
                dc.l    0                   ;font ptr (dflt)
                dc.l    g30txt              ;text pointer
                dc.l    0                   ;ptr to nxt txt structure

GTOP            set     GTOP+GHIGH+VGAP     ;set next gadget lower
GLEFT           set     GMINLEFT            ;initialize gadget left coord

Gadget31
                dc.l    Gadget32            ;pointer to next gadget
                dc.w    GLEFT               ;left edge
                dc.w    GTOP                ;top edge
                dc.w    GWIDE               ;width
                dc.w    GHIGH               ;height
                dc.w    GADGHCOMP           ;flags
                dc.w    RELVERIFY           ;activation flags
                dc.w    BOOLGADGET          ;gadget type
                dc.l    border1             ;ptr to border structure
                dc.l    0
                dc.l    g31itxt             ;ptr to text structure
                dc.l    0
                dc.l    0
                dc.w    35                  ;id
                dc.l    0

g31itxt
                dc.b    KEYCOL              ;front pen
                dc.b    0                   ;back pen
                dc.b    RP_JAM1             ;draw mode
                dc.w    1                   ;left edge
                dc.w    1                   ;top edge
                dc.l    0                   ;font ptr (dflt)
                dc.l    g31txt              ;text pointer
                dc.l    0                   ;ptr to nxt txt structure

GLEFT           set     GLEFT+GWIDE+HGAP    ;set next gadget rightward

Gadget32
```

```
            dc.l      Gadget33                    ;pointer to next gadget
            dc.w      GLEFT                       ;left edge
            dc.w      GTOP                        ;top edge
            dc.w      GWIDE                       ;width
            dc.w      GHIGH                       ;height
            dc.w      GADGHCOMP                   ;flags
            dc.w      RELVERIFY                   ;activation flags
            dc.w      BOOLGADGET                  ;gadget type
            dc.l      border1                     ;ptr to border structure
            dc.l      0
            dc.l      g32itxt                     ;ptr to text structure
            dc.l      0
            dc.l      0
            dc.w      17                          ;id
            dc.l      0

g32itxt
            dc.b      KEYCOL                      ;front pen
            dc.b      0                           ;back pen
            dc.b      RP_JAM1                     ;draw mode
            dc.w      1                           ;left edge
            dc.w      1                           ;top edge
            dc.l      0                           ;font ptr (dflt)
            dc.l      g32txt                      ;text pointer
            dc.l      0                           ;ptr to nxt txt structure

GLEFT       set       GLEFT+GWIDE+HGAP            ;set next gadget rightward

Gadget33
            dc.l      Gadget34                    ;pointer to next gadget
            dc.w      GLEFT                       ;left edge
            dc.w      GTOP                        ;top edge
            dc.w      GWIDE                       ;width
            dc.w      GHIGH                       ;height
            dc.w      GADGHCOMP                   ;flags
            dc.w      RELVERIFY                   ;activation flags
            dc.w      BOOLGADGET                  ;gadget type
            dc.l      border1                     ;ptr to border structure
            dc.l      0
            dc.l      g33itxt                     ;ptr to text structure
            dc.l      0
            dc.l      0
            dc.w      18                          ;id
            dc.l      0

g33itxt
            dc.b      KEYCOL                      ;front pen
            dc.b      0                           ;back pen
            dc.b      RP_JAM1                     ;draw mode
            dc.w      1                           ;left edge
            dc.w      1                           ;top edge
            dc.l      0                           ;font ptr (dflt)
            dc.l      g33txt                      ;text pointer
            dc.l      0                           ;ptr to nxt txt structure

GLEFT       set       GLEFT+GWIDE+HGAP            ;set next gadget rightward

Gadget34
            dc.l      Gadget35                    ;pointer to next gadget
            dc.w      GLEFT                       ;left edge
```

```
                    dc.w    GTOP                    ;top edge
                    dc.w    GWIDE                   ;width
                    dc.w    GHIGH                   ;height
                    dc.w    GADGHCOMP               ;flags
                    dc.w    RELVERIFY               ;activation flags
                    dc.w    BOOLGADGET              ;gadget type
                    dc.l    border1                 ;ptr to border structure
                    dc.l    0
                    dc.l    g34itxt                 ;ptr to text structure
                    dc.l    0
                    dc.l    0
                    dc.w    19                      ;id
                    dc.l    0

g34itxt
                    dc.b    KEYCOL                  ;front pen
                    dc.b    0                       ;back pen
                    dc.b    RP_JAM1                 ;draw mode
                    dc.w    1                       ;left edge
                    dc.w    1                       ;top edge
                    dc.l    0                       ;font ptr (dflt)
                    dc.l    g34txt                  ;text pointer
                    dc.l    0                       ;ptr to nxt txt structure

GLEFT       set     GLEFT+GWIDE+HGAP                ;set next gadget rightward

Gadget35
                    dc.l    Gadget36                ;pointer to next gadget
                    dc.w    GLEFT                   ;left edge
                    dc.w    GTOP                    ;top edge
                    dc.w    GWIDE                   ;width
                    dc.w    GHIGH                   ;height
                    dc.w    GADGHCOMP               ;flags
                    dc.w    RELVERIFY               ;activation flags
                    dc.w    BOOLGADGET              ;gadget type
                    dc.l    border1                 ;ptr to border structure
                    dc.l    0
                    dc.l    g35itxt                 ;ptr to text structure
                    dc.l    0
                    dc.l    0
                    dc.w    39                      ;id
                    dc.l    0

g35itxt
                    dc.b    KEYCOL                  ;front pen
                    dc.b    0                       ;back pen
                    dc.b    RP_JAM1                 ;draw mode
                    dc.w    1                       ;left edge
                    dc.w    1                       ;top edge
                    dc.l    0                       ;font ptr (dflt)
                    dc.l    g35txt                  ;text pointer
                    dc.l    0                       ;ptr to nxt txt structure

GTOP        set     GTOP+GHIGH+VGAP                 ;set next gadget lower
GLEFT       set     GMINLEFT                        ;initialize gadget left coord
Gadget36
                    dc.l    Gadget37                ;pointer to next gadget
                    dc.w    GLEFT                   ;left edge
                    dc.w    GTOP                    ;top edge
```

```
            dc.w    GWIDE                   ;width
            dc.w    GHIGH                   ;height
            dc.w    GADGHCOMP               ;flags
            dc.w    RELVERIFY               ;activation flags
            dc.w    BOOLGADGET              ;gadget type
            dc.l    border1                 ;ptr to border structure
            dc.l    0
            dc.l    g36itxt                 ;ptr to text structure
            dc.l    0
            dc.l    0
            dc.w    6                       ;id
            dc.l    0

g36itxt
            dc.b    KEYCOL                  ;front pen
            dc.b    0                       ;back pen
            dc.b    RP_JAM1                 ;draw mode
            dc.w    1                       ;left edge
            dc.w    1                       ;top edge
            dc.l    0                       ;font ptr (dflt)
            dc.l    g36txt                  ;text pointer
            dc.l    0                       ;ptr to nxt txt structure

GLEFT       set     GLEFT+GWIDE+HGAP        ;set next gadget rightward

Gadget37
            dc.l    Gadget38                ;pointer to next gadget
            dc.w    GLEFT                   ;left edge
            dc.w    GTOP                    ;top edge
            dc.w    GWIDE                   ;width
            dc.w    GHIGH                   ;height
            dc.w    GADGHCOMP               ;flags
            dc.w    RELVERIFY               ;activation flags
            dc.w    BOOLGADGET              ;gadget type
            dc.l    border1                 ;ptr to border structure
            dc.l    0
            dc.l    g37itxt                 ;ptr to text structure
            dc.l    0
            dc.l    0
            dc.w    16                      ;id
            dc.l    0

g37itxt
            dc.b    KEYCOL                  ;front pen
            dc.b    0                       ;back pen
            dc.b    RP_JAM1                 ;draw mode
            dc.w    1                       ;left edge
            dc.w    1                       ;top edge
            dc.l    0                       ;font ptr (dflt)
            dc.l    g37txt                  ;text pointer
            dc.l    0                       ;ptr to nxt txt structure

GLEFT       set     GLEFT+GWIDE+HGAP        ;set next gadget rightward

Gadget38
            dc.l    Gadget39                ;pointer to next gadget
            dc.w    GLEFT                   ;left edge
            dc.w    GTOP                    ;top edge
            dc.w    GWIDE                   ;width
            dc.w    GHIGH                   ;height
```

```
                dc.w    GADGHCOMP               ;flags
                dc.w    RELVERIFY               ;activation flags
                dc.w    BOOLGADGET'             ;gadget type
                dc.l    border1                 ;ptr to border structure
                dc.l    0
                dc.l    g38itxt                 ;ptr to text structure
                dc.l    0
                dc.l    0
                dc.w    15                      ;id
                dc.l    0

g38itxt
                dc.b    KEYCOL                  ;front pen
                dc.b    0                       ;back pen
                dc.b    RP_JAM1                 ;draw mode
                dc.w    1                       ;left edge
                dc.w    1                       ;top edge
                dc.l    0                       ;font ptr (dflt)
                dc.l    g38txt                  ;text pointer
                dc.l    0                       ;ptr to nxt txt structure

GLEFT           set     GLEFT+GWIDE+HGAP        ;set next gadget rightward

Gadget39
                dc.l    Gadget40                ;pointer to next gadget
                dc.w    GLEFT                   ;left edge
                dc.w    GTOP                    ;top edge
                dc.w    GWIDE                   ;width
                dc.w    GHIGH                   ;height
                dc.w    GADGHCOMP               ;flags
                dc.w    RELVERIFY               ;activation flags
                dc.w    BOOLGADGET              ;gadget type
                dc.l    border1                 ;ptr to border structure
                dc.l    0
                dc.l    g39itxt                 ;ptr to text structure
                dc.l    0
                dc.l    0
                dc.w    14                      ;id
                dc.l    0

g39itxt
                dc.b    KEYCOL                  ;front pen
                dc.b    0                       ;back pen
                dc.b    RP_JAM1                 ;draw mode
                dc.w    1                       ;left edge
                dc.w    1                       ;top edge
                dc.l    0                       ;font ptr (dflt)
                dc.l    g39txt                  ;text pointer
                dc.l    0                       ;ptr to nxt txt structure

GLEFT           set     GLEFT+GWIDE+HGAP        ;set next gadget rightward

Gadget40
                dc.l    0                       ;pointer to next gadget
                dc.w    GLEFT                   ;left edge
                dc.w    GTOP                    ;top edge
                dc.w    GWIDE                   ;width
                dc.w    GHIGH                   ;height
                dc.w    GADGHCOMP               ;flags
                dc.w    RELVERIFY               ;activation flags
```

```
                 dc.w      BOOLGADGET                  ;gadget type
                 dc.l      border1                     ;ptr to border structure
                 dc.l      0
                 dc.l      g40itxt                     ;ptr to text structure
                 dc.l      0
                 dc.l      0
                 dc.w      5                           ;id
                 dc.l      0

g40itxt
                 dc.b      KEYCOL                      ;front pen
                 dc.b      0                           ;back pen
                 dc.b      RP_JAM1                     ;draw mode
                 dc.w      1                           ;left edge
                 dc.w      1                           ;top edge
                 dc.l      0                           ;font ptr (dflt)
                 dc.l      g40txt                      ;text pointer
                 dc.l      0                           ;ptr to nxt txt structure


g1txt            dc.b      'DEC',0
g2txt            dc.b      'HEX',0
g3txt            dc.b      'OCT',0
g4txt            dc.b      'BIN',0
g5txt            dc.b      'CLR',0
g6txt            dc.b      'STO',0
g7txt            dc.b      'RCL',0
g8txt            dc.b      'SUM',0
g9txt            dc.b      ' (',0
g10txt           dc.b      ' )',0
g11txt           dc.b      'SHF',0
g12txt           dc.b      ' D',0
g13txt           dc.b      ' E',0
g14txt           dc.b      ' F',0
g15txt           dc.b      ' K',0
g16txt           dc.b      'NOT',0
g17txt           dc.b      ' A',0
g18txt           dc.b      ' B',0
g19txt           dc.b      ' C',0
g20txt           dc.b      ' /',0
g21txt           dc.b      'OR',0
g22txt           dc.b      ' 7',0
g23txt           dc.b      ' 8',0
g24txt           dc.b      ' 9',0
g25txt           dc.b      ' *',0
g26txt           dc.b      'AND',0
g27txt           dc.b      ' 4',0
g28txt           dc.b      ' 5',0
g29txt           dc.b      ' 6',0
g30txt           dc.b      ' -',0
g31txt           dc.b      'XOR',0
g32txt           dc.b      ' 1',0
g33txt           dc.b      ' 2',0
g34txt           dc.b      ' 3',0
g35txt           dc.b      ' +',0
g36txt           dc.b      'CE',0
g37txt           dc.b      ' 0',0
g38txt           dc.b      ' .',0
g39txt           dc.b      '+/-',0
g40txt           dc.b      ' =',0
```

```
numstr          dcb.b    9,0                     ;space for numeric string
errstr          dc.b     ' Error '               ;string to display error
dispstr         dcb.b    18,0                    ;space for displayed string
                dc.b     0                       ;terminal null for string

wtitle          dc.b     'Programmer Calc',0

INT_Lib         dc.b     'intuition.library',0
DOS_Lib         dc.b     'dos.library',0

msg             dc.b     'This program must be run from the Workbench.',$0a
msglen          equ      *-msg

        end
```

Appendix:

The Library Routines

What follows is a list of the library routines available to Amiga software developers. Each routine is listed along with the library that contains it. Except for the **exec** library, all libraries must be opened before their routines are available to a programmer. For the purposes of clarity, the _LVO prefix has been omitted, but should be affixed when you are using these routines from assembly language code.

Below each routine's name is a list of mnemonics showing the parameters required (if any) for its operation. These mnemonics serve only to provide a reminder of what each parameter actually represents. Next to each mnemonic is the register that should be used to send it to the routine.

AbortIO   exec.library
  ioRequest
  a1

AddAnimOb   graphics.library
  obj,animationKey,rastPort
  a0 a1   a2

AddBob   graphics.library
  bob,rastPort
  a0 a1

AddDevice
device
a1

exec.library

AddFont
textFont
a1

graphics.library

AddFreeList
freelist,mem,size
a0   a1   a2

icon.library

AddGadget
AddPtr,Gadget,Position
a0   a1   d0

intuition.library

AddHead
list,node
a0 a1

exec.library

AddIntServer
intNumber,interrupt
d0   a1

exec.library

AddLibrary
library
a1

exec.library

AddPort
port
a1

exec.library

AddResource
resource
a1

exec.library

AddTail
list,node
a0 a1

exec.library

AddTask
task,initPC,finalPC
a1 a2   a3

exec.library

AddTime
dest,src
a0 a1

timer.device

AddVSprite vSprite,rastPort a0 a1	graphics.library
Alert alertNum,parameters d7 a5	exec.library
AllocAbs byteSize,location d0 a1	exec.library
AllocCList cLPool a1	clist.library
AllocEntry entry a0	exec.library
AllocMem byteSize,requirements d0 d1	exec.library
AllocRaster width,height d0 d1	graphics.library
AllocRemember RememberKey,Size,Flags a0 d0 d1	intuition.library
AllocSignal signalNum d0	exec.library
AllocTrap trapNum d0	exec.library
AllocWBObject No Parameters	icon.library
Allocate freeList,byteSize a0 d0	exec.library

AlohaWorkbench   intuition.library
  wbport
  a0

AndRectRegion   graphics.library
  rgn,rect
  a0 a1

Animate   graphics.library
  animationKey,rastPort
  a0   a1

AreaDraw   graphics.library
  rastPort,x, y
  a1   d0 d1

AreaEnd   graphics.library
  rastPort
  a1

AreaMove   graphics.library
  rastPort,x, y
  a1   d0 d1

AskFont   graphics.library
  rastPort,textAttr
  a1   a0

AskSoftStyle   graphics.library
  rastPort
  a1

AutoRequest   intuition.library
  Window,Body,PText,NText,PFlag,NFlag,W, H
  a0   a1   a2   a3   d0   d1   d2 d3

AvailFonts   diskfont.library
  buffer,bufBytes,flags
  a0   d0   d1

AvailMem   exec.library
  requirements
  d1

BeginRefresh   intuition.library
  Window
  a0

BeginUpdate   layers.library
layer
a0

BehindLayer   layers.library
li,   layer
a0 a1

BltBitMap   graphics.library
srcBitMap,srcX,srcY,destBitMap,destX,destY,sizeX,sizeY,minterm,mask,tempA
a0   d0 d1 a1   d2   d3   d4   d5   d6   d7 a2

BltBitMapRastPort   graphics.library
srcbm,srcx,srcy,destrp,destX,destY,sizeX,sizeY,minterm
a0   d0 d1 a1   d2   d3   d4   d5   d6

BltClear   graphics.library
memory,size,flags
a1   d0 d1

BltPattern   graphics.library
rastPort,ras,xl, yl, maxX,maxY,fillBytes
a1   a0 d0 d1 d2   d3   d4

BltTemplate   graphics.library
source,srcX,srcMod,destRastPort,destX,destY,sizeX,sizeY
a0   d0   d1   a1   d2   d3   d4   d5

BuildSysRequest   intuition.library
Window,Body,PosText,NegText,Flags,W, H
a0   a1   a2   a3   d0   d1 d2

BumpRevision   icon.library
newname,oldname
a0   a1

CBump   graphics.library
copperList
a1

CMove   graphics.library
copperList,destination,data
a1   d0   d1

CWait   graphics.library
copperList,x, y
a1   d0 d1

Cause   exec.library
interrupt
a1

ChangeSprite   graphics.library
vp,simplesprite,data
a0 a1   a2

CheckIO   exec.library
ioRequest
a1

ClearDMRequest   intuition.library
Window
a0

ClearEOL   graphics.library
rastPort
a1

ClearMenuStrip   intuition.library
Window
a0

ClearPointer   intuition.library
Window
a0

ClearRegion   graphics.library
rgn
a0

ClearScreen   graphics.library
rastPort
a1

ClipBlit   graphics.library
srcrp,srcX,srcY,destrp,destX,destY,sizeX,sizeY,minterm
a0   d0   d1   a1   d2   d3   d4   d5   d6

Close   dos.library
file
d1

CloseDevice   exec.library
  ioRequest
  a1

CloseFont   graphics.library
  textFont
  a1

CloseLibrary   exec.library
  library
  a1

CloseScreen   intuition.library
  Screen
  a0

CloseWindow   intuition.library
  Window
  a0

CloseWorkBench   intuition.library
  No Parameters

CmpTime   timer.device
  dest,src
  a0   a1

ConcatCList   clist.library
  sourceCList,destCList
  a0   a1

CopyCList   clist.library
  cList
  a0

CopySBitMap   graphics.library
  l1, l2
  a0 a1

CreateBehindLayer   layers.library
  li, bm, x0, y0, x1, y1, flags,bm2
  a0 a1 d0 d1 d2 d3 d4   a2

CreateDir   dos.library
  name
  d1

CreateProc   dos.library
  name,pri,segList,stackSize
  d1   d2 d3   d4

CreateUpfrontLayer   layers.library
  li, bm, x0, y0, xl, y1, flags,bm2
  a0 a1 d0 d1 d2 d3 d4   a2

CurrentDir   dos.library
  lock
  d1

CurrentTime   intuition.library
  Seconds,Micros
  a0   a1

DateStamp   dos.library
  date
  d1

Deallocate   exec.library
  freeList,memoryBlock,byteSize
  a0   a1   d0

Debug   exec.library
  No Parameters

Delay   dos.library
  timeout
  d1

DeleteFile   dos.library
  name
  d1

DeleteLayer   layers.library
  li, layer
  a0 a1

DeviceProc   dos.library
  name
  d1

Disable   exec.library
  No Parameters

DisownBlitter
No Parameters
graphics.library

DisplayAlert
AlertNumber,String,Height
d0   a0   d1
intuition.library

DisplayBeep
Screen
a0
intuition.library

DisposeLayerInfo
li
a0
layers.library

DisposeRegion
rgn
a0
graphics.library

DoCollision
rasPort
a1
graphics.library

DoIO
ioRequest
a1
exec.library

DoubleClick
sseconds,smicros,cseconds,cmicros
d0   d1   d2   d3
intuition.library

Draw
rastPort,x, y
a1   d0 d1
graphics.library

DrawBorder
RPort,Border,LeftOffset,TopOffset
a0   a1   d0   d1
intuition.library

DrawGList
rastPort,viewPort
a1   a0
graphics.library

DrawImage
RPort,Image,LeftOffset,TopOffset
a0 a1 d0 d1
intuition.library

DupLock　　　　　　　　　　dos.library
　lock
　d1

Enable　　　　　　　　　　　exec.library
　No Parameters

EndRefresh　　　　　　　　　intuition.library
　Window,Complete
　a0　　　d0

EndRequest　　　　　　　　　intuition.library
　requester,window
　a0　　　a1

EndUpdate　　　　　　　　　layers.library
　layer,flag
　a0　d0

Enqueue　　　　　　　　　　exec.library
　list,node
　a0　a1

ExNext　　　　　　　　　　　dos.library
　lock,fileInfoBlock
　d1　d2

Examine　　　　　　　　　　dos.library
　lock,fileInfoBlock
　d1　d2

Execute　　　　　　　　　　dos.library
　string,file,file
　d1　　d2　d3

Exit　　　　　　　　　　　　dos.library
　returnCode
　d1

FattenLayerInfo　　　　　　layers.library
　li
　a0

FindName　　　　　　　　　exec.library
　list, name
　a0　a1

FindPort   exec.library
name
a1

FindResident   exec.library
name
a1

FindTask   exec.library
name
a1

FindToolType   icon.library
toolTypeArray,typeName
a0   a1

Flood   graphics.library
rastPort,mode,x, y
a1   d2   d0 d1

FlushCList   clist.library
cList
a0

Forbid   exec.library
No Parameters

FreeCList   clist.library
cList
a0

FreeColorMap   graphics.library
colormap
a0

FreeCopList   graphics.library
coplist
a0

FreeCprList   graphics.library
cprlist
a0

FreeDiskObject   icon.library
diskobj
a0

FreeEntry   exec.library
entry
a0

FreeFreeList   icon.library
freelist
a0

FreeGBuffers   graphics.library
animationObj,rastPort,doubleBuffer
a0   a1   d0

FreeMem   exec.library
memoryBlock,byteSize
a1   d0

FreeRaster   graphics.library
planeptr,width,height
a0   d0   d1

FreeRemember   intuition.library
RememberKey,ReallyForget
a0   d0

FreeSignal   exec.library
signalNum
d0

FreeSprite   graphics.library
num
d0

FreeSysRequest   intuition.library
Window
a0

FreeTrap   exec.library
trapNum
d0

FreeVPortCopLists   graphics.library
viewport
a0

FreeWBObject
WBObject
a0
icon.library

GetCC
No Parameters
exec.library

GetCLBuf
cList,buffer,maxLength
a0   a1   d1
clist.library

GetCLChar
cList
a0
clist.library

GetCLWord
cList
a0
clist.library

GetColorMap
entries
d0
graphics.library

GetDefPrefs
preferences,size
a0   d0
intuition.library

GetDiskObject
name
a0
icon.library

GetGBuffers
animationObj,rastPort,doubleBuffer
a0   a1   d0
graphics.library

GetIcon
name,icon,freelist
a0   a1   a2
icon.library

GetMsg
port
a0
exec.library

GetPrefs
preferences,size
a0   d0
intuition.library

GetRGB4   graphics.library
  colormap,entry
  a0   d0

GetSprite   graphics.library
  simplesprite,num
  a0   d0

GetWBObject   icon.library
  name
  a0

IEEEDPAbs   mathieeedoubbas.library
  integer,integer
  d0   d1

IEEEDPAdd   mathieeedoubbas.library
  integer,integer,integer,integer
  d0   d1   d2   d3

IEEEDPCmp   mathieeedoubbas.library
  integer,integer,integer,integer
  d0   d1   d2   d3

IEEEDPDiv   mathieeedoubbas.library
  integer,integer,integer,integer
  d0   d1   d2   d3

IEEEDPFix   mathieeedoubbas.library
  integer,integer
  d0   d1

IEEEDPFlt   mathieeedoubbas.library
  integer
  d0

IEEEDPMul   mathieeedoubbas.library
  integer,integer,integer,integer
  d0   d1   d2   d3

IEEEDPNeg   mathieeedoubbas.library
  integer,integer
  d0   d1

IEEEDPSub   mathieeedoubbas.library
  integer,integer,integer,integer
  d0   d1   d2   d3

IEEEDPTst   mathieeedoubbas.library
integer,integer
d0   d1

IncrCLMark   clist.library
cList
a0

Info   dos.library
lock,parameterBlock
d1 d2

InitArea   graphics.library
areaInfo,vectorTable,vectorTableSize
a0   a1   d0

InitBitMap   graphics.library
bitMap,depth,width,height
a0   d0   d1   d2

InitCLPool   clist.library
cLPool,size
a0   d0

InitCode   exec.library
startClass,version
d0   d1

InitGMasks   graphics.library
animationObj
a0

InitGels   graphics.library
dummyHead,dummyTail,GelsInfo
a0   a1   a2

InitLayers   layers.library
li
a0

InitMasks   graphics.library
vSprite
a0

InitRastPort   graphics.library
rastPort
a1

InitRequester
req
a0
          intuition.library

InitResident
resident,segList
a1   d1
          exec.library

InitStruct
initTable,memory,size
a1   a2   d0
          exec.library

InitTmpRas
tmpras,buff,size
a0   a1 d0
          graphics.library

InitVPort
viewPort
a0
          graphics.library

InitView
view
a1
          graphics.library

Input
No Parameters
          dos.library

Insert
list,node,pred
a0 a1   a2
          exec.library

IntuiTextLength
itext
a0
          intuition.library

Intuition
ievent
a0
          intuition.library

IoErr
No Parameters
          dos.library

IsInteractive
file
d1
          dos.library

ItemAddress   intuition.library
MenuStrip,MenuNumber
a0   d0

LoadRGB4   graphics.library
viewPort,colors,count
a0   a1   d0

LoadSeg   dos.library
fileName
d1

LoadView   graphics.library
view
a1

Lock   dos.library
name,type
d1   d2

LockIBase   intuition.library
dontknow
d0

LockLayer   layers.library
li,   layer
a0   a1

LockLayerInfo   layers.library
li
a0

LockLayerRom   graphics.library
layer
a5

LockLayers   layers.library
li
a0

MakeFunctions   exec.library
target,functionArray,funcDispBase
a0   a1   a2

MakeLibrary   exec.library
funcInit,structInit,libInit,dataSize,codeSize
a0   a1   a2   d0   d1

MakeScreen   intuition.library
Screen
a0

MakeVPort   graphics.library
view,viewPort
a0   a1

MarkCList   clist.library
cList,offset
a0   d0

MatchToolValue   icon.library
typeString,value
a0   a1

ModifyIDCMP   intuition.library
Window,Flags
a0   d0

ModifyProp   intuition.library
Gadget,Ptr,Req,Flags,HPos,VPos,HBody,VBody
a0   a1 a2 d0   d1   d2   d3   d4

Move   graphics.library
rastPort,x, y
a1   d0 d1

MoveLayer   layers.library
li,   layer,dx, dy
a0 a1   d0 d1

MoveLayerInFrontOf   layers.library
layer__to__move,layer__to__be__infront__of
a0   a1

MoveScreen   intuition.library
Screen,dx, dy
a0   d0 d1

MoveSprite   graphics.library
viewport,simplesprite,x,   y
a0   a1   d0 d1

MoveWindow   intuition.library
window,dx,dy
a0   d0 d1

MrgCop   graphics.library
view
a1

NewLayerInfo   layers.library
No Parameters

NewRegion   graphics.library
No Parameters

NotRegion   graphics.library
rgn
a0

OffGadget   intuition.library
Gadget,Ptr,Req
a0   a1 a2

OffMenu   intuition.library
Window,MenuNumber
a0   d0

OldOpenLibrary   exec.library
libName
a1

OnGadget   intuition.library
Gadget,Ptr,Req
a0   a1 a2

OnMenu   intuition.library
Window,MenuNumber
a0   d0

Open   dos.library
name,accessMode
d1   d2

OpenDevice   exec.library
devName,unit,ioRequest,flags
a0   d0 a1   d1

OpenDiskFont   diskfont.library
textAttr
a0

OpenFont   graphics.library
textAttr
a0

OpenIntuition   intuition.library
No Parameters

OpenLibrary   exec.library
libName,version
a1   d0

OpenResource   exec.library
resName,version
a1   d0

OpenScreen   intuition.library
OSargs
a0

OpenWindow   intuition.library
OWargs
a0

OpenWorkBench   intuition.library
No Parameters

OrRectRegion   graphics.library
rgn,rect
a0 a1

Output   dos.library
No Parameters

OwnBlitter   graphics.library
No Parameters

ParentDir dos.library
lock
d1

PeekCLMark clist.library
cList
a0

Permit exec.library
No Parameters

PointerColors intuition.library
Screen,Red,Gren,Blue
a0   d0   d1   d2

PolyDraw graphics.library
rastPort,count,polyTable
a1   d0   a0

PrintIText intuition.library
rp, itext,left,top
a0 a1   d0 d1

Procure exec.library
semaport,bidMsg
a0   a1

PutCLBuf clist.library
cList,buffer,length
a0   a1   d1

PutCLChar clist.library
cList,byte
a0   d0

PutCLWord clist.library
cList,word
a0   d0

PutDiskObject icon.library
name,diskobj
a0   a1

PutIcon icon.library
name,icon
a0   a1

PutMsg   exec.library
  port,message
  a0 a1

PutWBObject   icon.library
  name,object
  a0 a1

QBSBlit   graphics.library
  blit
  a1

QBlit   graphics.library
  blit
  a1

Read   dos.library
  file,buffer,length
  d1 d2   d3

ReadPixel   graphics.library
  rastPort,x,   y
  a1   d0 d1

RectFill   graphics.library
  rastPort,xl, yl, xu, yu
  a1   d0 d1 d2 d3

RefreshGadgets   intuition.library
  Gadgets,Ptr,Req
  a0   a1 a2

RemDevice   exec.library
  device
  a1

RemFont   graphics.library
  textFont
  a1

RemHead   exec.library
  list
  a0

RemIBob   graphics.library
  bob,rastPort,viewPort
  a0 a1   a2

RemIntServer   exec.library
intNumber,interrupt
d0   a1

RemLibrary   exec.library
library
a1

RemPort   exec.library
port
a1

RemResource   exec.library
resource
a1

RemTail   exec.library
list
a0

RemTask   exec.library
task
a1

RemVSprite   graphics.library
vSprite
a0

RemakeDisplay   intuition.library
No Parameters

Remove   exec.library
node
a1

RemoveGadget   intuition.library
RemPtr,Gadget
a0   a1

Rename   dos.library
oldName,newName
d1   d2

ReplyMsg   exec.library
message
a1

ReportMouse   intuition.library
Window,Boolean
a0   d0

Request   intuition.library
Requester,Window
a0   a1

RethinkDisplay   intuition.library
No Parameters

SPAbs   mathffp.library
float
d0

SPAcos   mathtrans.library
float
d0

SPAdd   mathffp.library
leftFloat,rightFloat
d1   d0

SPAsin   mathtrans.library
float
d0

SPAtan   mathtrans.library
float
d0

SPCmp   mathffp.library
leftFloat,rightFloat
d1   d0

SPCos   mathtrans.library
float
d0

SPCosh   mathtrans.library
float
d0

SPDiv   mathffp.library
leftFloat,rightFloat
d1   d0

SPExp float d0	mathtrans.library
SPFieee integer d0	mathtrans.library
SPFix float d0	mathffp.library
SPFlt integer d0	mathffp.library
SPLog float d0	mathtrans.library
SPLog10 float d0	mathtrans.library
SPMul leftFloat,rightFloat d1 d0	mathffp.library
SPNeg float d0	mathffp.library
SPPow leftFloat,rightFloat d1 d0	mathtrans.library
SPSin float d0	mathtrans.library
SPSincos leftFloat,rightFloat d1 d0	mathtrans.library

SPSinh
float
d0
mathtrans.library

SPSqrt
float
d0
mathtrans.library

SPSub
leftFloat,rightFloat
d1   d0
mathffp.library

SPTan
float
d0
mathtrans.library

SPTanh
float
d0
mathtrans.library

SPTieee
float
d0
mathtrans.library

SPTst
float
d1
Mathffp.library

ScreenToBack
Screen
a0
intuition.library

ScreenToFront
Screen
a0
intuition.library

ScrollLayer
li, layer,dx, dy
a0 a1   d0 d1
layers.library

ScrollRaster
rastPort,dX,dY,minx,miny,maxx,maxy
a1   d0 d1 d2   d3   d4   d5
graphics.library

ScrollVPort   graphics.library
vp
a0

Seek   dos.library
file,position,offset
d1 d2   d3

SendIO   exec.library
ioRequest
a1

SetAPen   graphics.library
rastPort,pen
a1   d0

SetBPen   graphics.library
rastPort,pen
a1   d0

SetCollision   graphics.library
type,routine,gelsInfo
d0 a0   a1

SetComment   dos.library
name,comment
d1   d2

SetDMRequest   intuition.library
Window,req
a0   a1

SetDrMd   graphics.library
rastPort,drawMode
a1   d0

SetExcept   exec.library
newSignals,signalSet
d0   d1

SetFont   graphics.library
rastPortID,textFont
a1   a0

SetFunction exec.library
library,funcOffset,funcEntry
a1 a0 d0

SetIntVector exec.library
intNumber,interrupt
d0 a1

SetMenuStrip intuition.library
Window,Menu
a0 a1

SetPointer intuition.library
Window,Pointer,Height,Width,Xoffset,Yoffset
a0 a1 d0 d1 d2 d3

SetPrefs intuition.library
preferences,size,flag
a0 d0 d1

SetProtection dos.library
name,mask
d1 d2

SetRGB4 graphics.library
viewPort,index,r, g, b
a0 d0 d1 d2 d3

SetRast graphics.library
rastPort,color
a1 d0

SetSR exec.library
newSR,mask
d0 d1

SetSignal exec.library
newSignals,signalSet
d0 d1

SetSoftStyle graphics.library
rastPort,style,enable
a1 d0 d1

SetTaskPri   exec.library
   task,priority
   a1   d0

SetWindowTitles   intuition.library
   window,windowtitle,screentitle
   a0   a1   a2

ShowTitle   intuition.library
   Screen,ShowIt
   a0   d0

Signal   exec.library
   task,signalSet
   a1   d0

SizeCList   clist.library
   cList
   a0

SizeLayer   layers.library
   li,   layer,dx, dy
   a0 a1   d0 d1

SizeWindow   intuition.library
   window,dx, dy
   a0   d0 d1

SortGList   graphics.library
   rastPort
   a1

SplitCList   clist.library
   cList
   a0

SubCList   clist.library
   cList,index,length
   a0   d0   d1

SubTime   timer.device
   dest,src
   a0 a1

SumLibrary   exec.library
  library
  a1

SuperState   exec.library
  No Parameters

SwapBitsRastPort-
ClipRect   layers.library
  rp, cr
  a0   a1

SyncSBitMap   graphics.library
  l
  a0

Text   graphics.library
  RastPort,string,count
  a1   a0   d0

TextLength   graphics.library
  RastPort,string,count
  a1   a0   d0

ThinLayerInfo   layers.library
  li
  a0

Translate   translator.library
  inputString,inputLength,outputBuffer,bufferSize
  a0   d0   a1   d1

TypeOfMem   exec.library
  address
  a1

UCopperListInit   graphics.library
  copperlist,num
  a0   d0

UnGetCLChar   clist.library
  cList,byte
  a0   d0

UnGetCLWord cList,word a0 d0	clist.library
UnLoadSeg segment d1	dos.library
Unlock lock d1	dos.library
UnPutCLChar cList a0	clist.library
UnPutCLWord cList a0	clist.library
UnlockIBase IBLock a0	intuition.library
UnlockLayer layer a0	layers.library
UnlockLayerInfo li a0	layers.library
UnlockLayerRom layer a5	graphics.library
UnlockLayers li a0	layers.library
UpfrontLayer li, layer a0 a1	layers.library

UserState
sysStack
d0

exec.library

VBeamPos
No Parameters

graphics.library

Vacate
semaport
a0

exec.library

ViewAddress
No Parameters

intuition.library

ViewPortAddress
window
a0

intuition.library

WBenchToBack
No Parameters

intuition.library

WBenchToFront
No Parameters

intuition.library

Wait
signalSet
d0

exec.library

WaitBOVP
viewport
a0

graphics.library

WaitBlit
No Parameters

graphics.library

WaitForChar
file,timeout
d1 d2

dos.library

WaitIO
ioRequest
a1

exec.library

WaitPort   exec.library
  port
  a0

WaitTOF   graphics.library
  No Parameters

WhichLayer   layers.library
  li, x, y
  a0 d0 d1

WindowLimits   intuition.library
  window,minwidth,minheight,maxwidth,maxheight
  a0   d0   d1   d2   d3

WindowToBack   intuition.library
  window
  a0

WindowToFront   intuition.library
  window
  a0

Write   dos.library
  file,buffer,length
  d1 d2   d3

WritePixel   graphics.library
  rastPort,x, y
  a1   d0 d1

XorRectRegion   graphics.library
  rgn,rect
  a0 a1

Glossary

address bus—The bits output by the processor that specify to memory the precise memory location that is currently being addressed.

algorithm—The method used by a routine to perform a computation.

assembler—A program that reads source code comprised of a list of mnemonics and symbolic addresses and outputs a binary version of it. This binary version may be directly executable or may have to be linked with other programs before execution. Some assemblers directly output executable code; others produce code that becomes executable only after being processed by a linker.

assembler directive—An opcode that is used within the source code program that, instead of producing an executable instruction for use by the processor, causes the assembler itself to perform some task.

assembly language—The text input to an assembler, consisting of opcode mnemonics and operands in the form of numbers or symbolic textual labels.

A-trap—An exception on the 68000 that begins with the bits 1010 (or hexadecimal A). This causes the processor to execute the *unimplemented instruction* exception vector number 10 at hexadecimal address 28.

BCD—Binary-coded decimal: a method whereby each four bits of a register or memory location are used to contain the digits 0 through 9 only.

binary point—The binary equivalent of a decimal point. For instance, 2.5 in decimal is the same as 10.1 in binary: the first contains a decimal point; the second, a binary point.

bit—A binary digit: 0 or 1.

byte—Eight bits; one quarter of a 68000 register; the number of bits required to hold one character.

data bus—The set of bits used by the processor to either send data to or read from memory.

double precision—A floating-point number stored with seven bytes for the mantissa and one byte for the exponent.

exception—An event that causes the 68000 processor to stop its current program execution and jump to an address in the exception table in low memory between 0 and 3FF.

exponent—The part of a floating-point number that locates the binary point.

extended precision—A floating-point number stored with nine bytes for the mantissa and one byte for the exponent.

FIFO—First-in, first-out: a method of storing numbers in a list such that the first number put in is the first taken from the list.

floating-point—A method of storing numbers whereby the number part and the location of its binary or decimal point are stored separately.

F-trap—An exception on the 68000 that begins with the bits 1111 (or hexadecimal F). This causes the processor to execute the *unimplemented instruction* exception vector number 11 at hexadecimal address 2C.

GIGO—Garbage-in, garbage-out: Not as frivolous as it sounds, this cynical little axiom is true of any program written by any person running on any computer anywhere.

heap—An area of memory used to store programs and/or data usually on a more permanent basis than a stack. In contrast with a stack, a heap grows upwards in memory.

hexadecimal—A numbering system that counts to the base 16 and uses the digits 0 through 9 and A through F.

I/O—Input/Output.

instruction—A set of bits that causes the 68000 to perform a particular operation.

interrupt—A condition that is detected by a processor, causing it to temporarily stop execution after its current instruction and jump to a special interrupt routine.

LIFO—Last-in, first-out (Like a stack.): a method of storing numbers in a list such that the last number stored is the first number retrieved.

linker—A program that takes special linkable output from an assembler to produce an executable binary version.

list—A connected set of memory structures used to provide a simple way to access each individual structure.

long word—32 bits: the whole of a 68000 register, twice the length of a word, and four times the length of a byte. As an unsigned quantity, it can hold quantities between 0 and 4,294,967,295.

machine code—The pure binary numbers used to drive the processor.

mantissa—The part of a floating-point number that stores the actual digits used in that number.

mnemonic—A short (usually three or four-letter) abbreviation for an opcode.

node—A structure used to denote and identify a member of a list.

NOP—No operation: a special instruction known to the processor; NOP causes it to do nothing (i.e., skip the NOP instruction). Used mainly in debugging to provide areas that can be patched with other opcodes.

object code—The output from a program such as an assembler or compiler. The object code may be directly executable or may itself become the source code for another program during the generation of an executable program.

octal—A numbering system that counts to the base 8 using the digits zero through seven.

opcode—Short for operation code, opcode refers to a mnemonic that an assembler understands and translates into a machine-code numeric instruction.

operating system—A low-level set of input/output routines in software; these are merged together to provide a working interface to the hardware. The Amiga provides calls into the operating system to enable use of these I/O routines.

processor—The central piece of hardware on a computer, the processor follows instructions written in machine code and thereby performs useful work.

pseudo-op—*See* assembler directive.

queue—A list that is maintained in a definite order.

R/W—Read/Write.

RAM—Random-access memory: used to hold data that is only used while power is applied to the computer.

ROM—Read-only memory. ROM on the Amiga is actually a write-protected area of RAM from address F8000000 to FFFFFFFF. This is written to once only from the kickstart disk at power up and contains the executive and operating system.

register—A set of predefined bits in the processor used to store and manipulate numbers. A register behaves like a RAM location internal to the processor.

routine—A set of instructions in a program that performs a task separate from other routines.

significand—*See* mantissa.

single precision—A floating-point number stored with three bytes for the mantissa (or significand), and one byte for the exponent.

stack—An area of memory used to temporarily save data in a form whereby the last number saved becomes the first one retrieved. Stacks increase in size from high towards low memory as they are filled.

structure—An area of data consisting of individual data elements kept in a known format.

subroutine—A routine that performs a stand-alone function and usually ends with an opcode, such as rts, that returns to the part of the program that called it.

trap—A 68000 operation whereby an exception that makes the 68000 jump to an address stored in a table in low memory is caused.

word—16 bits; half of a 68000 register. As an unsigned quantity, it can hold quantities between 0 and 65,535.

Index

Edited by Marianne Krcma